William Francis Finlason

A Brief and Practical Exposition of the Law of Charitable Trusts

With special reference to the jurisdiction of the commissioners of charities,

containing also all the Charitable Trusts Acts

William Francis Finlason

A Brief and Practical Exposition of the Law of Charitable Trusts
With special reference to the jurisdiction of the commissioners of charities, containing also all the Charitable Trusts Acts

ISBN/EAN: 9783337377182

Printed in Europe, USA, Canada, Australia, Japan

Cover: Foto ©Suzi / pixelio.de

More available books at **www.hansebooks.com**

A

BRIEF AND PRACTICAL EXPOSITION

OF THE

LAW OF CHARITABLE TRUSTS,

WITH SPECIAL REFERENCE TO THE

JURISDICTION OF THE COMMISSIONERS OF CHARITIES,

CONTAINING ALSO ALL

THE CHARITABLE TRUSTS ACTS;

With Notes,

AND THE RULES, MINUTES, AND ORDERS OF THE COURT OF CHANCERY AND THE COMMISSIONERS OF CHARITIES.

By W. F. FINLASON, ESQ.,

OF THE MIDDLE TEMPLE, BARRISTER-AT-LAW,
EDITOR OF THE CHARITABLE TRUSTS ACTS OF 1853 AND 1855.

"Summa charitas est, facere justitiam, omnibus personis, omni tempore quando necesse fuerit."—*Stat. Westm.* 1.

LONDON:
V. & R. STEVENS & SONS,
Law Booksellers and Publishers,
26, BELL YARD, LINCOLN'S INN.
1860.

TO

SIR RICHARD BETHELL,

HER MAJESTY'S ATTORNEY-GENERAL,

This Edition of

THE CHARITABLE TRUSTS ACTS

IS,

IN ACKNOWLEDGMENT OF HIS SERVICES IN PASSING THEM,

AND GENERALLY OF HIS LABOURS IN THE CAUSE

OF LEGAL REFORM,

RESPECTFULLY INSCRIBED.

CONTENTS.

	PAGE
I.—PRACTICAL EXPOSITION	1—122
1.—TRUSTS IN GENERAL	1—9
GRAMMAR SCHOOLS	10
PAROCHIAL AND MUNICIPAL CHARITIES	11—14
RELIGIOUS SOCIETIES	15
2.—OF THE CREATION OF CHARITABLE TRUSTS	18
THE PURPOSES OF SUCH TRUSTS AND THEIR VALIDITY	20—28
RELIGIOUS TRUSTS	29
ROMAN CATHOLIC TRUSTS	30—50
GENERAL AND DISCRETIONARY TRUSTS	50, 51
GIFTS ON TRUST: HOW VALID: MORTMAIN LAW	52
DECLARATION OF TRUST: HOW NECESSARY	55
AS AGAINST TRUSTEES	57
DISCLOSURE OF TRUSTS	60
3.—JURISDICTION OF CHANCERY OR OF THE COMMISSIONERS OF CHARITIES IN REGARD TO CHARITABLE TRUSTS	61—68
APPOINTMENT OF TRUSTEES	64

I.—PRACTICAL EXPOSITION (*continued*).

 4.—THE ADMINISTRATION OF CHARITIES . 68—98
  ADHERENCE TO PURPOSES . . . 68, 69
  RESTRICTION TO PLACES . . . 70, 71
  DISPOSITION OF SURPLUS . . . 71
  HOW FAR TRUSTEE ENTITLED . . . 78
  RECIPIENTS OF CHARITIES: THEIR RIGHTS
   AND REMEDIES 81
  RELIGIOUS QUESTIONS AS TO SCHOOLS . . 84
  LORD CHELMSFORD'S ENDOWED SCHOOLS ACT 85
  INTERNAL MANAGEMENT OF CHARITIES . . 86
  DISMISSAL OF OFFICERS, &C. . . . 87
    SCHOOLMASTERS . 88, 89
     MINISTERS OF CHAPELS . 91
  DISSENTERS' CHAPELS ACT . . . 92
  ROMAN CATHOLIC CHAPELS . . . 93

 5.—MANAGEMENT OF CHARITY PROPERTY 98—104
  INVESTMENT 99
  LETTING LANDS 101
  PARISH LANDS 102
  SELLING LANDS, &C. 103

 6.—SPECIAL JURISDICTION IN CHANCERY: RO-
  MILLY'S ACT 104

 7.—POWERS OF COMMISSIONERS OF CHARITIES . 108
  INQUIRY 108
  DIRECTION 111
  ARBITRATION 114
  LITIGATION 115
  ADJUDICATION 120

Contents. vii

	PAGE
II.—CHARITABLE TRUSTS ACT OF 1853	123
1.—POWERS OF THE BOARD GENERALLY	125
INQUIRY	126
PERSONS LIABLE TO BE SUMMONED	126
POWERS AS TO DIRECTION AND ADVICE	129
TO DIRECT OR RESTRAIN LITIGATION	130—133
TO SANCTION COMPROMISES	134
OR DISMISSALS	135
LEASES	136
SALES OR EXCHANGES	137
PURCHASES	138
2.—JURISDICTION IN CHANCERY AT CHAMBERS (IN CASES ABOVE 50*l.*)	140
3.—JURISDICTION IN THE COUNTY COURTS (IN CASES UNDER 50*l.*)	143
4.—PROVISIONS AS TO SPECIAL JURISDICTION	149
5.—LIMIT OF AMOUNT OF INCOME, HOW ASCERTAINED	154
6.—PROVISIONS FOR SECURING CHARITY PROPERTY	156
7.—APPLICATION TO PARLIAMENT FOR NEW SCHEMES	161
8.—ACCOUNTS OF TRUSTEES	163
9.—EXEMPTIONS	164
INTERPRETATION	168
III.—CHARITABLE TRUSTS ACT OF 1855	171
1.—ACCOUNTS AND INQUIRIES, FURTHER POWERS	172
2.—APPORTIONMENT OF CHARITIES	174, 183

III.—CHARITABLE TRUSTS ACT OF 1855 (*continued*).

    3.—FURTHER PROVISIONS FOR SECURING CHARITY PROPERTY 175
    4.—FURTHER POWERS AS TO SALES, LEASES, &C. 179
    5.—TAXATION OF COSTS 182

IV.—CHARITABLE TRUSTS ACT OF 1860 187
    1.—POWERS OF THE BOARD TO MAKE ORDERS . 187
    2.—PROVISIONS AS TO APPEAL . . . 189
    3.—FURTHER POWERS AS TO DISMISSALS AND REMOVALS OF OFFICERS OR RECIPIENTS . 191
    4.—AS TO INVESTMENT 194
    5.—ACCOUNTS 195
    6.—CUSTODY OF DEEDS . . . 195
    7.—ORDERS OF BOARD, HOW ENFORCED . 196

V.—ROMAN CATHOLIC CHARITIES ACT 198

APPENDIX.

ORDERS IN CHANCERY 204
RULES IN THE COUNTY COURTS 204
    OF THE COMMISSIONERS OF CHARITIES . . 211
FORMS OF ENQUIRY 216
    APPLICATIONS 224

A

BRIEF AND PRACTICAL EXPOSITION

OF THE

LAW OF CHARITABLE TRUSTS.

CHARITABLE TRUSTS are where property, real or personal, is held on trust for purposes which the law deems charitable; and charities are endowed foundations or institutions for such purposes. Gifts for purposes contrary to public policy the law does not give effect to; but gifts for purposes it deems charitable are upheld, when those purposes require it, in perpetuity. But the law has always defined the limits and conditions within which it will allow of this perpetuity; or of any alienations of property away from the natural heirs, especially when made by last will. Thus by the common law men could not, even while living in full health, dispose of more than a reasonable part of their property (*a*), and could not do so at all when labouring under a mortal disease, at least for a purpose not thought of in health. Thus

---

(*a*) Glanville.

also, ancient statutes restrain the alienation of land, for purposes of religion or charity in perpetuity (*a*); and thus a statute prohibits endowments to secure for the donors the special benefit of divine services (*b*). Before that last statute there was no restraint on the prerogative of the Crown at common law to confer the privilege of perpetual succession by incorporation, and to license the holding of lands in mortmain. And that privilege was exercised in favour of purposes not in law charitable, as well as for those which were. Thus there were "chauntries," or chapels, for the private benefit of the founders, as well as churches or chapels for the general benefit of the people. Thus also there were colleges, some educational, and therefore charitable, and others which held property only for the benefit of their members. Thus, too, there were hospitals, some for the benefit only of the members, some for the reception of strangers. It is the purpose or object to be carried out, not the mere motive, which in law makes a charity; and a gift for the benefit of the holder, though the motive may be charitable, is not a charity. There must be a purpose which the law deems charitable, and a trust for such purpose which the law will enforce. The law does not deem a purpose charitable if it be for the benefit of donor, or of any particular persons, donees. Thus the chauntries were not charities, being for the benefit of the souls of donors; nor are the parish churches so, because, though for the general benefit of the people, their endowments are estates absolute and not held on trust. Hence

---

(*a*) See the Statutes of Mortmain, 18 Edw. III. c. 3, and 15 Rich. II. c. 5.
(*b*) 33 Hen. VIII. c. 10.

the Charitable Trusts Act does not except parochial churches from its operation, for they do not come within its definition of charities; but property held in trust for the *augmentation* of benefices would do so, (whence Queen Anne's Bounty is specially excepted), and so would property held by ecclesiastical persons or bodies in trust for others than themselves. Hence, as cathedral and collegiate churches sometimes hold part of their estates on such trusts, they are specially exempted, though cathedral and collegiate schools are not so. Hence, also, to cure any doubt that might exist, the last Charitable Trusts Act specially provides that the jurisdiction created shall apply to corporate bodies enjoying property for their own benefit solely or jointly with other persons or bodies politic. Such corporate bodies, as colleges not educational, and hospitals not eleemosynary, have been by various statutes suppressed (*a*); but the ancient charitable foundations still with few exceptions subsist(*b*). By the last of these statutes—suppressing colleges not educational, and chapels or chauntries, or endowments for the support of priests for the benefit of the *founders' souls*,—provision was made that the Crown might, by commission, found grammar schools and endowments for the maintenance of priests or preachers, or the relief of the poor; and such foundations or endowments are or ought to be still subsisting, and are *charities*. And though by statute 23 Hen. VIII. endowments (of *land*) on trusts for the use of

---

(*a*) 27 Hen. VIII. c. 28; 31 Hen. VIII. c. 13; 37 Hen. VIII. c. 4. This last alone affected *charitable* hospitals; and was scarcely in force a year.

(*b*) The 1 Edw. VI. c. 14, does not affect hospitals, and excepts colleges educational.

churches or chapels, or fraternities, &c., or foundations intended for the benefit of the donors' souls, are void; this does not extend to endowments *not* of land, or for the support of priests or ministers for the cure of souls and the administering the sacraments: purposes which are not personal, but general, and so charitable. Nor does it prevent endowments for any uses deemed in law charitable, as for schools, or for the relief of the poor and needy (*a*). And by statute 39 Eliz. c. 5, any subjects are empowered to erect and incorporate hospitals and other institutions, so that they be charitable, *i. e.*, for the benefit not merely of those holding the estates, but of others (*b*), as the poor or the children of the poor (*c*), and may endow them with lands (*d*). By the 43 Eliz., the Statute of Charitable Uses, it was finally completely defined what those uses are which the law deems charitable, comprising hospitals, schools, and chapels, and endowments for their support, or the support of masters, ministers, &c. (*e*), and for which any persons or bodies corporate may hold property in trust, as charities, under the protection and government of the Court of Chancery and the Commissioners of Charities.

Thus, then, there are now subsisting charities corporate and un-incorporate; educational colleges or schools, whether free grammar schools or endowed

---

(*a*) Porter's Case, 1 Coke, 24.
(*b*) As in the case of Sutton's Hospital, the Charter House, 10 Coke, 24.
(*c*) See the 21 James 1, c. 1; and see 7 & 8 Wm. 3.
(*d*) By deed executed 12 months, and enrolled 6 months before death, 7 Geo. II. c. 36.
(*e*) So that the endowments of land are by licence and by deed, *ut suprà*.

free schools for the children of the poor; hospitals for the aged, the sick, or the poor; and endowments in aid of churches, chapels, or religious or charitable purposes, held either by corporate or other persons on trust for such purposes.

There are, first, the ancient hospitals and educational colleges, and other corporate charities, existing before the suppression statutes; there are the grammar schools and other foundations erected by the Crown, or subjects under royal charter, *since* those statutes; and there are also endowments held by persons or bodies corporate or *not* corporate, on trust for charitable purposes.

As regards foundations of the suppressed class, if they are still in the hands of the Crown or corporate bodies for charitable purposes, either not having been alienated by the Crown (*a*), or granted by the Crown on trust for such purposes (*b*), the Crown has the power of enforcing their due application to charitable purposes (*c*). In the case of corporate bodies holding such lands by grant or charter from the Crown, for charitable purposes, still, though the Limitation Acts would bar the right of the charities as to lands they had *lost*, it should seem that no length of time would bar a suit by the Attorney-General on behalf of the Crown, to enforce the due administration of the charities (*d*).

(*a*) *At.-G.* v. *Boston,* 1 De Gex & Smale, 519.
(*b*) *At.-G.* v. *Trevelyan,* 16 L. J., Ch., 54.
(*c*) *At.-G.* v. *Ironmongers' Company,* 12 Cl. & Fin. 908; *At.-G.* v. *Corporation of Newark,* ibid, 403; *At.-G.* v. *Lady Peyton's Hospital,* 14 L. J., Ch., 129; *At.-G.* v. *Wyggeston Hospital,* 12 Beav.
(*d*) *At.-G.* v. *St. Magdalen's College,* 23 L. J., Ch. 844.

As by statute 39 Eliz. subjects had power to erect hospitals which were thereby incorporated, and before then subjects might do so by licence from the Crown, any hospital even established *before* then may be presumed to have been rightfully and lawfully established, although no deed can be found relating to it, nor any evidence of enrolment, nor of any letters-patent, nor of any common seal the usual legal evidence of incorporation (*a*). The very object of the first Statute of Charitable Uses was the recovery of these ancient hospitals (*b*), and many were so recovered. The fact that at any time such hospital *existed* is *primâ facie* proof that it *exists*, as there is no period of limitation as against a charity. And therefore they are always, it should seem, fit subjects for inquiry by the Commissioners of Charities.

Free grammar schools likewise are, or ought to be, subsisting; and cathedral, collegiate, and chapter schools are not exempted from the operation of the Act. And though grammar schools, excepting the great schools of Eton, Harrow, &c., are under the Grammar Schools Act (3 & 4 Vict. c. 77), they are not the less, *including* those schools, under the operation of the Charitable Trusts Act.

The chartered foundations, hospitals, or grammar schools usually have provision made for their regulation by governors or trustees, and there is a visitatorial jurisdiction over the governors or trustees, either in the Crown, the bishop, or the patron, whether a corporate body or person, or the heirs of the

---

(*a*) *Simpson* v. *Wilkinson*, 7 Man. & Gr. 50.
(*b*) *Lady Peyton's Hospital*, 14 L. J., Ch., 129; *At.-G.* v. *Wyggeston Hospital*, 12 Beav.; *At.-G.* v. *Pretyman*, 4 Beav. 462.

founder (*a*). But they are not the less trusts under the protection and jurisdiction of the Court of Chancery (*b*).

Where there is a visitor, his power of visitation extends to the internal management, the dismissal of officers, and the disputes between the members, though not to adverse claims by or against the charity (*c*).

And where, though there is a local visitor as to the management of the charity, there is a trust as to the application of the funds, the Crown has jurisdiction in Chancery over that trust (*d*).

The proper performance of the spiritual duties of any officer in a charity of a spiritual character (as the chaplain of a school) is a matter for the jurisdiction of the visitor (*e*), not of the Court of Chancery. And where a person in holy orders has an endowed lectureship, though that is a charity, he is still in his spiritual duties under the control of his ordinary (*f*). The mere fact that a chaplain in holy orders is master of a hospital does not make it, however, a spiritual foundation, so as to place it wholly under spiritual visitation; and the general control of the revenues will be in Chancery (*g*). Where the relation of trustee and *cestui que trust* exists even between a corporation lay or spiritual, as a dean and chapter, or a college and any of its officers or members, the Court

---

(*a*) At.-G. v. *Catherine's Hall*, 4 Term. Rep. 243.
(*b*) At.-G. v. *Lubbock*, C. P. C., 15.
(*c*) At.-G. v. *Windham*, Cooper's Rep.
(*d*) *Ex parte Berkhampstead School*, 2 Vesey & Beames.
(*e*) At.-G. v. *Smythies*, 1 Keen's Rep. 289; 2 My. & Cr. 135; *Holdsworth* v. *Fairfax*, 3 Cl. & Fin. 115.
(*f*) At.-G. v. *Brown's Hospital*, 19 L. J., Ch., 73.
(*g*) At.-G. v. *St. Cross Hospital*, 22 L. J., Ch. 793.

of Chancery will interpose; otherwise, as in the case of the master of a cathedral or college grammar school, merely having a stipend out of the common fund, the jurisdiction is in the visitor (*a*).

Thus the due internal administration of the charity as it exists is a matter for the visitatorial jurisdiction (*b*); but the protection of the funds and their due application is under the general control of the Court of Chancery (*c*).

Hence the Charitable Trusts Act, which declares its scope to be the due administration of charitable trusts, and for the more beneficial application of charitable funds, in cases where the Court of Chancery may exercise jurisdiction, does not exempt hospitals and schools having visitors, although, like the Grammar-Schools Act, it recognises the visitatorial jurisdiction where it exists within its true scope—the internal management. As to that, there was no necessity for the exemption, as it is implied; as to anything beyond, there is no exemption, and all charitable foundations, corporate or not, are subject to the general jurisdiction of Chancery.

So, although the Charitable Trusts Act exempts the universities, and colleges thereto belonging, this does not extend to charities of which they are trustees, but only to the property they hold as their own:

(*a*) *At.-G.* v. *St. Mary Magdalen College*, 10 Beav. 412; *Whiston* v. *The Dean and Chapter of Rochester*, 18 L. J., Ch. 473.

(*b*) *At.-G.* v. *Dulwich College*, 4 Beav. 255. Harrow, Eton, Winchester, &c., are not exempted, but the jurisdiction of the Commissioners would not extend to their internal management. See *At.-G.* v. *Harrow School*, 2 Vesey, 551.

(*c*) *At.-G.* v. *Shrewsbury School*, 19 L. J., Ch., 287, 1 Macn. & Gord. Rep.; *At.-G.* v. *Brown's Hospital*, 19 L. J., Ch.; *At.-G.* v. *Sherborne Grammar School*, 24 L. J., Ch., 74.

any property held by any corporate body for charitable uses, as to which, or the *administration of the revenues or property* whereof, the Court of Chancery has or may exercise jurisdiction, is within the operation of the Charitable Trusts Act, and under the jurisdiction of the Commissioners of Charities.

The Charitable Trusts Act, 1853, contains an express exception of chapels or buildings registered and *bonâ fide* used as places of meeting for religious worship; and the amended Act of 1855 contains a similar exemption, which only applies to the places of worship of Dissenters (*a*), Jews (*b*), and Roman Catholics (*c*). But the definition of "Charity" in the principal Act clearly *includes* chapels, for which reason the *exemption* was inserted; and in the Roman Catholic Charities Act the *definition* is adopted without any exception. So that Roman Catholic chapels are under the Charitable Trusts Act. And even were it otherwise, the exception would not apply to gifts or bequests for the support of chapels or of priests, or of Roman Catholic religious worship or education.

But for the reasons above stated, the absence of the exemption (though probably a mistake) is not material, added to which only endowed chapels are within the Act, even when not exempted, and if partly supported by voluntary subscriptions, they are only within the Act as to the endowments. Therefore, if only supported by pew rents, or offerings at the doors, they are not within the Act — in the first case, not being charities; in the second, not being endowed charities.

(*a*) 15 & 16 Vict. c. 70; 18 & 19 Vict. c. 86.
(*b*) 9 & 10 Vict. c. 59.
(*c*) 2 & 3 Will. 4, c. 115.

Grammar Schools.

So with regard to the old grammar schools, founded chiefly for the teaching of Greek and Latin, there is a special Act (the 3 & 4 Vict. c. 77), making provision for any extension of these benefits which may be desirable: the patrons, visitors, and governors having no authority to establish any other system of education than is expressly provided for by the foundation, and the courts of equity being frequently unable to give adequate relief (*a*). But in this Act, even within its

---

(*a*) Whenever any question may come under consideration in *any court of equity* concerning the system of education thereafter to be established in any grammar school, or the right of admission into the same, whether such question be already pending, or *whether the same shall arise upon any information, petition, or other proceedings*, which may be now or at any time hereafter filed or instituted, for whatever cause the same may have been or may be instituted, according to the ordinary course of proceedings in courts of equity, or under the provisions of this Act, it shall be lawful for the court to make decrees or orders, as well for extending the system of education to other useful branches of literature and science in addition to or (subject to the provisions thereinafter contained) in lieu of Greek and Latin, or such other instruction as may be required by the terms of the foundation or of the then existing statutes, as also for extending or restricting the freedom or the right of admission to such school, by determining the number or the qualifications of boys who may thereafter be admissible thereto, as free scholars or otherwise, and for settling the terms of admission to or continuance in the same, and to establish such schemes for the application of the revenues of any such schools as may in the opinion of the court be conducive to the rendering or maintaining such schools in the greatest degree efficient and useful, with due regard to the intentions of the respective founders and benefactors, and to declare at what period and upon what event such decrees or orders, or any directions contained therein, shall be brought into operation, and that such decrees and orders shall have force and effect notwithstanding any provisions contained in the instruments of foundation, endowment, or benefaction, or in the then existing statutes: provided always, that in case there shall be any special visitor appointed by the founder, or other competent authority, opportunity shall be given to such visitor to be heard on the matters in question, in such manner as the court shall think

own scope—the establishment of new schemes—does not interfere with the jurisdiction of the Commissioners; on the contrary, as no application can be made to the Court of Chancery by any charity without their sanction, the provisions in the Grammar Schools Act are subordinate to those of the Charitable Trusts Act, which gives the Commissioners general powers as to new schemes for any charities.

Added to which the great grammar schools are exempted from the Grammar Schools Act (*a*) but *not* from the Charitable Trusts Act, which expressly provides that it shall not be deemed to exempt cathedral or collegiate schools.

Charities Municipal and Parochial.

Municipal corporations are often trustees of charities, either as such, or as separate bodies created by

---

proper, previously to the making of such decrees or orders.—C. 77, § 1.

Court of Chancery to have power to appoint mode of removing masters.—§ 17.

And in case of removal for incompetency from age, or other infirmity, governors, with the approbation of the visitor, may assign a pension.—§ 18.

Premises held over by masters dismissed, or ceasing to hold office, to be recovered summarily, as under the 1 & 2 Vict. c. 74.—§ 19.

Masters so dismissed, or ceasing to hold office, not to be permitted to question title of the trustees, &c.—§ 20.

Mode of Proceeding.]—Applications to court to be by petition—to be decided under the 52 Geo. 3, c. 101.—§ 21.

(*a*) *Saving of Rights.*]—Jurisdiction or power of ordinary not to be prejudiced; and the Act not to extend to the universities of Oxford or Cambridge, or to any college or hall within the same, or to the university of London, or any colleges connected therewith, or to the university of Durham, or to the colleges of St. David's or St. Bee's, or the grammar-schools of Westminster, Eton, Winchester, Harrow, Charter House, Rugby, Merchant Taylors', St. Paul's, Christ's Hospital, Birmingham, Manchester, or Macclesfield, or Louth, or such schools as form part of any cathedral or collegiate church—§ 24.

Construction of terms.—§ 25.

charter for the purposes of the charity; and the Municipal Corporations Act provided that "where the body corporate of any borough should stand seised of any estate or interest of any hereditament in trust for charitable uses, all their estate and powers in respect of such uses and trusts should continue in the persons who at the time of the passing of the Act were such trustees; and that the Lord Chancellor should make such orders as he should see fit for the administration subject to such uses and trusts of the trust estates." Under this Act the Lord Chancellor has power to appoint new trustees in lieu of those persons who were trustees at the time of the Act; but the provision in question applies, not to the legal estate, but the interest in the uses and trusts, and the legal estate would remain in the corporate body—at all events, where it had by a separate charter been created into another corporation for the purposes of the charity. Indeed it has been deemed doubtful whether the Act applies in such cases, as where a municipal corporation are made by another incorporation governors of a chartered hospital (a). Nor does the Act extend to charities of which the municipal corporation were only visitors (b), or as to which they have not the nomination, but only the approbation of trustees (c), nor as to which they have not the sole management but jointly with others (d). Where, however, the corporation is in substance identical with the trustees of the charity, the case comes within

---

(a) *Doe* d. *Governors of Bristol Hospital*, 11 M. & W. 913.
(b) *At.-G.* v. *Newbury*, 3 My. & K. 647
(c) *At.-G.* v. *Phillimore*, 9 L. J., Ch., 338.
(d) *In re Newark Charities*, 6 L. J., Ch , 216.

the provision of the Municipal Corporations Act (*a*). There is a provision in the Charitable Trusts Act of 1853, s. 65, that where the legal estate in the charity lands has not (in cases within the Municipal Act) been vested in trustees appointed by the Chancellor, it shall be so vested.

There are quasi corporations as to *parochial* charities. The 59 Geo. III. c. 12, s. 17, vests in the churchwardens and overseers of any parish lands and buildings for the purposes of the poor, and all other buildings and lands belonging to such parish. This Act vests the property in the churchwardens and overseers for the time being as a body, in the nature of a body corporate, and makes them *quasi* a corporation, for a particular purpose, of the care and management of the parish charity property; but it does not make them absolutely a corporation: and they still *act* as other bodies of persons not incorporate do; one or more acting for the others, but properly a majority for the whole (*b*). The Act, however, only applies to lands, &c., held *generally* on trust for the parish or its poor, not to lands held on *special* trusts of a parochial charity, as for repair of the church as well as the relief of the poor, or for binding poor children apprentices, &c., as well as generally for the relief of the poor; which, however, includes their instruction. Nor does it apply in cases of express trusts, as for the repair of the church and the relief of the poor, where there are trustees duly appointed under such trusts (*c*). Whoever are

---

(*a*) *At.-G.* v. *Mayor of Exeter,* 2 De Gex, Mac. & Gor. 507; *In re Northampton Charities,* 3 De Gex & Smale, 179.

(*b*) *Gouldsworthy* v. *Knight,* 11 M. & W. 337; *Ex parte Annesley,* 2 Y. & C. 356.

(*c*) *Re Paddington Charities,* 8 Sim. 620; *At.-G.* v. *Lewin,*

the trustees of course makes no difference as to the administration of the charity, nor the jurisdiction of Chancery or the Commissioners of Charities, who have special powers as to the framing of schemes, the appointment of trustees, and the apportionment of parochial charities.

Charities may be vested in any corporations, sole or aggregate, or vested in trustees, to be kept up by succession by the Court of Chancery. Hence, the Act defines "trustees" to mean any persons or corporations holding estates in trust or for the benefit of any charity.

There are no corporate persons, except the incumbents, chapters, and bishops of the Established Church, who are corporations, sole or aggregate, with perpetual succession, and can take, therefore, charitable trusts in their ecclesiastical character (a).

It is otherwise of Roman Catholic ecclesiastics, who, even in Ireland and apart from the Ecclesiastical Titles Act, have no legal *status*, nor any corporate character or succession (b), so that endowments for them and their successors can only take effect by means of trusts in equity; and so of all other religious bodies. Nor can there be any trusts for a *succession* of persons for purposes which the law does not recognise as charitable. Therefore neither the Roman Catholic nor any other clergy can take or hold property, except either solely for their own personal benefit, or under trusts for such purposes as are in law charitable; and they and all other persons

---

ibid. 366. *Churchwardens of St. Nicholas, Deptford,* v. *Sketchley,* 8 Q. B. 394; *At.-G.* v. *Blizard,* 25 L. J., Ch. 171.
(a) *Hopkinson* v. *Ellis,* 5 Beav. Rep. 34.
(b) *At.-G.* v. *Power,* 1 Ball & Beatty's (Irish) Rep. 145.

or bodies not incorporated can only take or hold property for religious purposes as individuals, and under charitable trusts. Other corporations than those of the Established Church are the creations of the Crown, either by charter under its prerogative, or with the assent of Parliament, as in the instance of the Commissioners of Queen Anne's Bounty, specially exempted from the Act. Except that ancient body and the Incorporated Societies for the Propagation of the Gospel, for Church Building, and the Sons of the Clergy, there are few *corporate* charities of modern foundation.

Religious or Charitable Societies.

It is only by a system of trusts and succession of trustees that permanence can be secured to any society or body not corporate, and which cannot have perpetual succession, in a legal sense; that is, as a legal incident or attribute of its nature.

There are many bodies, societies, institutions, or foundations of a charitable or religious nature, some of which are incorporated, and others not so—partly or chiefly supported by voluntary subscriptions, or endowments therefrom, as Queen Anne's Bounty, incorporated, but specially exempted from the Charitable Trusts Act; the Society for the Propagation of the Gospel in Foreign Parts, which also is incorporated, and is *not* exempted from the Act. Where these bodies are incorporated, they take as corporate bodies all gifts or bequests to their general funds, and in aid of their general purposes (a), and the Court of Chancery does not exercise its charitable

---

(a) See 39 Eliz. c. 5, allowing subjects to erect hospitals. *Vide At.-G.* v. *Corporation of Newcastle*, 5 Beav. 307.

jurisdiction over the application of such gifts, but merely directs the payment thereof to such body or society (*a*). Where, however, there is a gift or bequest to a body of persons having no corporate character, for *permanent* charitable purposes, the court will exercise its jurisdiction in directing the application of the fund, unless it is given *generally* and without any special directions as to its application (*b*). Where it is so given generally to a body or institution already established, the court will order it to be paid over thereto, without any directions as to its application (*c*), the *discretion* as to the application being in such cases confided by the constitution of the society or institution to the governing or managing body thereof, of which the donor must be supposed to have been aware, and which he has not at all fettered or withdrawn. But societies or institutions are not charitable, and so not within the Act, unless they are for the benefit of others than the subscribers or members; and hence donations to or endowments for them do not constitute charitable foundations, over which the Court of Chancery exercises its charitable jurisdiction, although it exercises *jurisdiction* as in all other cases in which questions of equitable right may arise. For a charity must be for the benefit of other than the donors. Thus endowments for support of chauntries or maintenance of priests for the benefit of souls of the donors and their children never were, are not, and never could be considered as

---

(*a*) *The Society for the Prop. of Gospel* v. *At.-G.*, 3 Russ. 142; *Corp. of Sons of Clergy* v. *Mose*, 9 Sim. 616.
(*b*) *Wellbeloved* v. *Jones*, 1 Sim. & St, 40.
(*c*) *Walsh* v. *Gladstone*, 1 Ph. 29.

charities. So, on the same principle, a private chapel(*a*), merely for the donor and his family, would not be considered a charitable foundation (*b*), although, if for the use of the persons on an estate, or even household, it might be so (*c*). On the same principle, a Dissenters' chapel, supported by pew rents, is not a charitable institution, for it is only for the benefit of the subscribers or pew-holders (*d*). So of any friendly societies; so that it was hardly necessary to except them from the operation of the Charitable Trusts Act. But, on the other hand, as it matters not from what source the fund which constitutes an endowment may come, if it is charitable, that is for the benefit of others than the donors (or any *particular* donees), funds supplied from the gifts of the Crown, of the legislature, or of private persons, for any purpose beyond their *own* benefit may be charitable endowments or foundations (*e*). Thus poor-schools, aided or established by grants from Parliament, *combined* with voluntary subscriptions, would be charities, under the jurisdiction of the Court of Chancery and the Commissioners of Charities.

It is to be observed that the Charitable Trusts Act, although it defines charities to be endowed foundations or institutions for charitable purposes, applies to all such charities, or the property, funds, or incomes thereof, *i.e.*, the charitable foundations, and the gifts or bequests thereto. But it declares that the Act is not to extend to any institution or society

---

(*a*) *Herbert* v. *Westminster*, 1 P. Wms. 774.
(*b*) *Ex parte Pearson*, 6 Price, 214.
(*c*) *Bristowe* v. *Bristowe*, 5 Beav.
(*d*) *Milligan* v. *Mitchell*, 4 L. J., Ch., 281.
(*e*) *At.-G.* v. *Heeles*, 2 Sim. & St. 17.

for religious or other charitable purposes wholly maintained by voluntary contributions; and where the institution is maintained partly by voluntary contributions aud partly by endowments, the Act is only to extend to the income from endowments; nor as to that or any donation or bequest thereto, if merely formed out of the general funds, and not from a donation or bequest of which any special application or appropriation is declared or directed by the donor. The jurisdiction of the Commissioners, therefore, extends to such institutions as are not wholly supported by voluntary subscriptions, and from these they are entitled to demand accounts of income, in order to see what portions are endowments derived from donations for special purposes, and what are not. They would have such jurisdiction over all chapels which are not entirely supported by pew-rents or voluntary subscriptions, were not Dissenters' chapels excepted. Roman Catholic chapels are not in terms exempted; they, as is well known, are always in part supported by the offerings of the congregations, so that it is only their endowments which come under the operation of the Act. And poor-schools, if endowed, are, *quoad* their endowments, whether derived from grants of Parliament or private donations, in the same position.

Of the Creation of Charitable Trusts.

Whether, however, for bodies corporate or unincorporate, or for private individuals, the Court will not carry into execution any other uses as charitable, than those which it deems so; and as it will not recognise any trusts which it cannot carry into execution, it will treat all others as void; and thus, if the donor has meant to execute such a trust, and has failed to do so, or if it be doubtful whether he has done so, as he has thus indicated, that the gift was not for the donee's personal benefit, the gift fails altogether, and the property passes to the heir, or next of kin, as the case may be (*a*); for it is a principle of law and equity that the heir is not to be disinherited but by *clear* declarations of intention, as he takes by virtue of a legal right, not to be displaced by a doubtful or invalid trust, which the courts will not carry into execution.

Now, the Statute of Charitable Uses declares such uses to comprise gifts for relief of aged, poor, and impotent persons; hospitals for the sick, support of orphans, marriages of poor maids, help of persons decayed, &c.; for the maintenance of schools and learning, free schools, and scholars in universities, &c.; and for the repairs of churches. The interpretation put upon this last use has extended it to gifts for the support of churches or chapels, or of preachers or ministers of religion, or of divine service, whether of the Church of England, Dissenters, or Roman Catholics. These are the charitable uses recognised in Chancery —religious, educational, and eleemosynary.

The gift or bequest may be to any class mentioned in the statute, as widows and orphans (*b*), or for any purposes within its scope, as hospitals or chapels; for the benefit of persons occupying a particular office or character (as that of schoolmaster, or minister, preacher, or teacher) exercised for the benefit

---

(*a*) *Vesey* v. *Jamison*, 1 Sim. & S. 69; *Ommaney* v. *Butcher*, 1 Turner & Rees, 290.
(*b*) *At.-G.* v. *Consher*, 2 S. & S. 93.

of others (*a*). Having this element, they may either be local or general, *i. e.*, the gift may be for the poor generally (*b*), or for the poor in an estate, district, or parish (*c*) ; and the field of application divides local charities into parochial or municipal. If general, any description of a class of poor is sufficient, as poor housekeepers, poor widows, poor Jews, poor priests or preachers, or schoolmasters, or the like; but to a man's poor relations, would be doubtful, as it would be construed to mean his next of kin, who are certain persons ascertained or ascertainable at a particular time ; and a gift for the relief of any among specific persons as may need it is not a charity, but simply a gift or legacy (*d*). The gift, if to persons, must either be to any class of persons mentioned in the statute, or included in its interpretation, or for any foundation or institution for their relief ; or it may be to the persons holding for the time being any office or character recognised by the statute or its interpretation, which includes augmentations of livings, endowments of curacies, lectureships, or for the support of priests, preachers, or the like.

Not only are gifts for any such purposes specially mentioned, valid charitable trusts, but general gifts for religious or charitable purposes so described, or for religion, or charity, or education, whether or not the particular objects of application are left to the discretion of the donee. If a trust is created but is not expressed effectually, the court will carry it out (*e*) ;

(*a*) Thus a bequest to support a schoolmaster is or may be in effect the same as to support a school.
(*b*) *Nash* v. *Morley*, 5 Beav. 177.
(*c*) *Bristow* v. *Bristow*, 5 Beav. 289.
(*d*) *Lilley* v. *Hayes*, 1 Hare, 58.
(*e*) *At.-G.* v. *Wilson*, 3 My. & K. 362 ; *Martin* v. *Maugham*, 13 L. J., Ch., 392.

but if the person taking has a discretion *whether to make the application or not,* it is an absolute gift and not a trust. So a gift for such purposes as the donee shall think fit, that is an absolute gift (*a*). But if a testator directs that property is to be employed in charity (*b*) or charitable purposes (*c*), even at the discretion of donee, these will be valid trusts, and they will be enforced and take effect. But again, if he directs his trustees to apply funds for such benevolent, charitable, and religious purposes they in their discretion think most advantageous and beneficial, the bequest will be held void for uncertainty; and as it is doubtful what the trust was to be, but plain that the donees were not to take beneficially, the *gift* is deemed to fail, as it is upon a *trust* that fails; and the property passes to the next of kin (*d*). So where a testator declared his will to be that his executors should apply certain personal property to such charitable *or other* purposes as they should think fit, without being accountable to any person whatsoever for such their disposition thereof, it was held too uncertain to be a charitable legacy, and not sufficiently extensive to give the donee the beneficial interest, so that the residuary legatee was declared entitled (*e*). So if the gift is declared to be *for any* specific purpose not for donee's own benefit, and that purpose fails for invalidity, then the property passes to the next of kin or residuary legatee (*f*).

(*a*) *Paice* v. *The Archbishop of Canterbury,* 14 Vesey, 370.
(*b*) *Legge* v. *Asgill,* 1 Turner, 265.
(*c*) *At.-G.* v. *Fletcher,* 5 L. J., Ch., 25; *Baker* v. *Sutton,* 1 K. 224.
(*d*) *Horde* v. *Earl of Suffolk,* 2 Myl. & K. 59; *Williams* v. *Kershaw,* 5 Clark & Fin. 111; *Stubbs* v *Sargon,* 5 K. 255.
(*e*) *Ellis* v. *Selby,* 1 Mylne & Craig, 286.
(*f*) *Pettingall* v. *Pettingall,* 11 L. J., Ch., 176; *Crockett* v. *Crockett,* ibid. 279; 1 Hare, 451.

But a bequest for such religious or charitable objects as the donee may think fit, or to such religious bodies, societies, or purposes as he may please (*a*), is a valid charitable trust, for it *binds* him to apply the whole fund to such purposes; and though the *selection* is in his discretion, he has no discretion as to the application; and the Court, in such cases, though it will not interfere in the exercise of his discretion, will enforce its exercise, or if necessary frame a scheme for the due application of the fund (*b*).

Where a fund was left to trustees to be disposed of at their pleasure, whether for charitable or public purposes, or to any person or persons as they should think proper, it was held that the trust was too general, and could not be executed by the Court; and that the executors could not take beneficially, because it was given expressly on trust, so that the next of kin were entitled (*c*). So if the fund is left generally in trust to be applied at the donee's discretion, the gift is on trust, the trust is too vague, so the gift fails with the trust (*d*). But it is otherwise if there is a charitable purpose indicated, and the carrying of it out is left to the donee (*e*). The general principle of law and equity is that when a gift as trust fails for uncertainty, the fund passes to the heir or next of kin, who take by law whenever there is no valid gift away from them (*f*). For which reason, even on a distinct bequest to executors, it must appear on the will that

---

(*a*) *Baker* v. *Sutton*, 1 Keen, 24.
(*b*) *Townsend* v. *Carus*, 3 Hare, 257.
(*c*) *Vesey* v. *Jamison*, 1 S. & S. 69.
(*d*) *Williams* v. *Kershaw*, 5 Cl. & F. 111.
(*e*) *Miller* v. *Rowan*, 5 Cl. & F. 99.
(*f*) *Johnson* v. *Johnson*, 4 Beav. 318.

they were to take beneficially or they will be deemed to take in trust for the next of kin (*a*). And a request to give handsome gratuities to them will be void for uncertainty (*b*), while a specific bequest will rebut any inference of an intention to give them the residue beneficially (*c*). And on a gift for charitable purposes, the residue to a donee, on failure of the gift for charitable purposes, the residue goes to the heir (*d*). If there is a gift to a person filling a particular office, as pastor, schoolmaster, preacher, &c., expressed to be for the support of the office or charity, and there is no intention indicated of mere personal benefit, then any surplus beyond a reasonable support of the office will be for the charity.

The most difficult class of cases of this kind, however, are those in which there is an entire gift to donee with an object, or purpose for the gift which he is to execute, and which is not inconsistent with but involves some personal interest; the question arising whether this is an interest in the whole or only part; whether it is only a life interest, or whether the whole is taken absolutely and beneficially under some trust, however general and discretionary. In these cases the relation of the parties, or the character and position, or functions of the donee with reference to the objects of the gifts, or to their claiming to be beneficially interested, is an important element of judgment as to whether there is a trust; and thus it is that the office of executors ordinarily being that of trustee for next of kin or for residue, it

---

(*a*) *Lowe* v. *Gaze*, 8 Beav. 472.
(*b*) *Tupper* v. *Tupper*, 9 Sim. 503.
(*c*) *Whitaker* v. *Tatham*, 7 Bing. 628.
(*d*) *Jones* v. *Mitchell*, 1 S. & S. 290.

is presumed that any gift to them is on trust for those parties (*a*). So as to the relation of parent and child, where moneys are given to the parent that she may dispose of them for the *benefit* of the children, then she does not take it as absolute interest, but there is a trust for the children to some extent with a large discretionary power (*b*). The great test is, whether the *object* of the gift as indicated requires for its carrying out that there should be a *continuance* of the fund beyond the life of the first taker; for if so, it is obvious that to allow the first taker an absolute interest, *i. e.* a right to dispose of it, would be to defeat the object of the gift; and, on the other hand, if there be a purpose which the court has to provide for, there can be only a life interest, whether the property be real or personal. And in the case of the parent just mentioned, though the discretion is large, she would not be permitted to apply the whole fund to her own purposes, or to dispose of it without maintaining the children. Thus, therefore, where legacies are given to parents for their own benefit and their children, they take for their *lives* only, the fund being secured in trust for their children; and they having only the interest (*c*).

The principle is equally applicable to real estate and personal; for as to real estate given for the purpose of making a provision for others beyond the first taker, he only has a life interest (*d*), the general principle of law being that a gift of real property not *expressed* to

---

(*a*) *Lowe* v. *Gaze*, 8 Beav. 472.
(*b*) *Raikes* v. *Wood*, 1 Hare, 465.
(*c*) *Bain* v. *Lescher*, 11 Sim. 397.
(*d*) *Inderwick* v. *Inderwick*, 13 Sim. 612.

be in fee is only for life (*a*) ; and a general gift in trust is only for such an estate as is necessary for carrying out the trust (*b*) ; and it being also, a general rule of equity as to personalty, that when property of a perishable nature is given to be enjoyed by persons in *succession*, and the object can only be attained by converting the property into permanent annuities, and giving each person in succession the dividends of the fund (*b*), the great test is, what is the object or purpose of the gift as indicated by the donor ? If it is only the personal benefit of donee, he takes absolutely and wholly ; thus while a gift for the mere maintenance of a child is for life, if the whole construction is for his *benefit*, then he takes absolutely (*d*) ; but this can never be the case where there is a purpose other than his personal benefit, and which extends beyond his life. There it is obvious that, for the purposes of continuance, the fund must be preserved beyond his life, and out of his disposition, in order that the object of the gift may be carried into execution (*e*).

This is a principle equally applicable, whether the purpose is the support of a charity or of a family ; it equally in either case negatives an absolute gift for the absolute personal benefit of the first donee. Thus it is that gifts for the benefit of wife and children are construed trusts for the children (*f*); and thus upon the same principle a gift in *terms* absolute to trustees

---

(*a*) *Doe* d. *Sams* v. *Garlick*, 14 M. & W. 698.
(*b*) Apart from the 7 Wm. iv. & 1 Vict. c. 26.
(*c*) *Morgan* v. *Morgan*, 14 Beav. 72.
(*d*) *Somes* v. *Martin*, 10 Sim. 287.
(*e*) *Bayne* v. *Crowther*, 20 Beav. 400.
(*f*) *Moore* v. *Cleghorn*, 10 Beav. 423 ; *Crockett* v. *Crockett*, 17 L. J., Ch., 230.

is construed to be for the purpose on which the whole estate or fund is given; and if those purposes are to extend beyond the life of the first taker, it is deemed a gift on trust (*a*). It is a general principle that wherever the object of the donor requires permanence it shall be carried out as far as possible; there being this difference in favour of a charity, that whereas for the sake of a mere family perpetuity is not allowed, in cases of charity it is provided for by the Court of Chancery (*b*); and that on a gift for a general object, as the relief of poor members of a religious body, that indicating an intention for permanence, the intention is carried out by the fund being invested and directed to be held in trust, the *interest* only being paid to the objects of the charity (*c*). This indeed is the great distinction between a private legacy and a charity; for a bequest to particular persons, however numerous, and whether mentioned *nominatim*, or as a class, as next of kin or the like, is not a *charity*, since it requires no permanence, and so is not an *endowed* institution or foundation (*d*).

It is otherwise where there is an intention indicated that the disposition or enjoyment of the benefits should be kept up beyond the lives of the first takers; there if the purpose is beyond a family it is entitled to perpetuity as a valid charity. And it matters not whether the intention is indicated by expression or by clear implication, by the use of terms or by the declaration of a purpose, which cannot be carried out without permanence. Thus of course if a gift is

---

(*a*) *Miller* v. *Rowan*, 5 Cl. & Fin. 99.
(*b*) *Blagrove* v. *Hancock*, 16 Sim. 371.
(*c*) *Gregory* v. *At.-G.*, 2 Beav. 366.
(*d*) *Lilley* v. *Hayes*, 1 Hare 58.

to preachers or ministers and their *successors*, that involves permanence, and the fund is to be invested, and the successive donees only have the dividends (*a*) ; but the intention would be equally clear without the use of those words, if the object were declared to be to support and keep up divine worship or instruction. Whenever the intention is a prolongation of the benefits of the gift beyond the life of the first taker, and for purposes beyond his personal benefit, he takes only a life interest (*b*). And such a purpose requires in personalty investment of the fund in order to preserve it and place it under the control of the court: so that if a fund is to be invested for the use of a person and his children, that itself implies a trust ; and *e converso* if it is for such a purpose it ought to be invested, and any allusion to investment of property will on the same principle indicate a trust (*c*).

And, though when a fund has thus been invested for such a purpose the first taker may have the beneficial interest or the *income* for his life, subject only to a charge for the purposes of the gift (as the maintenance of children or the like), it must not be taken that in such cases he could appropriate even the *income* entirely to his own purposes without meeting such charges (*d*). The party to whom trustees are directed to pay the dividends is clearly bound to apply a competent sum to the object; and the court holds that the amount is capable of being ascertained,

---

(*a*) *At.-G.* v. *Goddard*, 1 Turn. & Russ. 348.
(*b*) *Middleton* v. *Gould*, 10 Beav. 527.
(*c*) *Mason* v. *Clarke*, 22 L. J., Ch., 956.
(*d*) *Hadow* v. *Hadow*, 9 Sim. 438 ; *Berkeley* v. *Swinburn*, 6 Sim. 613; *Brown* v. *Paul*, 20 L. J., Ch., 75.

and will compel the party to do what is right; so that, if the object of the gift be *neglected*, however large the *discretion* may be, he will be held answerable. And in such cases, as regards the *corpus* of the fund, if personal, the first taker is only a bare trustee; and if it is real property, he is only tenant for life. The court in such a case does not interfere with the exercise of a fair discretion as to the allocation of the fund to the benefit of the donee and the objects of the gift; but if the objects are disregarded, the court will compel the donee to provide for them; and for the purpose of securing the fund in cases of personalty, will direct it to be invested (*a*).

Where endowments are for support of preachers or lecturers, or of lectureships or preacherships, or the like, there is clearly a trust for religious ministers in such character or office, and therefore only applicable to them while in that character or office, generally, or in particular places. And even though the gift is in the first instance to particular preachers, &c., if it is indicated that it is also to be for the support or benefit of their successors in the same place, this will create a trust in the first takers, and give them only a life interest. All endowments for the support of dissenting or Roman Catholic worship, or of ministers or ecclesiastics in that character, are, and can only be, maintained and kept up as charitable *trusts*. As regards Protestant ministers, gifts or bequests to or for any specific ministers by name and not by office, and not pointed expressly to their official character, would be considered to be for their personal benefit, and so not

---

(*a*) *Hart* v. *Tribe*, 23 L. J., Ch., 462.

charitable. But the case of Roman Catholic ecclesiastics may in that respect be different on many accounts, and the gifts of funded or landed property even to *individual* ecclesiastics, if their ecclesiastical character is mentioned, may be construed to be for the support of them and their successors in that character, and so charitable trusts, in which they only have a life interest. Otherwise, not having direct heirs, the property would go on their decease to their more distant kindred, which could not be supposed to have been the intention of the donor (*a*).

Bequests, either for the support of chapels or congregations, the assistance of Dissenters, or for the support of Dissenting ministers and their successors, or of particular ministers and their successors, or for the support of the worship or education of any denomination of Dissenters—including Unitarians—are valid charitable trusts (*b*); and all means for the permanent support of any worship but that of the Established Church, are only charitable trusts, there being no corporations or corporate persons, or bodies, for such objects. Places of worship registered, *i. e.*, those of Dissenters (*c*), are excepted from the operation of the Charitable Trusts Act; but the endowments attaching thereto are not, and it is only the application of the endowments that come within the jurisdiction of Chancery, or of the Commissioners of Charities. Hence, although the Roman Catholic Charities Act

---

(*a*) *Greaves* v. *Cox*, 4 Bro. C. C.; *Thornber* v. *Wilson*, 24 L. J., Ch. 6647.

(*b*) *Shrewsbury* v. *Hornby*, 5 Hare, 406; *At.-G.* v. *Lawes*, 8 Hare, 32. So of Jews, *Strange* v. *Goldsmid*, 8 Sim. 614; but it is otherwise of gifts to enable persons to propagate opinions opposed to Christianity.

(*c*) 15 & 16 Vict. c. 70; *vide ante*, p. 9.

does not except chapels, the omission is of no practical importance.

With regard to Roman Catholic religious charities, all their endowments for religious purposes are Charitable Trusts, and until and except the *penal* laws (long since repealed) there was never any law against any such endowments if charitable. The Statute of 33 Henry VIII. c. 10, prohibits endowments for the support of particular services, or of priests to have the benefit of such services, *i. e.* for the donors' souls; and the statute 1 Edward VI. c. 10, suppressed all such existing endowments because not deemed charitable, being only for the benefit of the donors; and because also found subject to abuses, and deemed superstitious. But that very statute provides for the maintenance of priests; and the next year a statute was passed requiring the celebration of the "Lord's Supper, commonly called the Mass" (a); so that these laws were not nor are directed against endowments for the support of Roman Catholic worship in general (b), which is charitable.

The Roman Catholic Charitable Bequests Act, 2 & 3 Will. IV. c. 115, provides that "Roman Catholics, in respect of their schools, places for religious worship, education, and *charitable purposes*, and the property held therewith, and the persons employed in and about the same," *i. e.* priests or schoolmasters, "shall in respect thereof be subject to the same laws as Dissenters;" and there is a clause expressly doing away with the declaration against the sacrifice of the mass, *i. e.* the

---

(a) *La messe*, or "the supper:" *i. e.* the Roman Communion Service.
(b) *Breeks* v. *Woolfrey*, 1 Curt. Eccl. Rep. 880.

Roman liturgy, which is offered, as it in terms expresses, for living and dead ; gifts or endowments for the support of Roman Catholic *worship* (*a*), *places* of worship (*b*), or ministers of worship, are legal (*c*), and have accordingly been held to be so.

It is otherwise of gifts for the celebration of divine services for the souls of donors or their family, which would merely be for their personal benefit, and so, even if legal, would not be charitable. The Roman law lays down that, in order to avoid the taint of avarice or charge of simony, they are to be regarded as gifts for the maintenance of the priests (*d*), and as such they would be, according to the English law, charitable—the benefit being *general*, not special and personal. And if the donors had so regarded them, the object being permanent, and extending beyond the personal benefit or the life of particular ecclesiastics, the English law would recognise and could and would enforce such gifts as trusts for the support of priests or the maintenance of divine worship in general, according to the Roman Catholic liturgy, although it is offered for living and the dead; that alone not being by the English law, nor even in the view of the English Church, superstitious. But in the cases referred to, the donors have not so regarded them; and have declared, on the contrary, the object of the gift to be purely special and personal. This the English law deems not charitable; and even if it were,

---

(*a*) Though it is always in terms offered for the dead—*pro vivis et defunctis*.

(*b*) *De Windt* v. *De Windt*, 23 L. J., Ch., 776.

(*c*) Sacerdos non accipit pecuniam quasi pretium consecrationis encharistiæ, hoc enim simoniacum, sed quasi stipendium sustentationis.—S. Thomæ. II. 29, 110, art. 2, ad. 2.

(*d*) *Walsh* v. *Gladstone*, 1 Ph. 29 ; *At.-G.* v. *Gladstone*, 13 Sim. 7.

it would create a trust impossible for any human law to enforce, seeing that it is rested on the intention and application of particular services for the benefit of individuals. And the attempt to secure this by gifts for such services, not the services themselves, is deemed superstitious. In this view the Roman law is much more in accord with the English than is generally supposed; and though upon the view taken in common by both, that these gifts are in substance for the support of priests, they would hardly be prohibited by the Roman Church, they are to the utmost restrained; and they are no otherwise recognised than by the rules of moral theology, enforcing, as *against the ecclesiastics accepting them,* their rigid observance, which tends indirectly to limit them, by enhancing the weight of their obligation. The English law, upon the grounds above stated, and not having any means of dealing with the conscience, deeming it dangerous to allow of men's accepting pecuniary endowments upon trusts, their fulfilment of which no one can enforce, not only regards these gifts as not charitable, but condemns them as contrary to public policy, and, in the legal sense, superstitious; and as these gifts are avowedly not for the benefit of the donees, considers them to fail altogether. It is clear that they are intended as trusts, and not for the mere personal benefit of the donees; and hence, especially as they are usually coupled with bequests for alms to the poor, the Roman law regards them as trusts, taking care that the funds be not applied by clerics or laymen to their own private use. And though in countries where the Roman Catholic Church is established, and the law recognises the right of the Roman Catholic ecclesiastics to receive such gifts, the execution of these spiritual trusts is committed to the prelates of that Church, even there it is impossible that they can enforce them in any other way than by seeing that the funds are placed in proper hands for the purpose of application, either to distribution of alms or maintenance of divine services, or the support of pious and proper priests and ministers of divine worship; nor could they do that without the aid of the civil or secular law; added to which, in this country, the bishops themselves are often the recipients of such gifts. And in this country, the law, for the reasons above stated, does not allow ecclesiastics to take such gifts, the reasons being all the stronger in that by the canons of the Council of Trent the Roman Catholic bishops—themselves the chief recipients of such gifts—have power to commute such trusts for the very reason, on which, among others, the English law regards them as contrary to public policy; viz., their inevitable tendency to an accumulation of obligations likely to render performance impracticable (a), especially when, as is always more or less the object, the obligation imposed is perpetual.

For this reason, the decrees of the Council of Trent give the Roman Catholic bishops authority to commute such trusts (b), warning the faithful, at the same

---

(a) Thus no priest can, save on an emergency, and by special leave, celebrate more than once on the same day; and all bishops and priests having cure of souls are bound to offer for their flocks on all Sundays and holidays; and the same service will not satisfy more than one obligation. Thus Innocent XII., "Omne damnabile lncrum ab ecclesia removere volens, prohibit sacerdoti qui missarum suscepit celebrandum, cum certa eleemosyna, ne eamdem missam alteri parte ejusdem eleemosynæ sibi retenta celebrandum committat." See on the whole subject Benedict XIV., *De sac. missæ*.

(b) Contingit sæpe in quibusdam ecclesiis vel tam magnum missarum celebrandum numerum ex variis defunctorum relictis impositum esse, ut illis pro singulis diebus a testatoribus præ-

time, of their tendency not only to an inconvenient accumulation of obligations, but to abuse, to avarice, to simony, or superstition (*a*), and especially warning them against reliance on any particular *number* of divine services (*b*), and to understand whence and from whom it is that the value of the efficacy of divine services must be derived (*c*), and denouncing as simony the celebration of such services for the *sake* of stipend or reward (*d*), plainly indicating the danger of superstition; not, indeed, in the object (which the law of England and of Rome alike recognise), but in the particular mode adopted for attaining it; and in imagining

---

scriptis nequeat satisfieri vel eleemosynam hujusmodi pro illis celebrandis adeo tenuem esse, ut non facile inveniatur qui velit huic se muneri subjicere, unde depererunt præ testantium voluntates, et eorum conscientias ad quos prædicta spectant onerandi occasio datur, sancta synodus, cupiens hæc ad pios usus relicta quo plenius et utilius potest impleri, facultatem dat episcopis, ut in synodo . . . possint statuere circa hæc quicquid magis ad Dei honorem et cultum atque ecclesiarum utilitatem viderunt expedire ita tamen ut eorum semper defunctorum commemoratis fiat qui pro suarum animarum salute legata ea ad pios usus reliquerunt.

(*a*) Quum igitur multa irrepsisse videantur quæ a tanto sacrificii, aliena sunt—decerunt—ut episcopi ea omnia prohibere quæ vel avaritia vel superstitio, veræ pietatis falsa imitatrix, induxit," "quod ad avaritiam pertinet cujusvis generis mercedem conditiones pacta et quicquid *pro missis novis celebrandis* datur; nec non importunas atque et illiberales eleemosynarum exactiones potius quam postulationes, atque hujusmodi quæ a simoniaca labe vel certe a turpe quæstu non longe absint, omnino prohibeant.

(*b*) Ne *superstitionis* locus aliquis detur, caveant, &c. quorundam vero *missarum certum numerum* qui magis a superstitioso cultu quam a vera religione inventus est, omnino ab ecclesia removeant."

(*c*) "Doceant populum quis sit, et a quo, potissimum proveniat sanctissimi hujus sacrificii tam pretiosis ac celestis fructus."—Ibid. "Quamvis virtus Christi quæ continetur sub sacramento sit infinita tamen determinatus est *effectus* ad quem illud sacramentum ordinatur.—St. Thom. 24, dist. 45, 9, 2; art. 4, 9, 3; ad. 2. And to that, "Sacerdotes quanto digniores fuerint tanto facilius pro quibus clamavit exaudiuntur."—Pope Alexand. I, can. 91, c. 1.

(*d*) Est simonia temporale dare pro spirituali non solum quando temporali datur tanquam pretium, sed etiam tanquam *motivum* conferendo vel efficiendi spirituali. Decretum Innocent. XII.

that to offer money to priests to celebrate divine services, or offer prayers for the donors, is so likely to obtain it, as simply to provide for the celebration of divine services along with other charitable works, leaving the celebration of such services to their spontaneous piety or charity. There is the obvious distinction between these endowments and endowments for those which the Roman law insists on regarding as their legitimate objects, viz., the support of ministers or places of worship: that there the gift is not necessarily made conditional on the actual celebration of divine services; whereas in the former they *are*, and so are open to the possible danger on one side of simony, and on the other of superstition.

It is to be observed that the modern endowments for the object alluded to are far more open to danger of those abuses, temptation to avarice and simony, than those which existed in ancient times. For in the ancient endowments, as chauntries, the donation or foundation was not to the priest, who offered the divine services, the selection of whom was the subsequent act of the donor or founder, or his heirs; and upon the presentation of a priest to a foundation already established and existing, he became legally entitled to it, and could not be deprived of it, except for *a total cesser* of divine services. So that there was little danger of suspicion that these foundations had been induced by promises of such services, or of the divine services being rendered for the sake of receiving the stipend—he having a legal estate independent of the celebration of any particular services, and at liberty to celebrate as often as piety might dictate. But in the modern endowments, funds or estates are left to ecclesiastics for the sake of special divine services, and, as to laymen, in trust or with a request to secure the benefit of such services: and in either case there is the appearance of holding out money as the *motive* of the services, and the services are regarded as the consideration for the money, whereas if the money received were simply for the support of the priest or place of worship, without any such request, condition, or stipulation, any services or prayers offered by the recipients of the donor's bounty, would be offered from motives of gratitude and with those feelings of piety and charity which influence the prayers of the faithful in general. And the Court of Chancery can only alter the disposition of the property, and cannot affect or interfere with the effects of those motives of piety or charity.

It is not surprising, therefore, that, even before the separation from Rome, by the legislature (*a*), and since then by our Courts, these endowments should have been deemed superstitious; and although in Roman Catholic countries, where the Roman Catholic Church is established, the bishops of that Church alone have the power of commuting such trusts, the law giving the funds absolutely to their disposition; in this country, on the contrary, they having no legal status, and taking these funds only on condition of their submission to the jurisdiction of Chancery, it is for that Court to commute these trusts into such as it can recognise and execute, *i.e.*, into charitable trusts.

A charitable trust, in the view of the Court of Chancery, to which it will lend its power to confer a perpetuity, is one which is for the benefit of *others*

(*a*) 31 Hen. viii. c. 10. "Vain opinions of masses satisfactory, and abuses of chauntries and trentals"—a *particular number* of masses. 1 Ed. vi., c. 14. *Vide* p. 34, note (*b*).

than the donor or his family, and is not merely for personal but *general* objects. So that whether or not these endowments are superstitious, they are certainly in that sense not charitable, and are not considered so by the Roman law, save as endowments for the support of priests. But if the donor does not give them that character, but manifests his own intention to be merely his own benefit, the English law will not take that view of them, but viewing them according to the intention of the donor declares them not charitable gifts entitled to the privilege of perpetuity.

Thus, where the will bequeathed certain sums to the ministers of certain Roman Catholic chapels, to have the benefit of their prayers, the *remainder* to be appropriated to " promote the knowledge of the Catholic religion," the Lord Chancellor, while holding the latter bequest valid, held the former to be void; because " the sums given to the priests were not intended for the benefit of the priests personally, *nor* for the support of the chapels for general purposes, but were given for the benefit of their prayers :" *i. e.*, not to benefit the priests, nor to support the chapels, but to secure a supposed benefit for the testatrix herself (*a*). And it is impossible not to see that this was so (*b*) ; and that therefore those bequests were not valid charitable bequests (*c*).

(*a*) *West* v. *Shuttleworth*, 2 Mylne & Keen, 697.

(*b*) Else, how was it that the *remainder* was expressly dedicated for the support of the Catholic religion ? Plainly implying that the previous bequests were *not* so. Had the testatrix simply given all the money to support the Catholic worship, she would have secured both objects every whit as well so far as the substance was concerned.

(*c*) That this was the real ground of the decision is shown by the later case, where a bequest for the use of Roman Catholic priests in and near London, was upheld (*At.-G.* v. *Gladstone*,

In such cases, there being an entire gift for an object, and coupled with a request for a use which, if granted, would create a trust, that object being invalid, vitiated the whole gift. Supposing it valid, there would arise a trust, even supposing the sum too small for an endowment, by the gift to an ecclesiastic; for he would be bound to find a fitting place in which to offer the divine services requested; and, supposing the sum large enough for an endowment, and even supposing it only large enough to afford a reasonable stipend for one priest, there would be indicated an intention for an object requiring permanence, and therefore there would be a trust to *invest* the fund, on the principle already elucidated. If the fund were more than large enough for the finding of a reasonable stipend for more than one priest, there would be a necessity to find others fit to discharge the sacred duties of the trust, and pay them their proportions of the dividends or rents accruing from the investment. All this could and would be done by the Court of Chancery, supposing the object were merely the support of ministers or places of divine worship; but the actual celebration of divine service, coupled with a special application, it could not execute; nor could or ought any court, civil or ecclesiastic; and it must be left to the devotion or gratitude, or conscience, of the ecclesiastics, with the warning above alluded to—

---

13 Simons' Rep. 7). There, the *object* was clearly the support of the *priest* (as such) and the support of Catholic worship, although who can doubt that practically, though incidentally, the benefit of their religious services was acquired ? So in *Heath* v. *Chapman*, 23 L. J., Ch., 950, though some expressions *obiter*, point to the supposed superstitiousness of prayers for the dead, the real ground of the decision is as above stated.

not to celebrate the services for the sake of the stipend. The court therefore not being able to carry out what is declared by the donor to be the object of his gifts, cannot recognise the trusts, and the gifts being *upon* trusts, the gifts failed with the trusts.

That being so, the Roman Catholic Charities Act provides, " that no gift or disposition on any lawful or charitable Roman Catholic trust shall be invalid, by reason that the same estate or fund is also subjected to a trust deemed to be superstitious ; but the Court of Chancery or the Commissioners of Charities may apportion the estate or fund, so that a proportion of it may be subject to the lawful or charitable trusts declared, and the residue, to such lawful charitable trusts as the Court or Commissioners may consider most just." The effect of which is, that the Court or Commissioners may declare the trusts to be, either in the hands of the present holders alone, or along with others, to be for the very objects which the Roman law regards as their own legitimate objects ; the only ones which any law can enforce the application of at all, viz., the support of places or ministers of the Roman Catholic worship.

As already shown, these gifts, whether to ecclesiastics or laics, are trusts, in substance, for support of divine services and the ministers thereof, because, though general in terms, the request for divine services indicates *that* as the great object, and negatives the object of mere personal benefit of the donors. Although, when the donee is an ecclesiastic, he will be entitled to a *primary* interest (not beyond his own life—the object being permanent) to the extent at least of a reasonable maintenance or stipend for the celebration of divine service, the residue, if any, being applicable to similar or other religious or charitable purposes, eleemosynary or otherwise. The possession or application of the fund will not therefore necessarily be altered, so far as any law can affect it; so that the ecclesiastic who now holds or receives the fund *may* be allowed still to retain it, the difference being that he will retain it so far his legal title goes, either as an endowment for his support as a minister of Roman Catholic worship, or for the maintenance of such worship, or his place of worship. The law does not, and no law could, interfere with such services as he may celebrate, still less with his motive or intention; but the law has done all in its power to enhance their purity, and therefore their value and efficacy, by doing what the donors *ought* to have done, *i.e.*, conferring the fund without any condition, and so providing that the services, if offered, shall be offered from the sole motives of piety and charity. It is not the object of the law to deprive the donors of the benefit of prayers offered from such motives; which the law, as already shown, deems lawful and laudable (a), but to free them from all taint of superstition or simony. And whatever may be the actual application of the fund, as it must be to *charitable* objects, and, on that express principle will doubtless be to *religious* objects, the donors must have the benefit of such prayers or services as *such* motives may inspire, and which alone are of any value. Nor is this all. For, not only will the law tend to enhance the purity and value of services

---

(a) *Breeks* v. *Woolfrey*, 1 Curt. Eccl. Rep. 880.

offered, but it will likewise tend to increase their number. Even where, from any particular donor, an ecclesiastic may have only a sum sufficient and reasonable as a stipend for his support, he may have similar endowments from others; or he may have from the same donor a far larger income than requisite for his own reasonable and sufficient support, in which case— supposing a *general* gift coupled with a general request for divine services—unless a specific sum is assigned to him by the disposer, or unless otherwise an intention is manifested to secure him the beneficed interest in the whole at least for his life, he will be deemed a trustee for the residue, which will be applicable on the same principle. It appears impossible that there can be an intention in such cases to give the beneficial interest in *any* part beyond the life of the first taker, for the *object* is permanent; and would be defeated by a power of alienation, or by its transmission to next of kin. It would be the duty of the first taker, on the principle already elucidated, to provide for the permanence of the endowment by investment, and this duty will be enforced by the Court or the Commissioners of Charities, in order to provide for the permanent application and distribution of the fund to such religious and charitable purposes as it can recognise and deal with upon the principle above explained.

By another clause in the Act, it is provided that where no document declares the trust, the consistent usage of twenty years shall be conclusive; and by another clause it is provided that the Act is not to "affect" any property held or enjoyed beneficially by any person adversely to such trust; *i.e.*, for his or their own use and benefit *against* and in denial of any obligation to apply it to any other purpose.

By the former of these clauses, if in the absence of a declaration of trust in any deed or document, the ecclesiastics who enjoyed the fund have been used for twenty years to celebrate divine services for the donors' souls, that will be deemed conclusive as to there being a *trust* so to do; but if there has been no settled usage for that period, the Board must frame a scheme, unless the case comes within the other provision as to adverse enjoyment; as to which it is to be observed that the *former* clauses does not apply to enjoyment adverse to a trust, but usage *showing* a trust (so that twenty years' beneficial enjoyment is not conclusive), and next, that the beneficial enjoyment to be "adverse" to a trust must be inconsistent with it; and it will not be so in the class of cases supposed, merely from its having been a beneficial enjoyment of the fund (for even in the case of a trust there may be a beneficial enjoyment for the life of the donee); but it must have been an enjoyment in the nature of an absolute dominion or ownership over the whole estate or fund, unaccompanied by any acts acknowledging an obligation to render any services whatever.

Where the gifts in question have been to ecclesiastics, as no outward act would indicate their offering of services for particular persons, and their enjoyment of the fund would be quite consistent with the existence of a trust for such services, there can scarcely have been an adverse enjoyment in the sense supposed. Where the gifts have been to laics, with requests (amounting to trusts) for securing such services, the appropriation of the fund to their own personal benefit would not be an adverse enjoyment within the meaning of the Act, but a fraudulent and wilful misappropriation. The meaning of adverse enjoyment, clearly and according to all legal analogy, is an enjoyment really and *bonâ fide* adverse; upon a sincere belief of right and title to an absolute beneficial ownership, free from any trusts or obligation of any kind.

Whether there has been such an adverse enjoyment, it is of course in each case for the Court or Commissioners to determine. And even where there has been, it may be a question whether the result of the provision that nothing in *the Act* shall affect it (*i. e.*, that the disposition shall not be applied to any charitable trusts) will not be that, the trust having failed, the heir or next of kin will take the property. The practical application of the law will probably not be much affected by the provision as to adverse enjoyment, for the enjoyment would be the same whether there were a trust acknowledged and acted on or not. Supposing there is really no request, secret or otherwise, for the benefit of divine services; and a mere intention to confer a personal and beneficial interest, without any condition or obligation, expressed or understood, then of course the law as to uses deemed superstitious does not apply at all: and the question whether there is any trust for other religious or charitable purposes depends on the construction of the document of gift, in connection with the circumstances of the parties and especially the ecclesiastical character of the donee. But where there is any trust, condition, or obligation, expressed or understood, it is scarcely probable that a Roman Catholic ecclesiastic will set up a beneficial enjoyment adverse to, *i.e.*, in defiance and disregard of such trust, condition, or obligation; which, whether for the uses deemed superstitious or not, the Roman law recognises as sacred and binding on the *donees;* and the breach of which would beyond all doubt at Rome be a ground for suspension or censure, and indeed, according to our own law, it is probable that it would be deemed fraudulent and wilful, and to entail a liability for restitution.

The only probable application of the clause as to adverse beneficial enjoyment will be in cases of gifts to ecclesiastics without any trust, condition, or obligation, express, implied, or understood. In such cases, however, if the ecclesiastic sets up a beneficial enjoyment as adverse, the question may arise whether it *can* be adverse, as the *enjoyment* would be the same, for his own life at least, whether there were a trust or not. And there may be a question whether a gift to an ecclesiastical person, who can have no direct heirs, and whose next of kin can scarcely have been intended to benefit, could be intended as an absolute gift, or for the support of him and his successors in his office, according to the principles already elucidated (*a*).

The law of the Roman Catholic Church is very strict in presuming that gifts or bequests to ecclesiastics are not for their own benefit, but for pious uses (*b*); and in the only class of cases in which gifts

---

(*a*) *Vide ante,* p. 25, and see *Thornber* v. *Wilson,* 24 L. J., Ch., 667.

(*b*) "Ut unus quisque presbyter res quos post dies consecrationis acquisivit propriæ ecclesiæ relinquat, inquirendum est si que Presbyterorum de reditibus ecclesiæ vel oblationibus vel votis fidelium, alieno nomine res comparavit; quia sicut nec suo ita nec alieno nomine Presbyter fraudem facere de facultatibus ecclesiaticis debet. De bonis per ecclesiam acquisitis clerici testari non possunt.

are likely to be made for their personal benefit, viz., by their penitents, their acceptance of such gifts have been forbidden. It is believed that by the law of all Roman Catholic countries, priests or ministers of religion are prevented from personally profiting by bequests of persons they attend (*a*), though the principle is also applied impartially to physicians, &c. In our own law there is no such prohibition, but the spirit of our courts of law and equity is strongly against such gifts, and they are regarded with great suspicion (*b*).

De bonis propriis vel acquisitis intuitu personæ clerici testari possunt: de acquisitis intuitu ecclesiæ non. Quod licet clerici de his quæ paternæ successionis vel cognationis intuitu, seu dono consanguineorum aut amicorum *non habito respectu ad ecclesiam*, pervenerunt ad ipsos libere disponere valeant, de his tamen quem consideratione ecclesiæ perceperunt, nullum de jure possunt facere testamentum."—Dec. Greg. Lib. iii. c. 9.

Sed considerandum est diligentur utrum testator leget hoc modo. Relinquo istud episcopo, an Relinquo istud ecclesiæ: vel Relinquo illud episcopo et ecclesiæ. In primo casu distinguendum est utrum relinquatur episcopo ab extraneo, an a propinquo. Si ab extraneo generaliter verum est, quod presumitur esse relictum intuitu ecclesiæ, non personæ; et hoc verum est nisi testator exprimat quod velit illud tantum esse episcopo, non ecclesiæ. Si vero relinquatur illud episcopo a propinquo, presumitur esse relictum non intuitu ecclesiæ sed personæ, nisi forté contrarium probatur. Quod si relinquatur episcopo, et ecclesiæ de illo canonica inter ipsos est diversio. Ilud enim est generalitur observandum circa eum, qui potest proprium possidere prelationem vel administrationem ecclesiæ non habentem; quod si ei aliquid specialiter relinquatur, non solum a propinquo verum etiam ab extraneo intelligitur esse relictum, non intuitu ecclesiæ sed personæ; nisi probatio in contrarium appareret.—Dec. Greg. Lib. iii. Tit. 26, c. 15.

(*a*) Thus by the law of France, "Les docteurs ou les pharmaciens qui auront traité une personne pendant leur maladie dont elle meurt, ne pourront profiter des dispositions entre vifs ou testamentaires qu'elle aurait faites, en leur faveur pendant le cours de cette maladie. *Les mêmes regles seront observées à l'égard du ministre du culte.*"—Code Civil. Liv. iii. Tit. ii. 909. And, although most persons think otherwise, this code was but a compilation from previous codes, showing the old law of France. And is so in other countries.

(*b*) If a clergyman or any person in the habit of imparting reli-

The statute does not mention gifts *wholly* for the uses deemed superstitious, and only mentions gifts partly for such uses and partly for charitable objects; but in point of fact such gifts are never made *simpliciter*, but are left to particular persons—usually ecclesiastics—or for particular purposes, as chapels or schools, with a request for the special application of divine services, which (the object being certain and definite) would be construed as a *trust*. The gifts are perhaps more generally of the former than the latter kind; *i.e.*, to persons, not purposes. And it should seem that the framers of the Act conceived that gifts, especially endowments to Roman Catholic ecclesiastics, as such, coupled with requests for the exercise of their functions, would be construed as charitable, *i.e.*, not personal, nor solely for their personal benefit, but for their maintenance in their ecclesiastical office and character, and so in trust for their successors therein, and for the exercise of the functions thereof; for which reason, as already mentioned, the Roman law regards these gifts as in substance for the support of the ecclesiastics; and in that view such gifts would be deemed trusts, because, although in terms absolute, they are coupled with a request implying a trust for a purpose requiring *continuance*. And the case would be in substance the same whether the gifts were to the ecclesiastics themselves or to laics to provide them; with this distinction, that in the latter case the laics would have *no* interest, and in the other the ecclesiastics would have only a *life* inte-

---

gious instruction, takes from the person who has so placed confidence in him a gift, there is strong ground for suspicious inquiry as to undue influence. *Middleton* v. *Sherburn*, 4 Y. & C. 4; *Dent* v. *Bennett*, 7 Simons, 539; *Roworth* v. *Marriott*, 1 Myl. & Keen, 643.

rest. Such gifts may be either of a fund or estate, coupled with a request for masses *generally;* in which case the whole fund would probably be deemed applicable to religious uses, and the donee only entitled to retain a reasonable part or sufficient stipend. Or, the gift would be general, and the request for a particular number of masses, in which case, though there were no allusion to other charitable purposes, the gift would be on an implied trust for such a number of services, and so the case would still be within the Act. And as to the surplus, its application would depend on the circumstances of the contract, and the existence or absence of personal friendship, which might indicate either an intention for personal benefit, or for the support of the dignity or office, and in the latter view the residue would probably be deemed a gift for that purpose, and so a charitable trust (*a*).

If the gift or bequest either to a layman or ecclesiastic of any church or sect be described as "for" religious or charitable purposes, however generally described, or even in those very words, or, on the other hand, for divine services — several or special — it will constitute an express *trust,* even although the word "trust" is not used, and it is expressly declared that the application to such purposes is to be at the discretion of the donee (*b*). For such a gift binds the donee to apply the whole

---

(*a*) As where an estate has been given to a schoolmaster, and no intention could be presumed of giving him an individual benefit beyond his stipend. *At.-G.* v. *The Master of Brentford School,* 1 M. & K. 377; *At.-G.* v. *Wilson,* 3 M. & K. 362. See also the *At.-G.* v. *The Dean and Canons of Windsor,* 27 L. J., Ch., 320, where all the cases are cited.

(*b*) *Townsend* v. *Carus,* 3 Hare, 257.

fund of the endowment to such purposes, although the selection is at his discretion; and if he does not so apply it, the Court will compel him to do so, and frame a scheme for its application (*a*). And even if the gift be absolute in terms, if it is coupled with a *request* to the donee to apply the fund to some definite object, although at his discretion, as divine services specially to be applied, or the support of divine service generally, there will be equally a *trust*.

The absence of any express indication of intention for an ecclesiastical application of the property is in such cases of the gifts before the statute of Wm. IV., legalising Roman Catholic worship, of course easily accounted for; since the expression of such an intention would have invalidated the gifts. And the least indication of intention to keep up or support the ecclesiastical office, or of a purpose extending beyond the donee's life (*vide ante*, p. 28), would be sufficient in such cases to show a trust, and even personal friendship hardly would account for the gift of permanent property for the *services* of an ecclesiastic. In such a case even the heirs might be construed successors; or the heirs might be deemed to take only the legal estate in trust for the successors. In that case there would, according to principles already explained, be a *trust*. The mere relation of *penitent*, so far from accounting for a gift for the absolute benefit of his spiritual director, would tend, according to Roman and English law, to raise the inference that the gift was in trust for charitable purposes, for it would be highly improper for a priest to take from a penitent any gift for his own benefit, or even for any religious

---

(*a*) *Heneage* v. *Andover*, 10 Price, 269, *vide ante*, p. 28.

purpose with which he is at all connected (*a*). Indeed the Roman law is very strict in construing gifts to priests or prelates to be for religious purposes, and strictly prohibits them from dealing with such gifts for their own benefit. And if there were no evidence not only of an intention to give personal benefit, but that the gift should be *solely* for that purpose, and be absolutely disposable for mere private expenditure, and either-saleable for such purposes, or at death bequeathed or left to next of kin, the gift would probably be held to have been on an implied trust for its application to the support of Roman Catholic worship, or of the Roman Catholic priest or bishop of the place or chapel to which the donee or donor might have belonged (*b*).

If, though the general object be definite, the *particular* objects are unascertained, as a gift for Catholic priests or Protestant preachers, or the like, the court will, if there be no trustee to ascertain them at his discretion, or if he neglect to do so, construct a scheme of application (*c*). If the gift is to a specific institution, as a college or a chapel, it will be simply

---

(*a*) Hence, at a very early time there was a decree to this effect in Rome, said to have been issued at the request of the Pontiff. —See Cod. Theod. xvi. tit. 82. So there is a modern canon: "Cavendum est ne sacerdos in aliquam incidat avaritiæ suspicionem si testamentorum confectione immiscens : si saltem in commodum ecclesiæ vel vivorum bonorum partem moribundus cedat;" and of course a priest can scarcely fail to fall into suspicion of avarice if under such words he takes a gift for himself; and though it is added that he is not to be deterred from urging the duty of restitution or of almsgiving, in either case it would be properly to the poor, rather than to any ecclesiastic (unless in trust for them), and, to avoid the suspicion of an undue influence, in trust for charitable purposes with which the priest has no connection.

(*b*) *Thornber* v. *Wilson*, 24 L. J., Ch., 667.
(*c*) *Walsh* v. *Gladstone*, 1 Ch., 29.

transferred thereto (*a*). If it is to erect, establish, or endow an institution or foundation, the court will either (supposing the gift valid) see that the trustees, if any are appointed, carry out the purpose, or will carry it out itself.

It matters not how *general* the purpose for which a gift is declared to be made, if the court can see that it is charitable; nor does it matter that the selection of objects, or the distribution of the fund, is left absolutely in the discretion of the donee. A general gift for charitable purposes will be carried into effect by the court by means of a scheme, supposing the execution not confided to the discretion of trustees (*b*), and even a gift so general as for religion or education and learning, has been held valid as a charitable trust (*c*).

The court will satisfy itself whether the object can be attained and how; trustees will be appointed if necessary; the fund will be secured in court, and the income will be paid to them with directions for its application, consistent with the charitable purpose (*d*). And even if by the gift the application of the fund be left to the discretion of the trustees, the question will be whether it gives a mere discretionary power, or imposes upon them a trust; for there is a distinction in equity between a mere discretionary power in trustees, and a trust to be executed by them, though it may sometimes assume the form of a power. When there is a mere discretion in trustees, to be executed simply as they think fit, the court will not interfere

---

(*a*) *At.-G.* v. *Gladstone*, 13 Sim. 7.
(*b*) *Martin* v. *Maugham*, 8 Jur. 609.
(*c*) *Whicker* v. *Hume*, 1 De Gex, Macn. & Gord. 506.
(*d*) *Mortimer* v. *Watts*, 21 L. J., Ch., 169.

with their discretion. If the trustees do not execute the trust, the court will not execute in their place; but if there is a trust the court will compel them to execute it, or will order it to be executed under its directions. And the test whether there is such a trust is, whether they are bound to exercise the discretion, and for the benefit of the parties interested in the trust. If so, the court will compel them to do so. And in the case of charitable or religious trusts, this will no doubt be the case; for the very reason given for holding valid a bequest to be applied to such charitable or religious societies or purposes as the trustees may think fit is, that it binds the trustees to exercise that discretion, and apply the whole fund to such purposes (*a*).

Such being the *purposes* for which charitable trusts may be created, there must, to create such trusts, be valid trusts for such purposes. There may, as already mentioned, be trusts by implication; and though any disposition of property to take effect at or after death must be by last will in writing duly attested, and unless it be by declaration of trust accompanied by actual transfer to trustees, *inter vivos*, and a declaration of trust, if made after the disposition, and to take effect after death, is testamentary, and must be by will duly attested; and though the Statute of Frauds (29 Ch. II.) requires that all declarations or creations of trust of any *lands, tenements, or hereditaments* shall be manifested and proved by some writing signed by the party by law enabled to declare it, or by his last will, or be utterly void and of no effect, except where a trust arises or may result

---

(*a*) *Townsend* v. *Carus*, 3 Hare, 257; 21 L. J., Ch., 174.

D 2

by implication or construction of law, as the statute does not apply to trusts so arising; so neither does it exclude parol evidence to show that there was a secret understanding in fraud of the law (*a*): nor could a *trustee* safely set up as against the trust the want of written evidence to enable him to hold property free of trust for his own benefit; for if there were no trust mentioned in the disposition, and no circumstances to account for a disposition for his own benefit, it might be deemed either that there was a secret trust, or a failure of trust, or a resulting trust for the heir; and so if on the disposition *some* trust were mentioned, but not disclosed in the disposition itself, or in any separate document, there the mention of a trust of course would exclude the donee from personal benefit, and the trust failing the gift would fail, and the estate go to the heir.

So, as to the statute improperly called the modern Mortmain Act (of 9 Geo. II., c. 36), which provides that any disposition of land, &c., or money to be laid out or disposed of in land in trust for or for the benefit of any charitable use, shall be void, unless made by deed executed twelve months and enrolled six months before the death of the donor, and made to take effect immediately, absolutely, and without any reservation; that only applies to real estate; and so not to shares (*b*), and to real estate to be *held* for the charitable use, not to be *sold* for its benefit (*c*); or to personalty *directed* to be laid out in land, or in

---

(*a*) *At.-G.* v. *Poulden*, 8 Sim. 472; *Pilkington* v. *Boughey*, 12 S., 114.
(*b*) *Myers* v. *Perigall*, 22 L. J., Ch., 431.
(*c*) *Doe* d. *Chidgly* v. *Harris*, 16 M. & W., 617; but a charge on land for a charity is within the Act: *Currie* v. *Pye*, 17 Vesey, 412.

building, if no land is already or otherwise provided for the purpose (*a*), and though bequests to be applied in erecting or establishing charitable institutions not already possessing land for building, might be deemed to be a direction to buy land, this is not so where the direction is to *endow* charities (*b*); and, added to this, a trust to be within *this* Act must be declared in writing, signed by the donor, under the other statute, and if it be not referred to in the deed of gift, and then existing, it must be declared by deed, which, as well as the deed of gift, must be enrolled, for the two together make up a disposition to charitable uses (*c*). And not only so, but parol evidence may be admitted to show a secret trust in fraud of the law, and a bill in chancery would lie to disclose it adversely to the charity, as on the part of the heir or residuary devisee. But though even after money has been left to be laid out in land for a charity, and *has* been so laid out contrary to the statute, the court will not establish or carry the trust into effect as against the heir (*d*); yet as the only effect of the statute is that the

---

(*a*) *At.-G.* v. *Hodgson*, 15 Sim. 146.

(*b*) There is a distinction between bequests for erecting and *endowing:* supposing the endowment to apply to existing. buildings, they are not within the Act: *Edwards* v. *Hall*, 25 L. J., Ch., 82.

(*c*) There are exceptions to the operation of the Act created by various Acts (3 & 4 Vict. c. 93, and 4 & 5 Vict. c. 26) in favour of church-building and schools, the former only applying to the Established Church, and their scope is specific bequests of 500*l.* for particular churches, not general bequests for church-building: *Church-Building Society* v. *Coles*, 24 L. J., Ch., 713. There are likewise Acts for facilitating building of *schools* which apply *generally* to all religious bodies: see 5 Vict. c. 38, an Act allowing the bequest of an acre of land as a site for a school for the education of poor persons, or for the residence of a schoolmaster or mistress, or otherwise for the purposes of the education of such poor persons in religious and useful knowledge.

(*d*) *At.-G.* v. *Acland*, 1 Rus. & Myl. 243.

disposition, if within it, shall be void, if the trustees have actual possession of the property and admit the trust, *they* may be subject to the jurisdiction of the court or the Commissioners of Charities in respect of the trust (*a*), and trustees may even be *fixed* with a trust as between themselves and the objects of it by a deed void under the Mortmain Act, the provisions of which are as between the trustees and the *heir*, not as between trustees and *cestuis que trust* (*b*); and though in a suit in which any party may have an interest adverse to the trust the court cannot act on a deed so void (*c*), yet where the trustees have been in possession of the property dedicated to charitable uses under the deed, and have acted under it, they cannot be allowed to dispute its validity, and the liability of the lands to be recovered by title paramount is no objection to a suit for administration. A recusant or dishonest trustee cannot therefore set up the invalidity of the deeds under which he himself holds, and if he claims to hold adversely to a charity he must be prepared to show an absolute gift to him for his own personal benefit; and though, no doubt, to fix him with a trust adversely, a substantive suit is necessary (*d*), the Commissioners of Charities may direct such a suit, in which *secret* trusts may be disclosed.

It is important to bear in mind that as against a donee the question is not whether donor has declared a trust, but whether he has indicated an intention to do so. For a gift in that case depends

---

(*a*) *At.-G.* v. *Ward*, 6 Hare, 483.
(*b*) *At.-G.* v. *Gardner*, 2 De Gex & Smale, 102.
(*c*) *At.-G.* v. *Munroe*, Ibid. 122.
(*d*) *Hutchinson* v. *Stephens*, 5 Sim. 498; *Walton* v. *Nerry*, 6 Sim. 328; *At.-G.* v. *Poulden*, 8 Sim., 472.

upon the trust, and if there is no trust there is no gift; so if there is no trust, the heir or next of kin takes (*a*). The declaration of trust is only material as against the donee when the gift itself is by way of declaration of trust, which in equity is a disposition of personalty, provided there be some transfer of the fund from the hands of donor. In such case it is for the next of kin to show that there was not a valid declaration of trust, because made after the transfer and to take effect at death, and so testamentary, and not duly executed. Because if there is no valid declaration of trust, there was no disposition, and the right of the next of kin is not displaced. But in other cases—as of an absolute legal gift, whether of realty or personalty—it is enough to show that there was an *intention* to create a trust, although it may not have been sufficiently declared, because that shows there was no intention to confer a beneficial interest, and so the gift was not intended to take effect according to these terms, but as a trust; and though it is otherwise if there was no intention to create a trust, although the purpose is disclosed, but to leave it to the donee without a trust, a trust may be sufficiently indicated to exclude the devisee from taking a *beneficial* interest, though the purpose is not disclosed (*b*). Thus, a bequest to an individual for a purpose expressed elsewhere, and which purpose, from some unexplained cause,

---

(*a*) *Johnson* v. *Ball*, 5 De Gex & Smale, 85; *Gray* v. *Gray*, 21 L. J., Ch., 755; *Petty* v. *Petty*, 22 L. J., Ch., 1065; *Tierney* v. *Wood*, 23 L.J., Ch., 897.

(*b*) Or even though the trust fails. *Bernard* v. *Marshall*, 28 L. J., Ch., 649.

is not discoverable by the trust, creates such an uncertainty that the court cannot declare the intention of the testator, and therefore the property vests, not in the legatee or devisee, but the heir or next of kin. Though the court does not presume a trust, and ' precatory ' words do not create a trust, if the objects are indefinite, that supposes the whole intention of the testator, so far as it has been expressed, to be before the court, and that the uncertainty is occasioned by the intention which it declares, and does not apply to a case in which, from the terms of the bequest, it would appear that there was a written expression of the intention of the testator which is not before the court; as where he says that the bequest, though in terms absolute, is for a "purpose" named in a paper not to be found. In such a case it is held that the trust fails for uncertainty, and that as the bequest was for a trust, and not for the donee's benefit, the gift fails, and the property passes to the heir or next of kin, as the case may be (*a*). And it is to be observed that if the bequest is declared to be for an ultimate purpose, which goes beyond the mere personal benefit of the donee, even though for his life he is to have the enjoyment, it will create a trust, though the execution of that purpose is left to the "judgment" of the donee (*b*), or if there be divers objects, a power of selection and distribution is left to him, as where the bequest is to distribute among certain objects as he may think proper (*c*).

As between the commissioners in the interest of a

(*a*) *The Mayor of Gloucester* v. *Osborn*, 1 House of Lords Cases, 272, affirming a decree of the Court of Chancery ; 3 Hare, 131.
(*b*) *Batt* v. *Anns*, 11 L. J., Ch., 52.
(*c*) *Burrough* v. *Philcox*, 5 Mylne & Craig, 73.

charity and the trustees, it matters not that the declaration of trust is *invalid*. If there be a disposition of realty,—which requires to make a trust valid as against the *heir*, a declaration of trust,—not in terms absolute, as though for the persoual benefit of donee, but alluding to some trusts not mentioned, but kept out of the will for the purpose of concealment, not only can the donee by bill in chancery be compelled to disclose the nature of any secret trusts for charitable purposes (*a*), but if they are denied or not disclosed, then the allusion to *some* trust will indicate an intention that the donee was not to take for his own personal benefit, and the gift will pass to the heir or next of kin, whether it be realty or personalty, the court not being enabled to execute it, it not appearing to be for *charitable* uses (*b*). And even though the bequest be in terms absolute—as to the priest, or preacher, or minister, of such and such a chapel, and his successors, or any similar terms—as the minister for the time being of such a chapel for ever, or for continuance beyond the life of any particular minister named (so as to create a gift legally charitable in its nature), then the gift will be not absolutely to the first taker, but in trust for his successors (*c*).

(*a*) *Jackson* v. *Russell*, 21 L. J., Ch., 46.
(*b*) *Briggs* v. *Penny*, 21 L. J. Rep. (N. S.), Ch., 265, where the words in the will were—"well knowing that she (the devisee) will dispose of it according to my wishes."
(*c*) *Thornber* v. *Wilson*, 24 L. J. Rep. (N. S.), Ch., 667 : the Vice-Chancellor said : "There is no doubt on the face of the will that the testator meant to endow a chapel with a stipend for the minister. My opinion is, therefore, that there is no gift to the priests out of regard for them, but a devise for the benefit of the office, so that the devises were held *trusts*." It was impossible to come to any other conclusion.

Upon the cases it appears that if a will contains an absolute gift to an individual, that individual must take for his own benefit, unless by other parts of the will, or by some other evidence brought home to the knowledge of the donee in the testator's life-time, that absolute gift is with certainty reduced to a trust. And a gift which, uncontrolled by the context, would give an absolute interest, is not to be reduced to a trust by a mere recommendation to the legatee to give an unascertained part of the legacy to a particular object, or any part of the legacy to an unascertained object (*a*). It is otherwise, however, if it appears that the intentions of the testator *were* ascertained and described by him, but are not disclosed (*b*). In that case there is a trust which fails, and the legatee does not take for his own benefit, but it passes to the heir or next of kin (*c*). Where indeed the heir seeks to take real property on the ground that the disposition is invalid, because for charitable purposes and not duly made according to the Mortmain Act, there he must fix the disposition with a valid trust in writing—which, if after the disposition, must be by way of testament (*d*)—or he must fix donee with a secret trust in fraud of the law, which he can only do by bringing a knowledge of it home to donee in the life-time of donor (*e*). But even in those cases, if the disposition itself declare that it is to be on some trust, though that

---

(*a*) *The Corporation of Gloucester* v. *Wood*, 3 Hare, 131.
(*b*) *The Corporation of Gloucester* v. *Osborn*, 1 House of Lords Cases, 284.
(*c*) *Knight* v. *Boughton*, 11 Clark & Finelly's Rep. (House of Lords Cases) 513.
(*d*) *Lomas* v. *Repley*, 24 L. J., Ch., 254.
(*e*) *Wallgrove* v. *Tibbs*, 25 L. J., Ch., 240.

trust is not disclosed, that will be sufficient to take the property from the donee; but while he has it he may be fixed with a trust by actual usage, or by his own acknowledgments or acts.

Nor would the mere *absence* of any express declaration of trust, parol or written, be sufficient to secure the donee the personal title and enjoyment, for usage itself is *evidence* of it; and might be presumptive evidence even of a deed; and as against a party who has for years *acted* on a trust, however invalid, every presumption will be made, insomuch that in a suit merely for the administration of a charity against a trustee, and not by the heir, even though an invalid deed is produced, it will be presumed that some other mode had been resorted to for making a valid disposition (*a*). This being so, it is manifest that the Commissioners of Charities, in the exercise of their jurisdiction—which is declared to be the due *administration* of charitable trusts, and the more beneficial application of charitable funds—have nothing to do with the mere invalidity of dispositions to charitable uses: having no jurisdiction on the one hand to take property from a charity, nor on the other hand to interfere with any suit or claim adverse to a charity, but simply to secure the due application of funds which *de facto* it finds in possession of a charity. And hence their jurisdiction as to inquiry is defined to be, "to examine, as they in their discretion may see fit, into all charities . . . and the application of the funds belonging thereto," in order to do which they must inquire as to what are charities; and it is declared that they "may cause

---

(*a*) *At.-G.* v. *Moss*, 20 Beav. 119.

inquiries *in relation"* to these matters, which comprises and must necessarily and primarily require inquiry as to whether in any particular case there *is* a trust or not for any charity. And as the heir *against* a charity may set up a secret trust in fraud of the law, so may the Attorney-General or the Commissioners of Charities set up a secret trust in fraud of the law, as against the trustee, but in *favour* of a charity.

And though it is provided that the Act shall not extend to give the Commissioners power of requiring from any person claiming to hold any property adversely to a charity, or free from any trust or charge (*i. e.* for his own benefit), any information, or the production of any deed or document in relation to the property so claimed,—this, in the first place, does not preclude them from getting the information from any other source, except perhaps the attorney of the party (*a*); and as to wills proved, they can of course obtain copies. And in the next place it is clear, upon general principles of law and equity, that the party to be entitled to this exemption must be claiming really, and not colourably or merely to defeat the jurisdiction; and of this the Commissioners in the first instance must judge; and if they decide against the claimant, and he continues recusant, they may apply to the Court of Chancery for process of contempt, on which application the court will determine upon the whole matter whether the claim of title is real or colourable (*b*). For it is clear law that in no case is a jurisdiction ousted by a *mere* claim of title, unless

---

(*a*) *Russell* v. *Jackson*, 21 L. J., Ch., 146.
(*b*) *Thompson* v. *Ingham*, 19 L. J., Q. B., 189.

real and *bonâ fide* (a), otherwise it is obvious any jurisdiction might easily be defeated.

Nor is this all. For the Commissioners, even supposing the claim of exemption from *their* jurisdiction be upheld, may certify the case as fit for prosecution by the Attorney-General, and then in the Court of Chancery it may be that there will be no exemption from discovery, and certainly not from interrogatory on oath with a view to discovery. In such a suit the books of the party may be ordered to be produced, the entries in which may tend to prove a usage and a trust, as well as any deeds bearing upon the question or relating to the matter at issue (b). Even written communications between the party and his attorney relating to the matters which form the subject of the suit, if before or even after the suit, and not mere legal advice or opinion, may be ordered to be produced (c). And if the allegation is that the deeds were coupled with secret trusts in fraud of the law, the court may upon the whole of the circumstances order a production of the deeds under which the party holds (d).

So far as to the jurisdiction of the Court of Chancery in establishing or disclosing a charitable trust, or of the Commissioners of Charities in aiding the court so to establish or disclose it. It remains now to consider the jurisdiction of the court or of the Commissioners of Charities in regard to charitable trusts. Their jurisdiction is exercised chiefly in

---

(a) *Lilley* v. *Harvey*, 17 L. J., Q. B., 357.
(b) *Ord* v. *Fawcett*, 19 L. J., Ch., 487; *Beswick* v. *Murray*, 1 Macn. & Gord. 530; *Bassford* v. *Blakesley*, 6 Beav. 131.
(c) *Peile* v. *Stoddart*, 1 Macn. & Gord. 192.
(d) *Walsingham* v. *Goodrich*, 3 Hare, 122; *Mayor of Dartmouth*, v. *Holdsworth*, 10 Sim. 476.

regard to the appointment of trustees, the establishment of schemes, and the due security and application of the funds. The establishment of a scheme and appointment of trustees may be necessary to the very establishment of a charity in the first instance.

If, in the original donation, there were no trustees appointed, or the trustees became unfitted for their office, or fail, application must, if necessary be made to the commissioners, or, with their approval, to the Court of Chancery, which has always had a general jurisdiction thus to provide for the permanence as well as establishment of charitable trusts. If there is any provision in the original deed, &c., as regards the appointment of trustees, those provisions must, unless varied by Chancery upon special grounds, be adhered to (a). As regards the transmission of the legal property to new trustees, special provision is made for any buildings held by any congregation or society, or body of persons associated for religious purposes, or for the promotion of education as a chapel, school, dwelling-house, glebe, &c. (expressions which apply equally to Church of England, Dissenting, or Roman Catholic bodies, the latter being by the statute Wm. IV. placed, as regards their places of worship or schools, on the same footing as Dissenters), by the Act 13 & 14 Vict. cap. 28, which provides that without any new conveyance the property shall vest from time to time in new trustees to be appointed either according to the provisions of the deed, or if no mode of appointment be therein prescribed, or if the power of appointment has lapsed, then in such manner as may be agreed upon by the body. And the Trustees Acts 1850 and 1855 confer upon the

---

(a) *At.-G.* v. *Dalton*, 20 L. J., Ch., 569; 13 Beav. 141.

Court of Chancery special powers in a summary way, upon petition, to appoint new trustees in all cases in which it is expedient to do so, and it is inexpedient to do so without the aid of the court. These Acts apply to charities, and include chapels; so that an application may be made to the court, upon petition, to appoint new trustees of a chapel (*a*), or in other cases to the Board, or with the assent of the Board to the court. Chapels of Dissenters and Roman Catholics are specially excepted from the Charitable Trusts Act, and therefore, as to trustees of chapels, the commissioners have no direct jurisdiction, nor, it should seem, even to restrain applications to the court in respect to such charities. But as to any applications to the court under the Trustees Acts, as regards a charity, the consent of the Attorney-General, even where that of the board is not required, is necessary, and the application can only be under these Acts and in a summary way, where the matter of fact on which the application turns is admitted, and the unfitness or failure of trustees cannot be disputed, as where they are infant, or lunatic, or under the Bankruptcy Act, in cases of bankruptcy (*b*). In cases where the question is a far broader one, as to the unfitness of the trustees, either on account of misconduct, maladministration, or deviation from the trust, or especially in religious or educational charities on the ground of their religious belief, the application must be with the sanction of the board to the general jurisdiction of the Court of Chancery, or, except in the last case, to the Board itself.

(*a*) *In re the Vartey Wesleyan Chapel*, 10 Hare xxxvii.; *In re Rolles's Charity*, 3 De Gex, Macn. & Gord. 760.

(*b*) 12 & 13 Vict. c. 106.

The Charitable Trusts Act of 1860, while giving the board power in certain cases of removing or appointing trustees, except the removal of a trustee on the ground of his religious belief, which is therefore still a matter for the jurisdiction of chancery, though as to that or any other matter no application can be made to chancery without the sanction of the board, unless in the case of Dissenters' chapels or Roman Catholic places of worship. As to the removal of trustees of religious charities on account of their religious belief, the general principle of chancery is that trustees of such charities should be of the religious opinions of the founder, or of the body of Christians, for whom the charity is intended (a). And that principle can only be enforced by the Court of Chancery itself, being expressly taken out of the jurisdiction of the Commissioners of Charities (b).

Assuming a charitable trust to be either admitted or manifested, even although of the most general character, the Court of Chancery has jurisdiction to enforce its due execution, and therefore the Commissioners of Charities also have jurisdiction. If the objects are general, and the trustees have a discretion, as where it is to be for charitable or religious purposes or bodies at their discretion, though the court or the commissioners cannot interfere in their discretion as to the selection of objects and distribution of funds—provided it be exercised *bonâ fide*—they can and will compel the application of all the funds to the purposes described; and for the purpose of finding whether there has been or is such an application, the Commissioners of Charities have power in

---

(a) *Drummond* v. *At.-G.*, 14 Jur. 137.
(b) Act of 1860.

such a case, or in any other case of a charity, to call for such accounts and statements as they think fit as to past or present receipts or disbursements, and therefore, if not satisfactory, to examine the party upon oath. Should it appear that the whole of the fund has been applied in good faith to such or similar purposes as those described, though there may have been errors, and, as to the future, there may be need for order or direction, thêre will be no case of misapplication; but if all the fund has *not* been so applied, there will be a discretionary power to enforce restitution; and in either case the commissioners may, and in the latter probably will, either frame a scheme for the future application of the fund, or direct an application to the Court of Chancery for the purpose. And so where the original trust appears to have been general, *without* a discretionary power in the trustees, or with no trustees; and thus, though a gift to a chapel or college will be simply secured for that institution (*a*), a general gift for priests, preachers, or the like, will require a scheme. If the objects are defined either by the original donation or by a subsequent scheme, the commissioners, even though the trustees have some amount of discretion as to the distribution or application, the commissioners will, exercising their jurisdiction as to accounts and inquiries, ascertain whether the trustees have kept within the limits so defined, and, if not, can correct any deviation for the future, by the like order or direction, or by directing application to chancery for it; and in case of any wilful defalcation or corrupt misapplication or loss to the charity through gross neglect, have a discretionary

---

(*a*) *Walsh* v. *Gladstone*, Ph. 29.

power of enforcing restitution, under peril of an application to the court (*a*). But no application for this or any other purpose can be made to Chancery without their sanction.

Where there is a particular foundation or scheme for a charity, it must be followed by the trustees, like those as regards the application of the funds, or the election or appointment of new trustees, or of officers or recipients of the charity, unless varied by the Court of Chancery, the Commissioners of Charities, or Parliament. And though in the *absence* of any particular provision, usage may be resorted to either to explain or supply the nature of the trust or the mode of appointing trustees, this can never be admitted against the express, clear terms of the foundation (*b*). Hence this principle was distinctly recognised in the Grammar Schools Act, the Dissenters' Chapels Act, and by the Endowed Schools Act, and Roman Catholic Charities Act of 1860 (*c*).

Very lately the principle has been stated thus:—
"In ordinary cases some will or deed of foundation or charter of incorporation exists, by referring to which, and ascertaining the meaning of the words used, the question may be determined. In cases where the original deed of foundation has been lost, the intention of the founders must be inferred, as well as it can be, by the practice which has regulated the charity."

But the application of the principle having led to litigation in the case of Dissenters' chapels, and there being a great deal of controversy as to what duration of usage should be deemed sufficient in the

---

(*a*) *At.-G.* v. *Gladstone*, 13 Sim. 7.
(*b*) *At.-G.* v. *Murdoch*, 7 Hare 445; 119 L. J., Ch., 3.
(*c*) 22 L. J., Ch., 574.

absence of express evidence, an Act was passed, called the Dissenters' Chapels Act (*a*), which provides that when the deed is silent, twenty-five years' usage shall be decisive. And so the Roman Catholic Charities Act makes a similar provision as to twenty years' usage, that it shall be conclusive. Apart from those statutes, it was a principle of the courts of equity that while usage could not lend a sanction to a clear breach of trust (*b*); practically usage might relieve the trustees from the responsibility for the past; so that if they had followed a usage they would not be deemed guilty of a breach of trust, although as to the future they might be decidedly bound to depart from the usage and adhere to the trust (*c*). But these Acts, where they apply, make the usage decisive as to the trust, only however where there is no deed declaring the trust; when there *is*, the old principle prevails, that usage may protect the trustees as to the *past*, though it will not alter the trust. Generally speaking, however, the whole internal management of a charity is left by the court to the trustees or persons acting in its administration. It is not the practice of the court, after settling a scheme, to retain the administration or the management of the charity; but the scheme being settled, it is for the *trustees* to administer the charity according to the course approved of by the court (*d*). And in charity cases the court will withhold its interference in the *execution* of the trusts, save where such interference is necessary to prevent a *breach* of trust (*e*). It has already been

---

(*a*) 7 & 8 Vict. c. 45.
(*b*) At.-G. v. *Drummond*, 14 Jur. 137.
(*c*) At.-G. v. *Mayor of Rochester*, 6 Sim. 223.
(*d*) At.-G. v. *Solly*, 5 L. J., Ch., 5.
(*e*) At.-G. v. *Bosanquet*, 11 L. J. Rep., Ch., 43.

seen that not only does the court respect the jurisdiction of a visitor, but by analogy thereto refrains from interfering in the *internal* management of a religious or educational charity (*a*), or indeed of any charity, leaving details to the discretion of the trustees, or of the officers whom they may appoint under their before-mentioned powers of appointment and dismissal. Thus the court never itself distributes the benefit of an endowment to its objects (though it hands over specific gifts to the parties entitled), but appoints the proper parties to do so, and frames a scheme where necessary.

The Administration of Charities.

The administration of charitable trusts is left by the Court of Chancery in the hands of the trustees, the court not interfering in the internal management of charities. Questions of administration of a charity refer either to the purposes to which, or to the places within which, the funds are to be applied, or to the disposition of any surplus. As to the *purposes*, whether as regards the benefits to be administered, or the person or class of persons to be recipients, there can be no *change* without the sanction of the Court of Chancery, or the Commissioners of Charities, by means of a new scheme. Nor can a trustee for a particular purpose intermix the fund for that purpose with trust funds for other purposes, and apply the whole in such proportions as he pleases (*b*). Nor can the instruction in a school, nor the persons whose children are admitted, be varied, save in the *absence* of express

---

(*a*) *At.-G.* v. *Sherbourne School,* 24 L. J., Ch., 74.
(*b*) *At.-G.* v. *Goldsmiths' Company,* C. P. C., 292.

direction, by usage (*a*). Thus the exhibitions of a free grammar school are confined to the *poor* boys on the foundation, and cannot be given to the boarders taken by the head-master (*b*), nor, indeed, can the master always receive boarders, and the Grammar Schools Act carefully provides that even in settling new grammar school schemes, no class of scholars shall be deprived of any right they at present possess.

Not only is an application of trust funds to an *entirely different* purpose a departure from a trust (*c*), but a substantial *variation* from it may be so, supposing it not excused by usage, although if the whole of the fund has been applied honestly to the purposes of the charity or of charity, and especially if the trust has been performed, and the question is only as to the application of a surplus (*d*), there will be no breach of trust. Thus it is a breach of trust to apply funds for the support of a school chapel, to making it large enough for the parish (*e*). So, where a chapel was pulled down, and the burial ground converted to a different purpose. And so, where the trust was for the maintenance of ten poor householders, and the fund was applied to the poor of the parish generally, it would seem that this was no *breach of trust, provided ten poor householders were relieved.* Neither can the place within which the benefits of the charity should be applied be varied without the sanction of the court.

(*a*) *At.-G.* v. *Christ School*, 1 Jacobs, 744; *At.-G.* v. *Hillard*, 2 Y. & C. 683; *At.-G.* v. *Mansfield*, 2 Russ. 50.

(*b*) *Solr.-G.* v. *Bath*, 18 L. J., Ch., 275.

(*c*) *In re Manchester College*, 22 L. J., Ch., 571. It was long ago held that, if there be an endowment for a priest at one place, to remove him to another would be a breach of trust. Not so to apply the surplus to another place.

(*d*) *Ex parte Gresham*, 1 Madd. 92.

(*e*) *Ex parte Fowler*, 1 Jac. & W. 70.

Thus if a trust be for the benefit of a particular town, county, or parish, it must be so applied (*a*). Thus if the trust is for a town, it cannot be applied only for the benefit of particular parishes (*b*). On the other hand, if the trust is for poor of a particular parish, it must not be applied in aid of the funds of a charity extending over that and other parishes (*c*). So closely is this principle adhered to, that where a particular institution, of which there are more than one in the particular town mentioned, is described by its locality, that particular institution alone can benefit by the gift (*d*). So, where it is for the benefit of the poor or a particular estate (*e*). Hence, where parishes are divided into districts a necessity arises for the apportionment of the benefits of the charities for the entire parish (*f*); in which case the same rule of appropriation as to the proportions of the different objects of the charity is to be adhered to in the districts as in the original parish (*g*).

Where funds are given to trustees to apply as *they* shall in their discretion think fit for the benefit of a particular town, district, or other place or locality, the court will not interfere with the exercise of that discretion, so far as it is exercised within and for the benefit of such place or locality, and will not entertain an information praying for a scheme for the distribution of the charity benefits within such locality (*h*).

(*a*) *At.-G.* v. *Lonsdale*, 1 Sim. 105; *In re Upton Warren*, 1 My. & K. 410.
(*b*) *At.-G.* v. *Mayor of Rochester*, 6 Sim. 273.
(*c*) *At.-G.* v. *Brandreth*, 1 Y. & C. 200.
(*d*) *Wilson* v. *Squire*, 1 Y. & C. 654.
(*e*) *Bristowe* v. *Bristowe*, 5 Beav. 289.
(*f*) *Westham Charities*, 2 De Gex & Smale, 218.
(*g*) *In re Lambeth Charities*, 22 L. J., Ch., 959.
(*h*) *At.-G.* v. *Gaskell*, 9 L. J., Ch., 188.

But, on the other hand, the rules of chancery are somewhat strict as to the extension of the benefits of a charity beyond the limits of the particular locality to which it is limited by the trust (*a*), unless the funds prove more than adequate for the fully satisfying its claims, when there may be a new scheme for the extension of the charity, on the express principle. Thus, where a chapel had been granted to trustees of a school for the sake of the *school*, and the inhabitants of the hamlet had been long accustomed to attend the performance of divine service there, it was held, with reference to its history and the particular language of the instruments, that as the chapel was not for the accommodation of the hamlet, but the school, the trustees had no right to apply the revenues of the charity in enlarging the chapel for the accommodation of the inhabitants of the hamlet. But that was a case of a Church of England charity, there being of course a parish church; and the application of the case to a Roman Catholic or Dissenting college or school would depend no doubt upon the circumstances. Moreover, it did not appear that the funds were more than sufficient for all the purposes of the *school*.

With respect to parochial charities, a difficult question often arises as to their apportionment, when the parishes have been divided into separate parishes or districts. An Act of Parliament (*b*) gave the Court of Chancery a discretionary power to direct an apportionment of charitable gifts in such cases, between the new district and the remaining portion of the parish (*c*). Under the 22nd section of the 8 & 9 Vict.

(*a*) *At.-G.* v. *The Earl of Mansfield*, 2 Russell's Ch. Rep. 50.
(*b*) *At.-G.* v. *Dalton*, 13 Beav. 141.
(*c*) 8 & 9 Vict. c. 70, s. 22. It has been held that, in applica-

c. 70, the court has a discretion whether or not to direct an apportionment of charitable gifts made for the benefit of a parish, between a district parish and the remaining part of the parish, and it is not imperative on the court to make such apportionment. Another Charitable Trusts (Amendment) Act, of 1855, contains a provision that in respect of all charities, the gross annual income whereof does not exceed thirty pounds, the board may make the apportionment (*a*). As to charities above that amount, the board must sanction an application to chancery.

Notwithstanding the strictness of the rule of Chancery as to the application of charities exclusively for the benefit of the localities for which they were intended to be established, it is open to the court, upon a large and liberal construction of the deed or instru-

---

tions under this Act, which might be made under Romilly's Act, it was not necessary to allege any abuses in the past or present management of the charities.—*West Ham Charities,* 2 De Gex & Smale, 218.

(*a*) As where a testator bequeathed a sum of money to be employed for the good and benefit of the poor of the *town* of Kensington for ever, in such manner as A. and B. and the churchwardens of the said parish of Kensington should think fit to establish, it appeared that there was a place called the town of Kensington, but that such place had not any known or defined metes or bounds, and that there was no municipal corporate town or market town in the parish of Kensington. It appeared, also, that the rents had been always applied for the benefit of the poor of Kensington parish generally, and that, in all the deeds relating to the property, no distinction had been made between town and parish; and it was held, that the trust was for the benefit of the parish of Kensington generally, and not for any particular part of it.

Where the bequest is to trustees for the benefit of the poor of a parish, and a separate body of trustees had for about 200 years (with some slight exceptions) managed the property and applied the rents, it is held, that, notwithstanding this separate management, the charity came within the 22nd section of the 8 & 9 Vict. c. 70, and was apportionable between a district parish and the remainder of the parish : *Ex parte Incumbent and Churchwardens of Brompton,* 22 L. J., Ch., 281.

ment of foundation (aided by a consideration of all the circumstances of the times), to judge whether the benefit of the particular locality was the sole or even the principal object of the foundation; and if not, as, for example, if the *main* object appears to have been of a general character, as the supply of ministers for a particular religious sect or church, then the mere fact that the charity was originally located at a particular place will not preclude the court from removing it to another, even upon petition under Romilly's Act (*a*).

With regard to any surplus, the question as to its disposition may arise, either as regards the right of different objects or charities to it, or the claims of the trustees to a beneficial ownership. And it may arise either as to the fund or estate, as originally taken, or as to any subsequent increase of the proceeds.

Taking the case first as regards claims of different objects or charities: it may arise either as to the shares or proportions to be allotted to each object, or as to a surplus undisposed of. If it arises in the first way, the general rule is that the objects, in the absence of specific appropriation or apportionment, take equally (*b*), and the court, on petition under Romilly's Act, by way of "relief, order, or direction," can declare the proportions; or the Commissioners, or the County Courts, or the Chancery Judges at

---

(*a*) *In re Manchester College*, 22 L. J., Ch. (N. S.), 571. There the object was the training up of ministers for the Protestant Dissenters, and with that view a college was to be founded at Manchester. But the Master of the Rolls held that the place was not one of the main fundamental objects of the charity, but accessory only, and so he sanctioned the removal of the college to another place.

(*b*) *In re Hall's Charity*, 14 Beav. 115.

chambers, can do so. If it arises as to the *original* fund, the testator or donor not having disposed of the whole of it by residuary dispositions or otherwise, and there appearing to be an undisposed-of surplus, as to which there are no specific directions, and no intention of personal benefit to the trustees or donees, the surplus will either be disposed of under a new scheme for the charitable objects mentioned (*a*), or, in certain cases, may go to the heir or next of kin (*b*).

In the former class of cases, there may be a question whether the court or the commissioners are authorised to frame the scheme, or must direct an application to Parliament for the purpose (*c*); as to which the principle is thus laid down. When the question arises between different charitable objects, as to a subsequent increase of the rents, &c., the general principle as to the allotment of the increase, where all the objects are specified, is, that where a specific fund is given to one charity, and the residue to the others, the latter have the increase (*d*); but where there is a common fund for all the objects, or specific gifts to each, exhausting originally the whole, then all share alike in the increase; though if specific *property* is given to each, then of course each takes alone the increase of its own property. In the case of increase no question can arise as to a claim of the trustees to a share of it beneficially, unless they had some beneficial interest in the *original* disposition, whether by way of residue or other-

---

(*a*) At.-G. v. *Holland*, 2 Y. & C. 683.
(*b*) At.-G. v. *Wilson*, 3 M. & K. 362.
(*c*) In re *Shrewsbury Grammar School*, 1 Macn. & Gord. 324, 19 L. J., Ch., 207.
(*d*) At.-G. v. *Solly*, 5 L. J., Ch. (N. S.); At.-G. v. *Cooper's Company*, 3 Beav. 27.

wise (*a*); and where the trustee or donee is one of the objects of the charity, and is himself administrator, he cannot retain an increase, unless he has it by way of residue; specific sums being allotted to the other objects, and the residue to himself (*b*). Where there is no specific appropriation, the objects of the charity will take equally; and where the gift is to the repair of a church, the relief of the poor, and other things needful for a particular parish, at the discretion of the trustees, this discretionary power will only apply to the distribution of the share coming to the last-mentioned object; but each is equally entitled (*c*). It is otherwise in cases where the trustee has a *general* discretion.

The court has jurisdiction to extend the application of the income of a charity beyond the mere *literally* expressed intentions of the testator, provided the income be applied to subjects connected with that intention (*d*). But where a gift or bequest is made *exclusively* for a specific charitable purpose, and the fund is more than sufficient for satisfying *that* purpose, the court or board has no jurisdiction over the surplus, nor can it be disposed of by the crown under the sign manual; but application must be made to the legislature for its disposition by special Act of Parliament (*e*). Hence, under the Charitable Trusts Act, it is provided that, where a new scheme appears to the board desirable, and it is doubtful whether it

---

(*a*) At.-G. v. *Christ's Hospital*, 4 Beav. 75.
(*b*) At.-G. v. *Tufnell*, 12 Beav. 35.
(*c*) In re *Hall's Charity*, 14 Beav. 115.
(*d*) At.-G. v. *Dixee*, 2 Mylne & Keen's Rep. 342.
(*e*) At.-G. v. *The Ironmongers' Company*, 2 Mylne & Keen, 576.

can be carried out by the court or board, the board may approve a scheme for sanction by Parliament (*a*).

When the Court of Chancery is called upon to vary or direct the application of a charitable fund, either through failure of object, generality of trust, or increase of the fund, or other alteration of circumstances, it does so upon what is called the *cyprès* principle; that is, the principle of executing the trust as nearly as possible to the intentions of the founder or donor. The application of this principle it never allows to the trustees, but reserves to itself; and whether the necessity for variation or alteration may arise originally in the very terms of the foundation, or subsequently, it is the same principle which is applied,—to keep as closely as possible to the expressed or implied intention of the donor. Thus, if the necessity arose originally from the generality of his directions, they will be adhered to as far as they can be discerned (*b*). Thus, if a gift generally is for a "school," it can only be applied to a school; but if for a schoolmaster, it may be applied in founding a school. If a gift is for the purposes of a school, it cannot be applied to purposes parochial, as to enlarge the school chapel for the use of the parishioners, (*c*) but, as already mentioned, a trust for the relief of the

---

(*a*) S. 54 and following sections. Divers schemes have been so prepared by the commissioners and sanctioned by Parliament: as the Dulwich College Scheme (20 & 21 Vict. c. 84); the Folkstone Charity (21 & 22 Vict. c. 29); the Bristol Charities (21 & 22 Vict. c. 31); the Swineshead Charity (21 & 22 Vict. c. 81); the Bath Hospital (19 & 20 Vict. c. 45); the Moulton School (19 & 20 Vict. c. 53); the Stoke Pogis Hospital (19 & 20 Vict. c. 111).

(*b*) See the recent case of *Philpott* v. *St. George's Hospital*, 28 L. J., Ch., 657.

(*c*) *At.-G.* v. *Mansfield*, 2 Russ. 80.

poor comprises their education (*a*). So, if the fund is for a school in a particular district, and becomes impossible *there*, it will depend upon whether the intention of the testator was to benefit that district, or merely to promote education, whether the school will be established anywhere else, or some other charity established for the district (*b*).

When the question arises as to an *increase* in the funds of a charity, the rule, as already elucidated, is, as far as possible, to apply the increase equally to *all* the objects, or (supposing it a *common* fund) to as many of them as possible (*c*); thus, if the endowment be for support of a school and other charitable purposes, and the school requires no further support, the whole increase goes to the *other* purposes (*d*); and so, if the fund was for a purpose which has failed and other purposes, the fund should be applied to the other purposes (*e*).

Where it is possible to follow the directions of the testator, they will be adhered to; and charities cannot be confused (*f*), nor one charity converted into another (*g*), without the leave and sanction of the court, upon proved necessity; but if it be difficult or doubtful which of two charities is entitled, the court will admit both (*h*). So, where from any reason the literal performance of the trust becomes impossible, the court will direct what is a substantial performance,

---

(*a*) *Wilkinson* v. *Malins*, 2 C. J. 636.
(*b*) *At.-G.* v. *Glynn*, 12 Sim. 84.
(*c*) *In re Marlborough School*, 13 L. J, Ch., 3.
(*d*) *At..G.* v. *Tuffnell*, 12 Beav. 35.
(*e*) *At.-G.* v. *Ironmongers' Company*, 10 Cl. & F. 908.
(*f*) *At.-G.* v. *Goldsmid*, C. P. C., 292.
(*g*) *In re Reading Dispensary*, 11 Sim. 118.
(*h*) *Bennett* v. *Hayter*, 2 Beav. 81.

and such a performance, even without that sanction, would never be deemed a breach of trust so as to incur restitution for the past; however, it might be deemed an error, and be set right by such direction as to the future (*a*). Where there was a charity for the poor of the parish, and also for the relief of wayfares, it was held that the increase of the funds should be applied to *both* objects (*b*). So, where the objects were schools and pensions, it was held that *both* must be carried out (*c*).

When the question arises whether the trustee or donee is entitled beneficially to a residue, overplus, or surplus, it must depend, first, upon the *original* donation; for if by *that* he takes no beneficial interest, he can have none in any subsequent *increase* of the rents. And the question is always one of construction as to the intention of the donor or testator, as expressed or indicated by the terms employed, and the position or character of the donee. The general principle is, that if a fund or an estate is given to donee generally, for a charity or charitable purpose, the *whole* of the fund or the rents must be applied thereto. On the same principle, if the donor, after thus giving the whole for a charitable purpose or purposes, goes on to apportion the whole fund among them, but does it so as not to exhaust the whole, still, the general intention being clear, the actually remaining surplus would be so applied. Whether the

---

(*a*) *At.-G.* v. *Vint*, 19 L. J., Ch., 150. In that case there was a gift of *porter* to the poor in a workhouse, and it was not admissible by the regulations; it was referred to the vicar to distribute the gift as he should judge best.

(*b*) *At.-G.* v. *Corporation of Rochester*, 5 De Gex, Mac. & Gord. 797.

(*c*) *In re Lambeth Charities*, 22 L. J., Ch., 959.

same principle would apply in the case of a general gift or bequest, with an implied trust, by way of request, out of the fund to secure a certain charitable purpose, not saying to what extent, whether in such case the donee would have a right to retain the residue after satisfying to some extent that purpose, would depend upon the intention to confer a personal and beneficial interest, as to which much would depend on whether there was any *specific* gift or bequest to the trustee, which of course would tend to rebut the inference of a beneficial gift of the residue, or whether there is a gift of the residue to the trustee. And if the gift of the whole or the residue is to a person in particular character or office, negativing the idea of personal benefit otherwise than as a remuneration for service in the exercise of its functions, then (except to the extent of such remuneration) it will not be construed as a beneficial gift. Thus a specific bequest to an executor is understood to be for his own benefit; but a bequest of residue is generally understood as made to him not for his own benefit, but for the purposes for which he would hold the general personal estate, *i. e.*, for the next of kin (a). Thus, even on a general bequest of all to executors, with specific legacies, they do not take the residue for their own benefit (b). And on a bequest of specific property to certain purposes, and the residue to executors for charitable uses, with legacies to them, if the specific property produces a surplus beyond the purposes to which it was bequeathed, that would go to the next of kin (c).

(a) *Smith* v. *Barney*, 2 R. Prop. Cases, 262.
(b) *Lowe* v. *Gaze*, 8 Beav. 472.
(c) *Russell* v. *Clowes*, 2 R. Prop. Cases, 232.

Where, however, there is any sum or estate, or annual sum, given to donee, not saying as to *all*, for a particular purpose, but *specific* sums or portions are applied to particular charitable purposes, and there is a residue which the donee holds, that is deemed an evidence of an intention that the surplus should belong to the donee; but it is only evidence of that intention, and is liable to be repelled by any other circumstances in the case (*a*). If the donees and trustees are themselves parties to whom a gift would be charitable, or are themselves to perform services in carrying out the charitable object, but have no specific bequest, the inference will of course be stronger that they are to have the residue undisposed of. Thus where sums of money are given to charities and the surplus, expressly or impliedly, to the donee, with an evident intention to give him a beneficial interest, he takes the surplus (*b*). And where the testator or donor does not give the whole generally for a charity, or with an implied bequest generally for a charitable purpose (which would amount to the same thing), but gives a specific part for the charity, and the residue to the donee, of course the donee takes the residue beneficially (*c*). And if lands or goods are given to a person, subject to *specific* charges, the residue belongs to him (*d*).

If a fund is given for the support of the person who shall fill a particular office, as priest, school-

---

(*a*) At.-G. v. *Mercers' Company*, 2 Bligh, N. S. 165.
(*b*) At.-G. v. *Brazennose College*, 2 Cl. & Fin. 295; At.-G. v. *Smythies*, 2 R. & M. 717; At.-G. v. *Mayor of Bristol*, 2 J. & W. 294.
(*c*) At.-G. v. *South Molton*, 23 L. J., Ch., 567.
(*d*) At.-G. v. *Dean of Windsor*, 27 L. J., Ch., 320.

master, &c., and not for his individual benefit merely, but for securing the performance of his duties connected with the object of religion or charity which the donor had in view, if the revenues increase so as to exceed a reasonable compensation for the duties, the surplus must be applied to other charitable purposes, if any other are indicated by the gift or bequest (*a*); if not, there may be a question whether the surplus will go to the heir, next of kin, or residuary legatee. But if, in such latter case, there be enough to raise a presumption of intention that the *whole* income shall go to the priest or the schoolmaster, then it will be so decided (*b*).

Within the limits of the trust, its administration and internal management are left to the trustees, subject only to the control of the Court of Chancery in case of breach, or error, and the ancillary jurisdiction of the Commissioners of Charities.

With regard to the recipients of the benefits of a charity, their rights, as *cestuis que trust*, are under the care and protection of the Court of Chancery, and it is in their regard that the helping powers of the

---

(*a*) As, where property was given to a schoolmaster to be applied partly for the support of a school, and partly for other specified charitable purposes; and no intention could be presumed of giving individual benefit to the person filling the office of schoolmaster, the surplus income having increased beyond the extent of a reasonable compensation for the schoolmaster's duties, the court directed the surplus to be applied to the other charitable purposes: *At.-G.* v. *The Master of Brentford School*, 1 Mylne & Keen, 377. But it might have been otherwise had not the testator indicated other charitable purposes.

(*b*) As where there was a codicil to give an additional income to the schoolmaster of a school founded by the will; this was held to afford such a presumption of intention that the whole of the previously devised income should go to him: *At.-G.* v. *Wilson*, 3 Mylne & Keen, 362.

Commissioners of Charities are likely to be most useful, especially in cases of small parochial or other eleemosynary charities for the benefit of the poor, the sick, the aged, or the infirm, whose position is such as not to admit of any other than an easy and a speedy remedy. Whether their claim is to admission to the rights of asylums, almshouses, or the like, either as inmates or out-door recipients; or whether, being inmates or recipients, their claim is to increased benefits or allowances (*a*); they have an easy and a speedy remedy in the way of a simple letter to the Commissioners of Charities (*b*). So, in a great variety of parochial charities, as where churchwardens, on the part of the parish, receive the rents of lands for the use of the poor on special trusts, or have cottages in which poor persons are to be permitted to live rent free (*c*); or cases in which rectors or vicars and churchwardens have alms to distribute. In cases where the churchwardens have lands or houses upon special trusts for relief of poor persons, they are not parish property available for the union, the very object of the Act of Parliament vesting lands for parish charities in the churchwardens being to *prevent* that.

(*a*) As in the case of the Rugby Charity, where there was an attempt made by mandamus to compel the payment of increased alms to claimants on the funds; but, of course, the claim being only equitable the suit was refused, though the applicants were at an advanced age, and would probably be dead before relief could be had in Chancery: *Ex parte Rugby Charity Trustees*, 9 D & R. 214.

(*b*) See *post*, p. 112, practical directions as to the application for advice. It should be in plain writing, on foolscap paper (with a large margin), headed in the name of the charity, and addressed to the Commissioners of Charities.

(*c*) *Rumball* v. *Munt*, 8 Q. B. Rep., 394, *vide ante*, p. 13.

As to the rights of inmates of chartered hospitals they are legal, and in some cases amount to freehold interests (*a*), but there will generally be some power in the trustees or governors to expel them for misconduct, in aid of which the Charitable Trusts Act of 1855 contains a useful provision, that in case they are so lawfully deprived there shall be a summary power of expulsion from any houses or rooms they may have occupied as recipients of the charity.

With regard to the recipients or objects of a charity, the rule of law has lately been well illustrated. In the administration of charities, where the intention of the donor or founder is defined distinctly, of course it is followed, and any necessary alteration of it can be obtained only in chancery, through the advice of the Commissioners of Charities. Where the intention of the donor is *not* clearly defined, or where deeds are lost, and the object unknown or uncertain, the religion of the founder will be considered as an index of intention, if the foundation is ecclesiastical, but not so implicitly if it be educational, and still less so if it is eleemosynary. In educational charities, however, the tenets of the founder will be considered, if any doubtful directions have been given as to religious instruction, and thus the Courts of Chancery have allowed, according to usage, Dissenters' children to partake in the *general* benefits of Church of England Schools (*b*), a subject now regulated by Act of Parliament upon the same principle, by Lord Chelmsford's Act (*c*). In eleemosynary charities, the

---

(*a*) *Simpson* v. *Wilkinson*, 7 Man. & Gr. 50; *Davis* v. *Waddington*, ibid. 37.
(*b*) *In re Ilminster School*, 27 L. J., Ch., 496.
(*c*) 23 & 24 Vict. c. 11.

founder's opinions are not regarded; and even if the power of selecting objects is given to an incumbent of the Church of England, that will not necessarily confine the benefits of the charity to members of the Established Church (a). If any doubt arises on this head, the proper course is to apply to the commissioners for their advice and direction, and they can, if necessary, sanction an application to the court.

There is a clause in the Charitable Trusts Act which has special reference to. endowed *schools*, providing that "nothing shall diminish or detract from any right or privilege which by any rule or practice of the Court of Chancery, or by construction of law, now subsists for the preference or the exclusive or special benefit of the Church of England, or the members of the same Church, in settling any scheme for the regulation of any charity, or the appointment or removal of trustees, or generally in the application or management of any charity." (s. 46.) This rule or construction of law only applies where there is anything in the foundation to restrict its benefits to the members of the Church of England; if there is not, trustees need not be members of that Church (b); or if the usage has been to admit Dissenters, and there is nothing in the deed against it (c). But if there is anything to indicate it, then, though the children of Dissenters may be admissible, either by usage or by the recent statute, the *religious* teaching must be that of the Church of England, and the trustees and teachers must be members of that Church (d). And

---

(a) *At.-G.* v. *Calvert*, 26 L. J., Ch., 682.
(b) *Re Norwich Charities*, 2 Mylne & Keen, 275.
(c) *At.-G.* v. *Bishop of Worcester*, 9 Hare, 328.
(d) *At.-G.* v. *Cullum*, 1 Y. & C. (N. S.) 411.

accordingly, although by the Endowed Schools Act, 1860, it is provided that :—

"It shall be lawful for the trustees or governors of every endowed school from time to time to make, and they shall be bound to make, such orders as, whilst they shall not interfere with the religious teaching of the other scholars as now fixed by statute or other legal requirement, and shall not authorise any religious teaching other than that previously afforded in the school, shall nevertheless provide for admitting to the benefits of the school the children of parents not in communion with the church, sect, or denomination according to the doctrines or formularies of which religious instruction is to be afforded under the endowment of the said school : *provided that in the will or wills, deed or deeds,* or other instrument or instruments regulating such endowment, *nothing be contained expressly requiring the children educated under such endowment to learn or to be instructed according to the doctrines or formularies of such church, sect, or denomination—*"

Yet this Act leaves untouched the rule that the *trustees* in such cases must be members of the Church of England; and the Act does not apply to any of the institutions mentioned in the Act 3 & 4 Vict. c. 77, "*An Act for improving the condition and extending the benefits of Grammar Schools,* nor to any school established or to be established by or in union with or to be in union with the national society for promoting the education of the poor in the principles of the Established Church, nor to any institution maintained wholly by voluntary subscriptions, or partly by voluntary subscriptions and partly by school payments."

Which proviso excludes the poor schools established

with the aid of grants from the Privy Council for different religious bodies ; and which by the acceptance of such grants, and the trust deeds, are placed under the control of the Court of Chancery, though, unless endowed, they are not under the jurisdiction of the Commissioners of Charities. If endowed they are so, *quoad* their endowments, and, of course, to ascertain their endowments they must supply *accounts*.

The internal management of charities having visitors is a matter for their jurisdiction, which within its scope is final and conclusive (*a*). On a principle analogous to that which precludes the intervention of the court in the internal management of a corporate charity which has visitors (*b*), the court abstains from interference in the internal regulation or conduct of any religious or educational charity, corporate or incorporate, as a chapel or a school. For religious charities (and all schools are more or less deemed to be religious), are always supposed to be under some system of visitation, episcopal or otherwise ; and the jurisdiction of the court is exercised in such cases only to secure the due application of the funds by or subject to the control of the proper parties to exercise that visitation. The master of a grammar school, as well as the incumbent of a Church of England chapel, must be licensed by his bishop; and so of similar offices in charities of the Churches of Scotland or of Rome; and as to Dissenting bodies, as the Wesleyans, having a general system of discipline ; while as to others, the congregational system of control is equally recognised (*c*). Thus the

---

(*a*) *At.-G.* v. *Smythies*, 1 Keen, 289 ; *At.-G.* v. *Crook*, 1 Keen, 121.
(*b*) *In re Warrwick School*, 14 L. J., Ch., 338.
(*c*) *At.-G.* v. *Aked*, 7 Sim., 321.

court leaves it to these authorities to see that the duties of such offices are discharged, taking care that, if not so discharged, the parties shall not be permitted to enjoy the profits of their offices, and so defeat the object of the trust.

The general principle which describes the jurisdiction of Chancery in all cases, indeed, is, that it does not interfere in the internal management of a charity.

With regard to the dismissal or removal of officers or functionaries of charities, as masters of schools or ministers of chapels, they being at once in the position of recipients and administrators of the benefits of the charity, it is only under the jurisdiction of the Court of Chancery by way of *control*.

In order to enable the trustees to ensure the due adherence to the objects of the trust or foundation, they have, either expressly or by necessary implication, the power of appointing and removing officers or recipients of the charity, as masters, ministers, &c. The right of nomination, presentation, or election, is generally, either as regards the parties entitled to appoint or the parties appointed, a legal right (*a*), and the Commissioners have no control over suits at law. Where the relation of trustee and *cestui que trust* exists, the application must be to Chancery (*b*), and by their sanction. Where the party was wrongfully appointed and is in possession, it is usually a mere legal question; where he was rightly appointed, but does not carry out the trust, it is a question for the Court of Chancery (*c*). The mere right of dismissal

---

(*a*) *R.* v. *Kendall*, 1 Q. B., 366.
(*b*) *In re Orton Vicarage*, 18 L. J., 2 B., 312.
(*c*) *R.* v. *Mosley*, 17 L. J., Ch., 446, 2 De Gex. & S., 398.

or removal is generally a legal question, but it is always under the *control* of chancery, which makes its great object the due administration of the *charity*.

Even in the case of the master of a free grammar school, who has a freehold in his office (*a*), he may be dismissed for misconduct, usually by express provisions in the foundation (*b*). If he is not a freeholder the power of appointment or removal is in the majority of the trustees (*c*) ; but even where there is a power of removal at discretion, the Court of Chancery exercises a control, and sees that the discretion is not exercised arbitrarily, or so as to defeat the objects of the charity (*d*) ; but as this is often a matter of difficulty, special provision is made both in the Grammar Schools Act and the Charitable Trusts Act, as to masters of endowed schools, and in the latter Act as to all other officers.

Where the master or minister has not a freehold office, the power of dismissing him depends on the terms of the foundation, or the terms of his engagement, and he may be dismissed on such notice or for such cause consistent with those terms, as the majority of the trustees think fit (*e*) ; and as to ministers of Dissenting chapels, merely allowed or engaged by trustees to preach, &c., they have no estate nor title beyond what may be created by the terms of their engagement, and can be dismissed for such cause as the trustees or congregation think just (*f*). Chapels

---

(*a*) *Chipping Sodbury School*, 8, L. J., Ch., 13.
(*b*) *R. v. Darlington School*, 6 Q. B. Rep. 682.
(*c*) *Wilkinson v. Malins*, 2 C. & J., 636.
(*d*) *Willis v. Child*, 20 L. J., Ch., 113.
(*e*) *Wilkinson v. Malins*, 2 Crompton & Jervis, 636 ; *Brown v. Dawson*, 12 A. & E. 624.
(*f*) *Doe v. Jones*, 10 B. & C., 713 ; *Perry v. Shipway*, 28 L. J., Ch., 660.

of Dissenters are not within the Trusts Act, but endowments for the support of ministers are, and the commissioners therefore have jurisdiction.

With regard to the Churches of England, Scotland, and Rome, assuming that the right parties have nominated, if the minister is or has become disqualified by the sentence of his spiritual superior, or by refusal of his licence or "faculties," the Court of Chancery will not allow him to retain possession of his office, or the trust would thereby be defeated. The application to remove him must be made to that court, with the sanction of the commissioners, and in adjudicating upon it the court will not enter into the merits or demerits of the religious question at issue between the priest or preacher and his superiors, but will treat it as a question of fact, whether, according to the usage and discipline.

Under the Poor Schools Act (a) provisions are made for poor schools, in respect to the masters and mistresses, somewhat analogous to those made in the Grammar Schools Act as to grammar schools.

" No schoolmaster or schoolmistress to be appointed to any school erected upon land conveyed under the powers of this Act shall be deemed to have acquired an interest for life by virtue of such appointment, but shall, in default of any specific engagement, hold his office at the discretion of the trustees of the said school." Sect. 17.

" Justices of the peace or sheriffs to give possession of schoolrooms, &c., in case of the refusal of the master." Sect. 18.

With respect to schools receiving aid from the

(a) 4 & 5 Vict. c. 38.

Committee of Privy Council for Education, the trust deed provides fully for their regulation, under what is called "the management clause" of that deed, in accordance with the principles already stated, vesting the management of the religious instruction in the clergyman of the parish, if a Church of England school; or of the priest of the chapel, if a Roman Catholic school; or of the minister and members of the congregation if a Dissenting school; and vesting the management in all other respects in a committee of management, establishing a kind of joint direct visitatorial jurisdiction in the crown as to secular instruction and moral conduct, in the bishops, &c., as to religious belief or instruction. The Charitable Trusts Act contains exemptions of chapels, so that its provisions cannot be applied to dismissal of the ministers of chapels, and even as to the Catholic chapels which are not exempted, well established principles of equity would preclude any dismissal save by the proper ecclesiastical authorities. And though there is a provision in the Act, that if any question or dispute shall arise among the members of any charity (exempted from the operation of the Act or not) in relation to any officer, or the fitness or disqualification of any trustee or officer, or his election or removal (*a*), or generally in relation to the management of the charity, two-thirds of the members present at any special meeting, &c., may refer such question or dispute to the arbitration of the commissioners,—this cannot refer to chapel charities, for reasons already explained (*b*).

(*a*) Sect. 64.
(*b*) *Vide ante*, p. 86.

Where there is an endowment for the support of a chapel or school for religious worship or instruction, according to the doctrines or usages of a particular religious body, no others are eligible to be teachers of the school, or preachers of the chapel, but such as are members of that religious body, and if the worship or instruction is to be that of any particular Church, then no preacher or teacher can be eligible for the office of pastor who is not licensed by that church, and recognised as in full communion with it (*a*), and any one excluded from such communion will be removed by the Court of Chancery. The same principle, of course, would apply to a Roman Catholic priest suspended or deprived, not to say excommunicated, who, independently of any particular body of canons, might be proved by any bishop or ecclesiastical superior of the Roman Catholic Church, to be not in communion with it, or not competent to administer the rights or sacraments of that church (*b*).

Dissenters' chapels, being under congregational management, are regulated under the Dissenters' Chapels Act, which applies, it will be observed, not merely to the chapels (excluded from the Charitable Trusts Act), but the *endowments* thereof, or for the ministers, which are *not* excluded. That Act provides "That so far as no particular religious doctrines or opinions, or mode of regulating worship, shall on the face of the will, deed, or other instrument declaring the trusts of any meeting house for the worship of

---

(*a*) *At.-G.* v. *Murdoch*, 1 De Gex, Macn. & Gord, 86; *At.-G.* v. *Munro*, 2 De Gex & Smale, 122.

(*b*) Just as Dr. Wiseman was examined before the Lords in the Sussex Peerage Case (11 Cl. & Fin., 86) on a question of Roman law, as a matter of fact. And see *R.* v. *Howell*, 1 C. & K., 689.

God by persons dissenting, either in express terms, or by reference to some book or other document as containing such doctrines or opinions or mode of regulating worship, be required to be taught or observed, or be forbidden to be taught or observed therein, the usage for twenty-five years immediately preceding any suit relating to such meeting house of the congregation frequenting the same shall be taken as conclusive evidence that such religious doctrines or opinions or mode of worship as have for such period been taught or observed in such meeting house may properly be taught or observed in such meeting house, and the right or title of the congregation to hold such meeting house, *together with any burial ground, Sunday or day school, or minister's house attached thereto;* and any *fund* for the *benefit of such congregation,* or of *the minister or other officer of such congregation,* or of *the widow of any such minister,* shall not be called in question on account of the doctrines or opinions or mode of worship so taught or observed in such meeting house : provided nevertheless, that where any such minister's house, school, or fund as aforesaid shall be given or created by any will, deed, or other instrument, which shall declare in express terms, or by such reference as aforesaid, the particular religious doctrines or opinions for the promotion of which such minister's house, school, or fund is intended, then and in every such case such minister's house, school, or fund shall be applied to the promoting of the doctrines or opinions so specified, any usage of the congregation to the contrary notwithstanding (*a*)."

(*a*) But it has been held that a deed void under the Mortmain

The Act, it will be observed, does not apply to schools (if any) *not* attached to chapels, and which are under the Charitable Trusts Act, even (*quoad* the endowments) if partly supported by voluntary contributions.

It is to be observed that the above Act only declares the law as to the religious persuasion to be deemed entitled to the chapel or school. *Their* control of it is exercised according either to the deed or usage by the members or communicants, as the case may be. In the absence of any usage, it will be for the court or the Commissioners of Charities, in any case that may arise relative to the endowments of ministers, to decide in whom the management may be (*a*).

With regard to Roman Catholic chapels and schools, they are, as already observed, not excepted from the Charitable Trusts Act, which embraces all religious or charitable endowments of the Roman Catholic body; all its religious endowments being in law charities, and only held subject to the implied condition of responsibility to the Court of Chancery and now to the Commissioners of Charities.

The Roman Catholic Charities Act has applied the same principle to all Roman Catholic religious trusts:

" V. Where any real or personal estate, subject to any use, trust, gift, foundation, or disposition for any Charity relating to or connected with the Roman Catholic religion, shall have been applied upon any Charitable Trusts relating to or connnected with the same religion during any continuous period of twenty

---

law, may be sufficient evidence as against the *trustees* of the trusts of the endowment. *At.-G.* v. *Ward*, 6 Hare, 477.

(*a*) *At.-G.* v. *Aked*, 7 Sim., 321; *Shipway* v. *Perry*, 28 L. J., Ch., 660.

years, but the original trusts of such property shall not be ascertained by means of any written document, the *consistent* usage of the last preceding twenty years, or of the last period of twenty years during which any consistent usage in the application of such property shall have prevailed, shall be deemed to afford conclusive evidence of the trusts on which the same property shall have been settled."

It will be observed that the usage under this enactment must have been "consistent;" which, however, probably is implied in the previous Act as to Dissenters, for the very word usage implies consistency. If the same usage has not been followed for a given period, there has not been a usage,—certainly not a usage for that period. And if there has not been such a usage—that is, if there has sometimes been one application of the fund and sometimes another—then, if there is no deed or document declaring the objects of the trust definitely, it must be referred to the Commissioners, to frame a *scheme* for its management, unless the deed or document expressly or impliedly give the power to the donee, vesting it in his discretion. If *not* so left to his discretion, *he* has no power to frame a scheme, or carry the application at his discretion. And, on the other hand, it follows that from the terms of the trust, as ascertained, either by express documentary evidence or by usage, there can be no deviation except under the authority of the Court of Chancery, or the Commissioners of Charities; or if they doubt their authority, there must be an application to Parliament. The Grammar Schools Act contains no provision as to usage; the evil as to schools being generally, not in ascertaining the trusts, but in the necessity for departing or deviating from them; and that is a necessity which the Court of Chancery never leaves to trustees to determine upon, unless the trust leaves it to them expressly, or by necessary implication from the very nature of the trust, as in the case of an institution or charity formally established and with regular government.

Where there is no deed *regulating* the trust, but *a* trust is declared or implied, and there is no discretionary power given to the donees lay or ecclesiastical, and usage is resorted to under the statute, it is not quite clear whether it will be material how far the usage, if proved in *fact*, and in itself consistent, appears to have been objected to by the ecclesiastical authorities of the Roman Catholic Church; or whether by the word "consistent" it is meant to be implied that the usage must have been consistent with their discipline or authority. It should seem that if this was intended, it has not been duly expressed, and that a usage in *fact* will bind. But there is little probability of any usage of twenty years having been maintained against the expressed will of the Roman Catholic spiritual authorities; at all events, not against the law or discipline of the Roman Catholic church.

Supposing, however, that there is neither deed nor usage, nor discretion in the donees or the trustees, and that the court or the commissioners have to settle a scheme for a Roman Catholic religious charity, they will undoubtedly, by analogy to the well-settled principles of practice of the court in such cases, consult the proper Roman Catholic authorities as to the best mode of carrying out the objects of the trust, and will take their evidence as to the discipline of their Church as a matter of fact, like that of foreign law (*a*).

In no case, therefore, can the authority of the Court of Chancery or of the Commissioner of Charities be justly deemed to interfere with their spiritual authority or their right of property. The proper spiritual authority of every body of Christians in the country is consulted and deferred to by the court, within its true scope and limits, the *internal* administration of the endowment, its spiritual visitation so to speak, its discipline and conduct, according to the laws of the Church (*b*).

And with respect to rights of property, to assume such a right, precedent to or paramount to the determination of the court, would be a fallacy; for it is the province of the court to decide whether there *is* a property, whether with reference to the laws regulating the *rights* of subjects to dispose of their property, or with reference to the question of trust. If there has been an infraction of the law as to disposition of property for such purposes, there is no right of property. If there is a legal right, coupled with a trust, then there is no right of property in the plenary sense of the term, for that includes the legal and the equitable sense; and a trustee is not the equitable owner—that is, he is not the beneficial owner; and if so, then he can have no right of property, save subject to the jurisdiction of the Court of Chancery. For

---

(*a*) As in the Sussex Peerage Case, 11 Cl. & Fin. 86, where Dr. Wiseman was examined at the bar of the House of Lords with regard to the law of his Church as to marriage. So in *Regina* v. *Howett*, 1 C. & K. 689, where the evidence of a priest was taken as to the discipline and usage, with respect to one of the sacraments, of his Church.

(*b*) *Vide ante*, p. 88.

trusts are the creations of that court, and disposition upon trusts at all are only conditional upon its control, and trusts if pecuniary are equitable debts; so that there is no more reason to object to the authority of the courts of equity as to trusts, than of the courts of law as to debts. When the Court of Chancery decrees that property given for religious purposes is to pass to the heir or next of kin, it does not take any property from the church or religious body to which it was bequeathed, but pronounces that it never *had* a property in it.

Under the common law the bishops took the estates of their sees absolutely, and without civil responsibility in respect thereof. Under the law now the Roman Catholic prelates or priests take funds entrusted to them for pious purposes, only on the condition of civil responsibility; for only on such conditions could the law allow the donors to give or the donees to receive, especially as regards bequests or gifts by will: for a man has no *natural* right to leave his property as he pleases away from his natural heirs; and the right, being purely artificial, is subject to such conditions as the law imposes, not being *contrary* to the laws of the Christian Church. Now it is contrary to the law of the church to take away property which is once legally vested for its use; but not so, either to decree that property *never* was legally vested in it, or in trust for its purposes, or that it was vested subject to the conditions of lay or civil control (with the exception only of questions as to eligibility for, or the due discharge of, spiritual duties); and still less is it so, to enforce its administration for such purposes, according to the laws and discipline of that church itself. Therefore the see of Rome has sanctioned an appeal by a Roman Catholic bishop to the Privy Council (a) against a decree of a civil court, —not indeed as to his spiritual office or duties, but as to certain civil rights alleged to be founded upon or attached to such spiritual office, and which he could only have or exercise by the aid of that court, and therefore subject to its jurisdiction.

So the Roman Catholic bishops have voluntarily placed such of their poor schools, as have accepted the grants in aid of education, under the control of the Court of Chancery, which, according to the terms of the management clauses of the trust-deeds of such schools, would have to decide all disputes save such as are solely religious, and are to be determined by the Roman Catholic bishop.

The Management of Charity Property.

The scope of the jurisdiction of the Court of Chancery and the Commissioners of Charities is the due application of the revenues of a charity to its proper purposes; and with that view, the security and due management of the charity property is one great object of that jurisdiction. In this, as in every other respect, the general principle of courts of equity is that

---

(a) *Hughes* v. *Pownal*, 4 Moore's Privy Council Cases, 47. There the question was whether the Roman Catholic bishop, the appellant, was entitled to all the fees or emoluments received in this office; or whether a lay committee was entitled to half. The Privy Council received on both sides evidence of, and recognised as valid, *inter se*, the acts and measures of the Roman See as to the spiritual office of the bishop; but the council had to decide, and the Roman See did not object to its deciding, what are the legal or civil rights or emoluments annexed to the office; and the council decided that, according to usage, to which the bishop assented, the lay committee had a right to receive the general offerings, and that they were to be applied in certain proportions to different objects.

"the fair exercise of their judgment by trustees is a protection, whether the consequences be good or bad" (*a*). On the other hand, when they have a discretion, they are bound to exercise it, and the courts will not exercise it for them, as it is a personal trust (*b*); and in such case the test of a negligent breach of trust is what would have been the course of the court under similar circumstances (*c*). The principle of Chancery is to leave the trustees to exercise their discretion, on their own responsibility (*d*). But under the Charitable Trusts Act they may in this or any other case ask the advice and direction of the board, and act upon it with safety (*e*).

One of the most important duties of a trustee, in which he has often a discretion, is investment of trust-money. If, as is usually the case, he is authorised or directed to lay it out in real or government securities, he is bound so to do; and although, while waiting to find a mortgage security, he may invest in exchequer bills (*f*), yet not only if he invest in a security unauthorised he is answerable for the loss (*g*), but so even if, having an option, as for example between real and government securities, he elects the former and it fails, he is answerable to the trust (*h*). The proper course, therefore, is to apply

---

(*a*) *Garrett* v. *Noble*, 3 L. J. (N. S.), Ch., 159; *Haincett* v. *Smith*, 1 L. J. (N. S.), Ch., 218; *At.-G.* v. *Solly*, 5 L. J., Ch. (N. S.) 5.
(*b*) *Wain* v. *Egmont*, 3 Myl. & Keen, 445.
(*c*) *Warner* v. *Torkington*, 4 L. J., Ch., 193.
(*d*) *Potter* v. *Seymour*, 3 Young & Collyers, Eq. Rep. 708.
(*e*) Act of 1853, s. 16.
(*f*) *Mathews* v. *Bruse*, 6 Beav. Rep. 239.
(*g*) *Tyler* v. *Tyler*, 3 Beav. 550.
(*h*) *Arves* v. *Parkinson*, 7 Beav. 379.

to the board for advice and direction (*a*); and so where the power is to invest in some good and approved investment (*b*).

With regard to personalty not expressly *directed* to be invested, the purpose being one requiring permanence, the duty of the trustee is to invest (*c*); hence, as already explained, investment is one of the necessary incidents of trusts as to personalty. The trustee *may* be liable for its loss; as where he leaves the money for years in the hands of bankers, who fail (*d*); and so if the banker had directions to invest, the trustee would be answerable for his omission to do so. In any case, therefore, in which the trustee has uninvested funds, he should either apply to the Board for advice and direction as to its investment or disposition (*e*), or he should transfer it to the official trustees (*f*); first obtaining an order of a Judge of the Court of Chancery, or of some Judge having jurisdiction under the Act for that purpose, as money cannot be so transferred without some such order. The investment of trust personalty being necessary to the perpetuity of the trust, there are many careful provisions in the Charitable Trusts Act upon the subject.

The Charitable Trusts Act contains no provision as to the mode of investment; as to which a recent Act (*g*) provides that, " When a trustee, executor, or

---

(*a*) Act of 1853, s. 16.
(*b*) Although in that case the trustee will not be liable for a loss if he has acted honestly.—*Jones* v. *Lewis*, 18 L. J., Ch., N. S. 430.
(*c*) *Driver* v. *Maudsley*, 18 L. J., Rep. (N. S.), Ch., 273.
(*d*) *Challer* v. *Shippam*, 4 Hare's Rep. 555.
(*e*) Act of 1853, s. 16.
(*f*) S. 51.
(*g*) 23 & 24 Vict. c. 38, s. 32.

administrator shall not, by some instruments creating his trust, be expressly forbidden to invest any trust fund on real securities, in any part of the United Kingdom, or on the Stock of the Bank of England or Ireland, or on East India Stock, it shall be lawful for such trustee, executor, or administrator to invest such trust fund on such securities or stock; and he shall not be liable on that account as for a breach of trust, provided that such investment shall in other respects be reasonable and proper."

And another Act (*a*) provides that the Court of Chancery may direct by general orders for the conversion of any three per cent. Bank annuities now standing in the name of the Accountant-General of the court, in trust in any cause or matter, into any other stocks, funds, or securities specified in the orders, and trustees are empowered, where they have an option, to invest in any such securities.

With regard to the letting of charity lands, the principle in Chancery is, that the court will look only to the benefit of the charity, and expect, therefore, that the best possible terms be obtained (*b*), on which principle it is that it disapproves of leases for *long* terms, which amount substantially to alienations (*c*), although in consideration of fines or rent-charges (*d*), unless under circumstances which make it manifestly for the benefit of the charity (*e*). Still, where the lease is not beyond three lives, and for large fines, in accordance with long custom, the court will not deem

---

(*a*) 22 & 23 Vict. c. 35, s. 10.
(*b*) *At.-G.* v. *Gains*, 10 Beav. 63.
(*c*) *At.-G.* v. *Pilgrim*, 12 Beav. 57, 2 Hall & Twells, 186.
(*d*) *At.-G.* v. *Pargeter*, 6 Beav. 150.
(*e*) *At.-G.* v. *Kerr*, 9 Beav. 421.

it improper (a), nor will it lay down any rule that lettings should be by competition or by public tender (b). With regard to parish lands, provision is made by statute (c). But it is obvious that the

---

(a) *At.-G.* v. *Crook*, 1 Keen, 121.
(b) *At.-G.* v. *Cullum*, 1 Keen, 104.
(c) The 5 & 6 Vict. c. 18 (reciting 7 Wm. IV & 1 Vict. c. 50), authorised the sale, exchange, letting, and disposal, by the guardians of a union of any workhouse, tenements, buildings, land, effects, or other property belonging to any parish which shall be comprised in the union, and, in cases of the sale, exchange, letting, and disposal of workhouses, tenements, buildings, land, effects and other property belonging to a dissolved union to have applied and to apply to a majority of the persons who were the last acting guardians previous to the dissolution of such union: Provided always that nothing in the act shall be deemed to render valid or to authorise the sale, exchange, letting, or the disposition of any property whatsoever which shall have been given or bequeathed by way of charitable donation, or shall have been allotted in right of some charitable donation or otherwise, for the poor persons of any parish, and not for the general benefit of the rate-payers, parishioners, or inhabitants of such parish, nor to dispense with the consent of the rate-payers and owners of property required by the last-recited act to all sales, exchanges, lettings, or other dispositions of property belonging to any parish, except in the case next hereinafter provided.—s. 2.
Where several parishes shall have been or shall be jointly interested in any workhouse, tenements, buildings, lands, whether of freehold, copyhold, or customary tenure, effects, or other property, it shall be deemed to have been and shall be lawful for the commissioners, upon the application of the overseers of the major part of such parishes, and with the consent of the rate-payers and owners of property in the major part of such parishes, to be ascertained in the manner directed by the said Act, to order the same to be sold, let, exchanged, or disposed of by the guardians of the union in which such parishes or the greater part thereof shall be situate, in such manner and subject to such rules, orders, and regulations as the said commissioners shall deem fit; and it shall be deemed to have been and to be lawful for the said commissioners to direct the application of the produce arising from such sale, letting, or disposition, in the same manner and to and for the same purposes as the produce arising from the sales of property belonging to other parishes may be applied to.—s. 3.
As to what are parish lands, as distinct from parochial charity lands, see *Alison* v. *Stark*, 9 A. & E., 255; *Cantrell* v. *Windsor Union*, 4 B. N. C. 348. As to evidence that lands are such (as payment of rent to churchwardens), see *Doe d. Higgs* v. *Terry*, 4 A. & E., 274.

only proper course for trustees to take if they desire to let for long terms, for building, mining, &c., is to apply to the board for advice or authority (*a*).

With regard to the sale of charity lands, the principle of the court is, that though in a proper case trustees have the power of alienating the property (*b*), a very special case must be made out of *benefit* to the charity, even to induce the court to refer it to its officer to enquire as to whether it would be "proper" to permit the sale (*c*), and it cannot be sanctioned by the court without such reference. Even when the alienation is in consideration of a rent-charge, the burden is on the trustees of proving that it was for the benefit of the charity (*d*), and of course, this being so, it would be imprudent even to incur the risk of applying to the court upon the subject, and the proper course is to apply to the board for direction and advice under the Charitable Trusts Act (*e*) or for leave to sell or exchange (*f*).

The general jurisdiction of the court is exercised ordinarily, by a bill, by a private party, or information at the suit of the Attorney-General, who, as representing the Crown in its capacity as

---

(*a*) Act of 1853, s. 16.
(*b*) At.-G. v. the *South Sea Company*, 4 Beav. 453.
(*c*) At.-G. v. *Corporation of Norwich*, 1 Hare's Ch. Rep. 395.
(*d*) At.-G. v. *Brettingham*, 3 Beav. 91; At.-G. v. *Kerr*, 2 Beav. 421.
(*e*) Act of 1853, s. 16.
(*f*) Ib., s. 24. See 1 & 2 Geo. IV. c. 92, as to *exchange* of charity lands. Leases for long terms—beyond 99 years, the ordinary duration of a building lease—are virtually alienations of the worst kind, and will be set aside as such unless *manifestly* for the benefit of the charity. See At.-G. v. *South Sea Company, suprà*. So of a husbandry lease for 200 years at a fixed rent; which cannot possibly be supported.—At.-G. v. *Pargeter*, 6 Beav. 150; At.-G. v. *Pilgrim*, 2 Hall & Twells, 186; 12 Beav. 57.

parens patriæ, is a guardian of charities in which the public have an interest. Hence as corporate property is now applicable to public purposes, and the borough-fund is a trust fund, it has been held right that the Attorney-General should sue even in conjunction with the corporation (*a*). Where, however, the subject matter of the information does not immediately affect the *interest* of the Crown, as in the case of a public charity, the proceedings are carried on in the name and under the direction and at the responsibility of a "relator," who need not have a personal interest, and if he has, the proceedings are by "information and bill." This proceeding by bill or information is proper to *declare* a trust, and fix a party with a trust who denies it, and claims to hold the property adversely to the charity, and for his own benefit absolutely (*b*); or against a trustee for *breach* of trust. The *latter* is the scope of the Charitable Trusts Act, and was also the scope of the Act called by the name of Sir S. Romilly, which was passed to afford a more summary remedy in cases of charity.

Special Jurisdiction in Chancery for the Control or Relief of Trustees of Charities.

By Sir S. Romilly's Act, it is provided, "That from and after the passing of this act, in every case of breach of any trust, or supposed breach of any trust created for charitable purposes (*c*), or whenever the

---

(*a*) *At.-G.* v. *Wilson*, 9 Sim.

(*b*) *Hutchinson* v. *Stephens*, 6 Sim., 498; *Walton* v. *Newry*, 6 Sim., 328.

(*c*) That in a case of plain breach of trust committed by persons in their character as trustees, not foreigners or strangers. *Ex parte* Skinner, 2 Merivale, 453.

direction or order of a court of equity shall be deemed necessary for the administration of any trust for charitable purposes (*a*), it shall be lawful for any two or more persons (*b*) to present a petition (provided that every petition so to be preferred shall be submitted to and be allowed by his Majesty's Attorney or Solicitor-general, and such allowance shall be certified by him before any such petition shall be presented) to the Lord Chancellor, &c., stating such complaint and praying such relief as the nature of the case may require; and it shall be lawful for the Lord Chancellor, &c., and they are hereby required, to hear such petition in a summary way, and upon affidavits or such other evidence as shall be produced upon such hearing to determine the same, and to make such order therein and with respect to the costs of such applications as to him or them shall seem just."

This Act was intended to give a more easy and less expensive mode of bringing before the court a clear abuse of a charity, but not where there is any question with respect to the persons interested in the trust, or what is the nature of the trust, or in what manner the breach of the trust is to be dealt with, nor in what way the charity is to be carried into effect (*c*).

The scope of this Act very much resembles that of the Charitable Trusts Act, save that the jurisdiction is domestic rather than judicial. It has been truly

---

(*a*) Constructive trusts are not as the Act. *Ex parte, Brown* v. *Cooper*, 295.

(*b*) Having a direct interest in the charity. *In re Bedford Charity*, 2 Swanston, 518; but householders are allowed to petition on account of misapplication of parish charities. *In re Chertsey Market*, 6 Price, 261.

(*c*) *Ludlow Corporation* v. *Greenhouse*, 1 Bligh, N. S. 17.

said that, under Sir S. Romilly's Act, the court has no power to decide whether trustees have power to alter the regulations of a charity, if that is asserted or contested (*a*), but the court *has* power under that Act to decide, upon petition under that Act, whether there shall be an application to Parliament to sanction a new scheme (*b*).

Under the Act the court has jurisdiction to declare the proportions in which charitable objects are entitled, and frame new schemes of application within its authority; but not to repair a previous misapplication of the funds among the various objects (*c*); nor to enter into adverse claims.

The scope of this Act very nearly describes the jurisdiction of the Charity Commissioners, so far at least as regards their powers of direction, adjudication, or administration. The words, "relief, order, and direction," used in Romilly's Act, are the words used in the clauses of the Charitable Trusts Act conferring jurisdiction either on the Commissioners, or on the County Court, or the Judges in Chancery at chambers. Whatever before the Charitable Trusts Act could not be done by the court on petition under Romilly's Act, must be done now by the court on bill or information; and, except the Attorney-General, or person claiming adversely to a charity, no one can resort to the court for any relief or direction relating to or concerning a charity without the sanction of that Board.

The words, relief, order, or direction, are the words

(*a*) *At.-G.* v. *East Retford Grammar School,* 17 L. J., Ch., 450.
(*b*) *In re Shrewsbury Grammar School,* 1 Mac. & Gord. 324.
(*c*) *Re Hall's Charity,* 14 Beav. 115.

used in Sir S. Romilly's Act, allowing summary application to the court upon petition in charity cases. And under that clause the court has no jurisdiction to decide what powers the trustees have, but only to interpose where there has been an improper exercise of an acknowledged power (*a*). So on the other hand the Act has no operation between trustees and strangers, but only as between trustees and the objects of the trust; and it is in the discretion of the court to what extent its powers under this Act ought to be applied (*b*). Under this Act, again, though the court has jurisdiction to declare the proportions in which the charitable objects are entitled, it cannot repair previous misapplications of the funds (*c*). It has power under this Act, upon petition, to frame new schemes, which comes under the words in the Act (used in the Charitable Trusts Act, s. 11) "order and direction," provided there be not an entire departure from the plan of the founder, as where it was held that it had no jurisdiction to transfer the funds of a dispensary to a hospital, and amalgamate the two institutions (*d*). But the court has jurisdiction, upon petition, to enquire into the expediency of an application to Parliament to authorise a different application of the funds (*e*), a discretion, however, which the court exercises very sparingly (*f*).

The scope of this Act is rather the relief of the *objects* of a charity, than the *trustees* of charities.

The only application to Chancery which trustees or

(*a*) At.-G. v. *Corporation of Bristol*, 14 L. J. (N. S.), Ch., 457.
(*b*) At.-G. v. *Bishop of Worcester*, 21 L. J., Ch., 20.
(*c*) *Re Hall's Charity*, 14 Beav. 115.
(*d*) *In re Reading Dispensary*, 12 Sim. 329.
(*e*) *In re Shrewsbury Grammar Schools*, 1 Mac. and Gord. 324, 19 L. J., Ch., 287.
(*f*) Ibid.

parties can take in a charity case, without the sanction either of the board or the Attorney-General, is a course open to executors or trustees, under the Trustees' Relief Act; under which they can pay or bring into court any fund as to which there are adverse claims, and on which it is difficult to decide. The money being thus brought into court, it abides the orders of the court, and the trustee is relieved from responsibility; or the parties who are entitled to it must apply to the court for it. This, however, is obviously only a course likely to be available, not for trustees of a charity, but for executors or trustees having funds *claimed* by a charity, and also claimed adversely to it. They are not bound to determine on adverse claims of any difficulty; and this course throws the *onus* in such a case on the trustees of the charity, who, in their turn, may apply to the Commissioners of Charities, and cannot apply to have the money paid out of court to them without the sanction of the board; although executors, being also trustees for a charity, may pay money into court without such sanction; the obvious distinction being, that in the one case the fund is placed under, in the other withdrawn from, the control of the court and the commissioners.

Powers of the Commissioners.—Enquiry.

The powers of the Commissioners of Charities are powers of investigation, of direction, of administration, of arbitration, of litigation, and of adjudication.

I. As to powers of investigation :—

1. Trustees are yearly to furnish accounts of all income, or additions thereto, and all expenditure.—(Act of 1855, s. 44.)

2. The board may *require* from trustees, &c., accounts and statements in writing, as they in their discretion think fit.—(Act of 1853, s. 9, 10.)

3. The board have a general power, as they in their discretion think fit, to examine and enquire into all charities or the funds thereof, and may summon any persons connected with charities for the purpose, examine them on oath or otherwise, and call for the production of deeds, &c. (Act of 1853, s. 11, 14), and examine *any* persons voluntarily attending.

4. These powers of enquiry necessarily include the enquiry as to what *are* charities; and the only restriction is, that they cannot enforce information from any person claiming to hold adversely to the charity, or for his own benefit; but the scope of their enquiries may include claims of property for use on *behalf* of a charity, or claims against or adverse to a charity.

5. They have *special* powers of enquiry, either of their own motion, or on the application of others, as to new schemes, or as to sales, exchanges, and partitions of charity property, as to dismissals of masters, &c., as subsidiary or preliminary to their powers of direction, of administration, of arbitration, of litigation, or restraint of litigation, or of adjudication.

In order to exercise these powers and provisions, the commissioners are empowered to make enquiries, as they in their discretion shall deem fit, into all charities and their income or property. For the purpose of enabling the board the better to prosecute these powers of enquiry, the trustees, or persons acting in the administration of a charity, are every year to prepare accounts :—

1. Of the gross income arising from, or which *ought* to have arisen from the endowments.

2. An account of all balances in hand at the commencement of the year, and of all monies received during the same year on account of the charity.

3. An account for the same period of all payments.

4. An account of all monies owing to or from the charity, so far as conveniently may be.

"Which accounts shall be certified under the hand of one or more of the said trustees or administrators, and shall be audited by the auditor of the charity, if any; and the said trustees or administrators shall, within fourteen days after the day appointed for making out such accounts, deliver or transmit a copy thereof to the commissioners at their office in London, and in the case of parochial charities shall deliver another copy thereof to the churchwarden or churchwardens of the parish or parishes with which the objects of such charities are identified, who shall present the same at the next general meeting of the vestry of such parishes, and insert a copy thereof in the minutes of the vestry book; and every such account shall be open to the inspection of all persons, and any person may require a copy." — (Act of 1855, s. 44.)

And in addition to this, the board may call for any accounts and statements, to be verified, if they require it, upon oath, and may summon persons to be examined on oath, and to produce all deeds, papers, documents, vouchers, &c., for inspection and examination. Upon these accounts and statements, the commissioners may prosecute any enquiries, and call for any explanations on oath.—(s. 10.)

Powers of the Commissioners—Direction.

II. Under the Act of 1853, the board receive and consider all applications made to them by any trustee or other person having any concern in the management or administration of any charity, for their opinion, advice, or direction, respecting the charity, its management, or its estate or funds, or the application thereof, or any question or dispute relating to such matters; and if they *think fit*, may, upon such application, give such *opinion or advice* as they think expedient, subject to any judicial order or direction which may be subsequently made or given by any court or judge; and every trustee or other person, who shall act upon such opinion, shall be deemed, so far as respects his own responsibility, to have acted in accordance with his trust. (s. 16). If they do not think fit to give any opinion or advice, they may, if it appears to them that any such petition or other proceedings concerning or relating to the charity or its estate would be proper or expedient, they may direct such proceedings (s. 19); or if the gross annual income does not exceed 50*l.* the proceedings may be at chambers; or they may now determine the matter themselves upon the application of the trustees (Act of 1860, s. 2).

And as within that trust the board has power to give any relief, there may be an application for relief by any person claiming to be entitled as the recipient of a charity, and such an application will afford an easy and speedy remedy in cases of small parochial charities (*a*).

(*a*) It may not be out of place to suggest as the proper mode of

If the matter concerns some dispute with strangers, and the board do think fit to give opinion or advice, it may be to recommend a reference to their powers of arbitration or compromise.

But these applications for opinion or advice appear to be made by or on behalf of one of the trustees, managers, or governors of the charity; and the concurrence of the other party to any dispute with a stranger is of course necessary for the exercise of the powers of arbitration.

Besides the above general power of direction, there are special cases in which application may be made to the board for authority to do various acts involving responsibility in trustees—the sale, letting, or exchange of charity lands (s. 21), the investment of charity funds (Act of 1853, s. 24, Act of 1855, s. 32), and the like. And their consent is necessary to investment by way of endowment (*a*).

Moreover, they may apportion parochial charities

---

making an application to the commissioners for direction or relief. 1. Write on foolscap paper with an inch margin on each side. 2. Write a large clear hand. 3. Head the application in the name of the charity, with its parish (or town) and county ["In the matter of the —— charity, parish of —— county of ——."] 4. Commence it thus, "application on behalf of" —— ["one of the recipients" or " —— " claiming to be entitled as a recipient of the said charity] "to the commissioners of charity," for "relief" or "direction." 5. Write a clear simple statement, (1) of the nature of the charity, as regards benefits and objects ; (2) its known trustees or managers; (3) of the nature of the title of the applicant or recipient; (4) of his complaint or claim ; (5) of what has been done (if anything) upon it in the way of application to the trustees or otherwise, and any reply received ; (6) refer to any person of respectable position knowing the applicant, and ready to vouch for his character and the truth of his statements; (7) address it legibly "To the Charity Commissioners, York Street, St. James's (W.), London." *Vide* Forms of Applications ; Appendix.

(*a*) *Corp. of Sons of Clergy* v. *Sutton*, 29 L. J., Ch. 393.

(Act of 1855, s. 10), or charges on lands for the benefit of charities (Act of 1855, s. 33).

Under the Trustees Acts the Court of Chancery has power upon petition in any case in which it is expedient so to do, to appoint new trustees and vest the property in them; and the board may direct an application for the purpose in cases, for any reason not within their own power to deal with, which application may be at chambers (*a*).

And in any case where from any cause a valid appointment of new trustees cannot be made, or where by reason of the expense it shall appear desirable, to the Court of Chancery or any judge of the court, at chambers (in cases where under the Act they have jurisdiction at chambers), the court or judge may order that the estate be vested in the official trustee, who may hold until new trustees are appointed. (Act of 1853, s. 51.)

And when it appears desirable to any judge having jurisdiction under the Act, that stock, &c., held in trust for any charity, ought, for the purpose of security or convenient administration to be transferred to the official trustees, he may order it to be so transferred. And any trustee, executor, &c., may, on an order of the board, transfer any stock or pay any money to the official trustees in trust for any charity (s. 22, 1855).

All deeds or documents relating to charities may be deposited with the board for safe custody, and there is this important compulsory provision: "The board may require any person having the custody or control of any deed or document in which any charity or

---

(*a*) See Act of 1853, ss. 28 & 48; but see Act of 1860, s. 1.

charities shall be solely interested to transmit the same to the office of the said commissioners for examination; and where such deed or document shall not be held by any person entitled as a trustee or otherwise to the custody thereof, the board may either retain the same, for the security thereof, in the repository provided by them, or, as they may think most advantageous to the charity, may thereupon, or at any time thereafter, return or issue the same to the trustees, or persons acting in the administration of the charity, for the purposes thereof." (Act of 1860.)

Powers of the Commissioners—Arbitration.

III. Powers of Arbitration or Compromise. Under the Act of 1853, s. 23, the board may sanction the compromise of any claim against any person in " relation to " the charity : or *against* any charity.

Under s. 64, Act of 1853, it is also provided that if any dispute or question arises among the members of any charity exempted from, or under the jurisdiction of, the commissioners, in relation to its management, two-thirds of the members present at any special meeting may refer it to the arbitration of the commissioners. The language of the enactment clearly implies that it may apply to any corporate charity, or to any *society* or institution, endowed or unendowed.

And by the Act of 1860, s. 20, it is expressly provided that the power vested in the board may be exercised with reference to any charities vested in any corporation, sole or aggregate (which includes corporations ecclesiastical or civil, and charities municipal or parochial), who either solely or jointly with any other persons shall be also *recipients* of the benefits. And exempted charities may petition to have the benefit of the Act (s. 63).

Powers of the Commissioners as to Litigation.

I. Power of the board to direct delay or restrain proceedings in Chancery.

All the powers and jurisdiction of the Court of Chancery over charities continue as before; but subject to this important restraint, upon all private parties, trustees or others;—not applying, however, to the Attorney-General.

"Before any such petition or other proceeding (not being an application in any suit or matter actually pending), for obtaining any relief, order, or direction concerning or relating to any charity, or the estate, funds, property, or income thereof, shall be commenced, there shall be transmitted to the board notice in writing, &c., for explaining the nature and object, &c., and no suit, &c., for obtaining any such relief, &c., shall be entertained or proceeded with by the court except upon and in conformity with an order or certificate of the board (s. 17).

Now this only applies to any application for relief, order, or direction, concerning or relating to (*i. e.*, *only* concerning) *any charity*, or the estates, funds, or property thereof. It does not apply to any application not relating entirely to a charity or the funds of a charity, but to the administration of some estate in which a charity is partly interested. Thus it does not apply to the payment of money into court under the Trustees' Relief Act (*a*), which provides that trustees may pay money into court, to abide the order of the court, in

---

(*a*) 10 & 11 Vict. c. 96.

cases of difficulty and doubt. The payment of money into court under that Act is not a proceeding within the above clause requiring notice; for the term "proceeding" is used as synonymous with "application," and no *application* of the trustees is necessary, the trustees being at liberty to pay the money in at their own option; the only question being whether they shall be allowed their costs of the step, if it *turns out* to have been unnecessary (*a*); and the payment into court is not to obtain, although it is to *abide* the direction of the court. But on the other hand, as the transfer of money paid into court under the Trustees' Relief Act can only be directed by an order made upon petition (*b*), it would be within the *provision* in the Charitable Trusts Act, if not within the exception as in a matter pending, and has been so held (*c*). But an application for the payment of money into court, or for a scheme for its application, has been held not to be a proceeding requiring notice under the above provision (*d*), because it is an application while such a matter is pending.

That, however, *is* an application for *relief*, &c., concerning or relating to a charity, or the funds thereof, and if the restriction does not apply, it is only by its being an application in a matter pending under the Trustees' Relief Act (*e*).

But under that Act the money must be paid into court in the matter of a particular trust, not generally upon the trusts of a will; at all events to enable the

---

(*a*) *In re Woodburn's Trusts*, 26 L. J., Ch., 522.
(*b*) *Re Masselin's Trusts*, 21 L. J. (N. S.), Ch., 53.
(*c*) *Bangley's Trust*, ibid. p. 875.
(*d*) *Re Meynell's Charity*, 24 L. J., Ch., 669.
(*e*) *In re St. Giles' Bloomsbury*, 29 L. J., Ch., 560; *In re Lister's Hospital*, 6 De Gex Mac. & Gord. 184.

court to *distribute* the fund it must stand to an account which separates it from the other assets, and disconnects it from all the other trusts of the will (a). When it is so paid in, the remedy of a claimant, whether a charity trustee or other party, must be prosecuted by petition under that Act, not under the ordinary jurisdiction of the court (b); and the application to have money paid out is to be by the parties claiming to be interested, as trustees for a charity or otherwise, without prejudice to their right to enforce any other or further claims against the trustees according to the will or deed (c); the scope of the Act in cases of adverse claims, raising questions of a difficulty which the trustees are not bound to determine (d). And it applies as regards charities where, under a will or deed, there are charitable gifts or legacies along with others, and there are adverse claims, either as *between* charities or *against* charities.

The restraining clause in the Charitable Trusts Act does not appear to apply to applications by trustees or executors to the Court of Chancery under Sir G. Turner's Act (13 & 14 Vict. c. 35), either for administration of an estate, or by special case for the construction of any act of parliament, will, deed, or other instrument, unless the applications are referred to a charity, and not made by a trustee of a *charity* alone, in the matter of a charity. In such case it is provided—"That every executor, administrator, trustee, or other person making any payment or doing any act in conformity with the declaration

---

(a) *Re Everett*, 12 Beav. 485.
(b) *Goode* v. *West*, 21 L. J., Ch., 127.
(c) *Re Sharp*, 17 L. J., Ch., 345.
(d) *Re Headington's Trusts*, 27 L. J., Ch., 175.

contained in any decree made upon a special case, shall in all respects be as fully and effectually protected and indemnified by such declaration as if such payment had been made or act done, under or in pursuance of the express order of the same court made in a suit between the same parties instituted by bill, save only as to any rights or claims of any person in respect of matters not determined by such declaration."

But this is a course of procedure only for the purpose of obtaining the opinion of the court in cases of doubtful construction (*a*). It is not similar to a suit or claim, as the court has no power to bind the rights of parties; and upon a case stated the court will decline to give any opinion upon points which involve disputed rights (*b*). The Act may either comprise the case of the trustee of a charity or trustee bonds or will, embracing among others bequests to a charity. In the latter case the application may be made to the Court of Chancery without the sanction of the Commissioners of Charities, for it is not an application for "relief, order, or direction" concerning or relating to any charity, but relating to the general administration of an estate, although *inter alia* it may concern a charity.

In the case of a trustee of a charity, however, the application can only be with the sanction of the board, who have themselves power (Act of 1853 s. 16) to give advice or direction, with a clause of indemnity very similar to that given under Sir G. Turner's Act.

(*a*) As in a question whether a power of appointment has been executed.—*West* v. *Ray*, 23 L. J., Ch., 447; or whether there has been a valid declaration of trust.—*Turner* v. *Wood*, 23 L. J., Ch., 895.

(*b*) *Bailey* v. *Collet*, 23 L. J., Ch., 230.

An administration, suit, or a petition under Sir S. Romilly's Act, or an application under Sir G. Turner's Act, for the opinion of the court, or under the Trustees' Acts of 1850 or 1855 to obtain the appointment of a new trustee, or the transfer of a fund, or the conveyance of land to new trustees, or to the persons beneficially entitled, are clearly petitions or proceedings, *i.e.*, applications for relief, order, or direction, and cannot therefore be made or entertained by any judge or Court of Chancery, except under the order or certificate of the board. It was said by the Master of the Rolls in the case before cited (*a*), that they must, unless the matter is a mere form (which cannot be predicated), readily exercise a *judgment* on the matter; and such seems to be the clear intent of the provision, taken in conjunction with the proviso at the end, " that it shall not extend to any such (*query* suit?) petition or proceeding in which any person shall claim any property, or seek any relief adversely to any charity;" and taken also in connection with a subsequent proviso (s. 23)—" that if it appear to the board that the institution of legal proceedings is requisite, and that it is desirable under the circumstances thereof that such proceedings should be instituted by the Attorney-General, they may certify the case to *him*, and thereupon *he* may institute such proceedings." The practical importance of this provision may be illustrated by a very recent case (*b*), where in the first instance a decree was made against a charity, but the Attorney-General, considering that the parties who had refused the

---

(*a*) *In re St. Giles' Bloomsbury*, 29 L. J., Ch., 560.
(*b*) *Philpott* v. *St. George's Hospital*, 5 Jur. N. S., 664.

charity were not fitted to do so, himself took the case up, and obtained a decree in its favour.

II. Powers of directing proceedings in Chancery.

If it appears to the board, either on their own inquiries or reports or by the application of others, that any suit or proceeding concerning or relating to any charity or the estate or income thereof, would be proper or expedient, they may direct or authorise it, and, if they think fit, certify it to the Attorney-General, for him to prosecute it (ss. 19, 20). As to the appointment or removal of any trustee, or "any *other relief, order, or direction*" relating to any charity, the Attorney-General, or any person with the authority of the board, may apply for an application to a judge of the Court of Chancery at chambers, or if the gross annual income of the charity does not exceed £50, to a judge of a county court, or of a district court of bankruptcy, or in such case they may now, on the application of the trustees themselves, make order in such cases, provided the cases are not of a contentious character, nor raising questions of any difficulty; in that respect their jurisdiction resembles that of the Court of Chancery under Romilly's Act or the Trustees' Act. And it is expressly provided that they shall not entertain any question as to the removal of a trustee, on the ground of religious belief—a matter which could only be determined by the Court of Chancery upon bill or information; and on any such matters the board have only to direct litigation in that court.

Powers of the Board—Adjudication.

The most important of the powers and provisions of the Charitable Trusts Acts are those of the Act of

1860, which confers upon the commissioners for the first time certain direct administrative powers of making orders.

"An application to a judge of the Court of Chancery at chambers in cases where the gross annual income of the charity exceeds £50, or to a judge of the county courts, or of a district court of bankruptcy where the income does not exceed that amount, may be made either by the Attorney-General or, with the sanction of the board, by any one or more of the trustees or persons administering or claiming to administer, or interested in the charity, or any two or more inhabitants of any parish or place within which the charity is administered or applicable; and such judges may make, order, or give any relief, order, or direction, as the case may require;" or the board, of their own motion, in cases where the income does not exceed £50, or on the application of the trustees where it *does* exceed that sum, may make such orders, for the appointment or removal of trustees of any charity, or for the removal of any schoolmaster or mistress or other officer thereof, or for or relating to the assurance, transfer, payment, or vesting of any real or personal estate belonging thereto, or entitling the official trustees of charitable funds, or any other trustees, to call for a transfer of and to transfer any stock belonging to such estate, or for the establishment of any scheme for the administration of any such charity.

So that the board have original, independent, *quasi*-judicial powers, in all cases where the income does not exceed £50; and on the application of the trustees (or the majority of them), in *all* cases, whatever the income; and if in any cases of the latter class, trustees (or the majority of them) do not make such application, then the board may, on the application of one trustee, or one person interested, or any two *inhabitants*, direct an application to a judge of the Court of Chancery at chambers. And this in all cases where the court would, under Romilly's Act (as to which *vide ante*, p. 104), have jurisdiction to give relief, order, or direction ; that is, as to the appointment or removal of trustees, the vesting or securing of trust property, the administration of the charity, the alteration or establishment of a scheme, or, generally, in almost any other of those matters in which, as shown in this brief exposition, the Court of Chancery has heretofore exercised its jurisdiction over charities, now transferred, most beneficially, to the Commissioners of Charities. The great exception being that to declare or *enforce* a trust adversely to a trustee (*a*), the jurisdiction will still remain in the Court of Chancery.

(*a*) As to which *vide Russell* v. *Jackson*, 10 Hare, 204, where, notwithstanding a devise in terms absolute, yet, there being an oral intimation to one of the devisees that he had confidence, they would carry out his intentions—which were to further a religious object— held evidence of a secret trust in *both*—and *neither* of them allowed to enjoy beneficially.

16 & 17 VICT. C. 137.

An Act for the better Administration of Charitable Trusts. [20th August, 1853.]

WHEREAS it is expedient to provide means for securing the due administration of Charitable Trusts, and for the more beneficial application of charitable funds (*a*) in certain cases: Be it therefore enacted &c.

1. It shall be lawful for her Majesty and her successors, by warrant under the royal sign manual, to appoint four commissioners, and also one secretary and two inspectors, for the purposes of this Act, (*b*) and upon any vacancy by the death, resignation, or removal of any commissioner, secretary, or inspector under this Act, from time to time in like manner to appoint another person to succeed to such vacancy, and until a fresh appointment shall be made it shall be lawful for the surviving or continuing commissioners, in case of any vacancy, to act as if no such vacancy had occurred; and three of the said commissioners shall hold office during good behaviour; and the fourth, and every secretary and inspector to be appointed under this Act, shall hold office during the pleasure of her Majesty. *Her Majesty empowered to appoint Charity Commissioners, Secretary, and Inspectors.*

(Clauses as to salaries &c., omitted).

6. The said commissioners to be appointed under this Act shall be styled "The Charity Commissioners for England and Wales," and may have and use a seal for authenticating documents, and such commissioners shall sit from time to time as a board for carrying this Act into execution; (*c*) and any two of such commissioners *Style of Commissioners, who may sit as a Board.*

(*a*) The jurisdiction is in aid of, not adverse to, charities.

(*b*) By s. 1 of the Acts of 1853 and 1860, those Acts and this are to be construed together as *one* Act, which applies, to any of the enactments in either, any of the powers and provisions of either of the others capable of such application. See for example s. 9 of the Act of 1855.

(*c*) By the Amending Act of 1855 others may be appointed, but the clauses as to those appointments are omitted. And the Amending Act of 1855, 18 & 19 Vict. c. 124, contains these clauses :—

"IV. Every act of the board may be sufficiently authenti-

Charitable Trusts Act, 1853.

may form a board, and may exercise all or any of the powers conferred on the commissioners or the board by this Act.

Minutes &c., of the Board.

Board to frame General Minutes.

7. The said board shall, by general minutes, from time to time prescribe regulations for their proceedings, and the proceedings of their inspectors, and concerning the form and manner of applications to the said board, and the conditious to be performed by applicants, and for the guidance of applicants in relation thereto (*a*), and all such general minutes shall be signed by three of the said commissioners at the least; (*b*) and copies of all such general minutes shall be laid before both Houses of Parliament within fourteen days after the making thereof if Parliament be sitting, or if Parliament be not sitting, then within fourteen days after the next meeting thereof.

Minutes of proceedings and orders, &c. to be entered, and copies of entries signed by the secretary to be received in evidence.

8. The said board shall cause minutes of their proceedings, and all orders, certificates, and schemes, made or approved by them under this Act, to be entered in books to be provided and kept for such purpose, and all such entries shall be signed by their secretary, and all copies purporting to be extracted from the books of the said board, and to be certified by their secretary, of any such minutes, orders, certificates, and schemes entered as aforesaid, shall be received as evidence of the proceedings to which such minutes shall relate, and of such orders, certificates, or schemes, and of the making or approval thereof (as the case may require) by the said board, without further proof thereof.

---

cated by the seal of the commissioners and the signature of their secretary, or in his absence of the chief clerk.

" V. All orders, certificates, schemes, and other documents issued under the seal of the board shall be deemed and taken to be the originals, and copies thereof shall be entered in the books of the board, and all such entries may be sufficiently certified by the signature of the secretary, or in his absence of the chief clerk : every order, certificate, scheme, and other document purporting to be sealed with the seal of the board shall be received in evidence without further proof ; and any writing purporting to be a copy extracted from the said books, and to be certified as aforesaid, shall be received in evidence in like manner.

(*a*) See the minutes already issued in the appendix *post*.
(*b*) See ss. 4 and 5 of the Amending Act, *supra*, which make certified copies originals, which in accordance with 14

Powers of the Board.

Power of the Board and Inspectors as to Inquiries.

9. It shall be lawful for the said board from time to time, as they in their discretion may see fit, to examine and inquire into all or any charities in *England* or *Wales* (*a*), and the nature and objects, administration, management, and results thereof, and the value, condition, management, and application of the estates, funds, property, and income belonging thereto; and the said board may cause examinations and inquiries in relation to the matters aforesaid to be made and prosecuted by their inspectors, acting together or separately, in such cases and at such times as the said board may think fit; and all such inspectors shall from time to time report their proceedings to the said board. *Board to inquire into condition and management of charities.*

10. The said board may require all trustees or persons acting or having any concern in the management or administration of any charity (*b*), or the estates, funds, or property thereof (*c*), to render to the said board, or *Power to require accounts and statements.*

& 15 Vict. c. 99, s. 9 will as public documents prove themselves upon production.

(*a*) As to what are "charities" within the Act, see the interpretation clause, *post* s. 66. Of what are so the board must judge, and must of course make inquiries as to what they suppose to be so. The mere fact that a party denies a trust for a charity will not oust their jurisdiction (see s. 15 and note); they must try the question in the first instance, and in case of resistance it must be decided in Chancery, see s. 14. And though the commissioners can only *summon* trustees, &c., they can *examine* any one (s. 12; see s. 15); which does not, it will be observed, prevent them from acquiring such information from *any other* person.

(*b*) Governors of chartered charities, &c.

(*c*) By s. 6 of the Amendment Act of 1855, this is thus expounded and explained :—

"VI. The board, or any commissioner or inspector, such inspector acting under the authority of the board, may require written accounts and statements and answers to inquiries relating to any charity, or the property or income thereof, to be rendered or made to them respectively by all or any of the following persons ; that is to say,

"Trustees or persons acting or concerned in the administration of the charity, its property or income, or in the receipt or payment of any monies thereof :

" Agents of any such trustees or persons :

"Depositories of any funds or monies of the charity :

to their inspectors, or either of them, accounts and statements in writing in relation to such charity, or the funds, estates, property, income, or monies thereof, or the administration, management, and application thereof, and may also require such trustees and persons to return answers in writing to any questions or inquiries addressed to them by the direction of the said board relating to the matters aforesaid.

11. All officers having the custody of enrolments, decrees, reports, records, and other documents relating to or concerning any charity (*a*) shall furnish such copies or extracts as shall be required by the said board; and every inspector, secretary, and other officer of the said board for the time being employed for the purposes of this Act shall be at liberty, by the authority and under the directions of the board, and subject to such regulations as the board may make in that behalf, to examine and search the registers and records of every court of law and equity (*b*), and every ecclesiastical court, and every public registry and office of records, and to take copies of and extracts from any decree or document recorded or registered or deposited therein respectively, for any purpose contemplated by this Act, without fee or other payment in respect thereof.

12. Any inspector (*c*) acting under the authority of

"Persons in the beneficial receipt of any funds thereof or of any income or stipend therefrom:

"Persons having the possession or control of any documents concerning the charity or any property thereof:

"And the board or the commissioner or inspector may require the persons rendering or making any such account, statement, or answer to verify the same by oath or otherwise, and may administer such oath: Provided always, that nothing herein contained shall extend to give to the said board or their inspectors any power of requiring from any person holding or claiming to hold any property whatsoever adversely to any charity, or free or discharged from any charitable trust or charge, any information, or the production of any deed or document whatever, in relation to the property so held or claimed adversely, or any charitable trust or charge alleged to affect the same."

(*a*) *Vide* s. 9, n. (*a*).
(*b*) As the Probate Court for wills.
(*c*) By s. 7 of the Act of 1855, 18 & 19 Vict. c. 124, this clause is expounded thus:—

"VII. The board or any commissioner or inspector acting as

the said board may, by precept under his hand, subject to such regulations as the said board may make in that behalf, require any person, being a trustee of any charity (*a*) or otherwise acting or having any concern in the management or administration of any charity (*b*), or of the estates, funds, or property thereof, or in the receipt or payment of the income or monies thereof, or deriving any income or stipend therefrom, (*c*) to attend before such inspector (*d*) for the purpose of being examined by him touching or relating to such charity, or the estates, funds, property, or income thereof (*e*), at any time and place mentioned or appointed by such precept, and to bring and produce any deed, paper, writing, instrument, or other document, being in the custody, possession, or power of such person, and relating to such charity, or the estates, funds, property, or income thereof, and may examine upon oath all persons attending in pursuance of such precept, and all persons voluntarily attending before him (*f*), and may administer such oath: Provided always, that no person shall be obliged to travel in obedience to any such precept more than ten miles from his place of abode.

---

aforesaid (*i. e.* under the clause in the amended Act), may require all or any such trustees and persons as aforesaid (*i. e.* as described in the previous clauses as in the amended Act explained) to attend before them respectively at such times and places as may be reasonably appointed, for the purpose of being examined in relation to the charity, and to answer such questions as may be proposed to them, and to produce upon such examination any documents in their custody or power relating to the charity or the property thereof, and may examine upon oath or otherwise all such persons and all persons voluntarily attending, and may administer such oath : Provided always, that no person shall be obliged to travel in obedience to any such requisition more than ten miles from his place of abode.

"VIII. All requisitions made under the foregoing authorities shall be made respectively by the order of the board, or by precept, under the hand of the commissioner or inspector making the same."

(*a*) See s. 9, n. (*a*).
(*b*) As governors of chartered charities.
(*c*) As masters, ministers, &c.
(*d*) See the proviso at the end.
(*e*) As bequests or gifts thereto.
(*f*) This is very important, especially with reference to s. 9, and the provision in s. 15.

Charitable Trusts Act, 1853.

Persons giving false evidence guilty of a misdemeanor.

13. If any person wilfully give false evidence upon any examination under this Act, every person so offending shall be deemed guilty of a misdemeanor.

Person refusing to render accounts, &c. to be deemed guilty of a contempt of Court.

14. If any person from whom the said board, or any inspector, is authorised to require any account or statement or answers to any questions or inquiries (*a*), or whose attendance any inspector is authorised to require (*b*), shall refuse or wilfully neglect to render to the said board such account or statement (*c*), or to make answers to such questions or inquiries (*d*), or to attend in obedience to any lawful precept of any inspector, or to give evidence before him, or shall wilfully alter, destroy, withhold, or refuse to produce any deed, paper, writing, instrument, or other document which may be lawfully required to be produced before any inspector or the said board (*e*) every person so offending shall be deemed and taken to have been guilty of a contempt of the high Court of Chancery, and shall be liable to be attached and committed by such court on summary application by the commissioners to the same, and shall pay the costs of and attending such contempt as the said court shall direct(*f*).

Saving for

15. Provided always, That nothing herein contained

(*a*) By s. 9, 10, 12, &c.
(*b*) See s. 12.
(*c*) s. 10.
(*d*) That is shall refuse or wilfully neglect to make answers; but an answer which is evasive may be considered *no* answer.— See *re Bradbury*, 23 L. J., C. P. 25.
(*e*) s. 10, 12.
(*f*) By s. 9 of the Amended Act, 18 & 19 Vict. c. 124, this clause is thus amended :

"IX. Any person refusing or wilfully neglecting to comply with any such requisition, or with any order of the board, made under the provisions of this Act or the principal Act, or destroying or withholding any document required to be produced or transmitted by him, shall be taken to be guilty of a contempt of the High Court of Chancery, and shall be liable to be attached and committed by such Court, on summary application by the commissioners to the same Court *or to any judge thereof*, and shall pay such costs attending such contempt as the said Court or Judge shall direct: Provided always, that the Court may at any time discharge, on such terms as it may deem just, any person attached or committed on any such application, or on any application made under section fourteen of the principal Act."

shall extend to give to the said board or their inspectors any power of requiring from any person holding or claiming claiming to hold any property whatsoever adversely to any charity (*a*) or free or discharged from any charitable trust or charge, any information, or the production of any deed or document whatever in relation to the property so held or claimed adversely, or any charitable trust or charge alleged to affect the same (*b*). *persons claiming adversely to charities.*

Power of the Board to give direction.

16. The said board shall receive and consider all applications which may be made to them by any trustee or other person having any concern in the management or administration of any charity (*c*), for their opinion, advice, or direction respecting such charity, or the management or administration thereof, or the estate, funds, property, or income thereof, or the application thereof, or any question or dispute relating to the same respectively (*d*), and, if they so think fit, may upon any such application give such opinion or advice as they think expedient (*e*), subject to any judicial order or direction which may be subsequently made or given by a competent court or judge (*f*); and such opinion or advice shall be in writing, signed by two or more of the said commissioners, and sealed with the seal of the said commission: and every trustee and other person who shall act upon or in accordance with the opinion or advice given by the said board shall in respect of so acting be deemed and taken, so far as respects his own responsibility, to have acted in accordance with his trust (*g*), and no such *Board to entertain applications for their opinion or advice.* *Persons acting on advice of board to be indemnified.*

(*a*) That is, for his own benefit.
(*b*) They may obtain the information from *any other person*, which shows that they may entertain questions as to the property so withheld from charities.
(*c*) Where the property is vested in any other persons than the persons acting in the administration of the funds (s. 48), as governors of chartered charities: *strangers* have no right to apply.
(*d*) This embraces any applications as to new schemes for the regulation of charities.
(*e*) The application being for *direction*, the *direction* is given by way of *advice*: which, as it may be safely followed, has practically all the effect of a decree, until reversed in Chancery; under this clause the board may practically frame schemes.
(*f*) There being no breach of trust in following the advice, the trustees will not have to pay costs. See an instance of reversal, Chelmsford Schools case, 24 L. J., Ch. 742.
(*g*) Thus, if he have made an application of the trust funds

Charitable Trusts Act, 1853.

judicial order or direction subsequently made or given by any court or judge shall have any such retrospective effect as to interfere with or impair the indemnity by this Act given to trustees and other persons who have acted upon or in accordance with such opinion or advice of the said board (*a*) : Provided always, that nothing herein contained shall extend to indemnify any trustee or other person for any act done in accordance with the opinion or advice of the said board, if such trustee or other person have been guilty of any fraud or wilful concealment or misrepresentation in obtaining such opinion or advice (*b*).

Power of Board to direct or delay suits.

Notice of legal proceedings as to any charity by

17. Before any suit, petition, or other proceeding (not being an application in any suit or matter actually pending) (*c*) for obtaining any relief, order, direction (*d*), concerning or relating to any charity (*e*), or the estate,

---

not in accordance with the strict rules of equity or to the *cy près* doctrine.

(*a*) Substantially and fairly so ; of course in a court of equity no strict or strained interpretation would be placed upon their conduct.

(*b*) There is a similar exception in Lord St. Leonard's Act, 22 & 23 Vict. c. 35, s. 81. Such a protection does not apply as to payments or acts for the benefit of the trustees themselves. *Foster* v. *Mc Mahon*, 11 Ir. Eq. Rep. 287.

(*c*) That is, at the time of the application.

(*d*) As to get money paid into court under the Trustees' Relief Act, 10 & 11 Vict. c. 96, paid out to the trustees of a charity and applied thereto. But it has been held that trustees may *pay* money into court under that Act, *without* the order of the board, *vide ante*, p. 116. The words are the same as in Romilly's Act, as to which *vide ante*, p. 104.

(*e*) That is *only* concerning a charity. The words cannot be deemed to restrain proceedings concerning the distribution of assets, or the division of an estate in which some charity or charities may be *partly* interested, and as to which questions of administration arise as to abatement or otherwise. This is one reason why executors or trustees may pay money into court under the Trustees' Relief Act, without the sanction of the board ; for they do so at the risk of costs if there is no doubt or difficulty ; and if there be doubt or difficulty it must arise from adverse claims and because of other interests than those of the charity being involved. For the same reason the restriction cannot apply to applications by executors or trustees under Sir G. Turner's Act, 13 & 14 Vict. c. 35, or Lord St. Leonard's Act

funds, property, or income thereof (*a*), shall be commenced, presented, or taken, by any person whomsoever, there shall be transmitted by such person to the said board notice in writing of such proposed suit, petition, or proceeding (*b*), and such statement, information, and particulars as may be requisite or proper, or may be required from time to time by the said board, for explaining the nature and objects thereof; and the said board, if upon consideration of the circumstances they so think fit, may, by an order or certificate signed by their secretary, authorise or direct any suit, petition, or other proceeding to be commenced, presented, or taken with respect to such charity, either for the objects and in the manner specified or mentioned in such notice, or for such other objects, and in such manner and form, and subject to such stipulations or provisions for securing the charity against liability to any costs or expenses, and to such other stipulations or provisions for the protection or benefit of the charity, as the said board may think proper (*c*); and such board, if it seem proper to them, may by such order or certificate as aforesaid require and direct that any proceeding so authorised by them in respect of any charity shall be delayed during such period as shall seem proper to and shall be directed by such board (*d*); and every such order or certificate may be in such form and may contain such statements and particulars as such board shall think fit; and (save as herein otherwise provided) (*e*) no suit, petition, or other proceeding for obtaining any such relief, order, or direction as last aforesaid shall be entertained or proceeded with by the Court of Chancery, or by any court or judge, except upon and in conformity with an *any person, except the Attorney-General, to be given to the Board.*

Courts not to entertain proceedings as to charities, except upon certificate of the Board.

for relief of trustees, 23 & 24 Vict. c. 35, s. 2, where such applications relate not merely to a charity, but to the general administration of an estate, concerning, *inter alia*, some legacy or legacies to a charity.

(*a*) Not adverse to the charity; see the proviso *post*.
(*b*) See as to this the general minute, No. iv. *post*.
(*c*) And if the original promoters refuse, the board may by s. 20, resort to the At.-G. See above as to the nature of such application, see s. 28 and s. 32; and see the *administrative* powers of the Board in such cases under Act of 1860, s. 2.
(*d*) To afford an opportunity for arrangement, as the court sometimes does, in suits instituted by or with the assent of the At.-G. See *At.-G.* v. *Merchant Tailors' Company*, 5 L. J., Ch. 62. (*e*) That is, in the next section.

order or certificate of the said board: Provided always, that this enactment shall not extend to or affect any such petition or proceeding in which any person shall claim any property or seek any relief adversely to any charity (*a*).

Saving for the Attorney-General acting ex officio.

18. Provided always, That it shall be lawful for her Majesty's Attorney-General *ex officio* to make such applications, and take and prosecute such proceedings with respect to any charity, in the Court of Chancery or otherwise as to him may seem fit, as if this Act had not been passed (*b*), and that nothing in this Act contained shall be construed as dispensing with the fiat or allowance of her Majesty's Attorney-General, with respect to any proceeding not being an application under the jurisdiction created by this Act were such fiat or allowance was necessary before the passing of this Act (*c*).

Board may, upon the report of an inspector, authorise proceedings where no notice has been given to them, and may in other cases cause local inquiries by their inspector.

19. Provided also, That where upon any report of any inspector under this Act (*d*) or otherwise (*e*) it appears to the said board that any suit, petition, or other proceeding concerning or relating to any charity, or the estate, funds, property, or income thereof (*f*), would be proper or expedient, it shall be lawful for the said board by their order to authorise or direct such suit, petition, or proceeding to be commenced, presented, or taken, and to give such directions in relation thereto as the said board may think proper; and thereupon such suit, petition, or proceeding may be commenced, presented, or taken accordingly (*g*), without any such previous notice in writing as hereinbefore mentioned (*h*); and the said board, before giving any such opinion, advice, or direction upon any such application as aforesaid, or

---

(*a*) That is, free from any trust for his own benefit; see the same proviso, s. 15 and s. 41.

(*b*) See s. 42. Attorney-General may proceed without relators. *In re Bedford Charity*, 2 Swan. 520. *At.-G.* v. *Ashburnham*, 1 S. & S. 394.

(*c*) As under Romilly's Act, or the Trustees' Act, see 10 Hare, App. xxxix.

(*d*) *Vide ante.*

(*e*) Without any *notice* to them, under clause 171 of a suit actually being proposed.

(*f*) Which may be to recover property from persons claiming to hold it adversely to the charity; for their own benefit.

(*g*) If the parties directed decline, the board by next section may put the At.-G. in motion.

(*h*) s. 17.

making any such order or certificate after notice to them as aforesaid, may, where local inquiry appears to them to be requisite, cause such inquiry to be made by one of their inspectors (a); and the said board may, in any case where they see fit, before acting upon the report of any inspector, cause such report to be deposited for local inspection, and give notice of the same being so deposited, and consider any statements or objections which may be transmitted to them in relation thereto.

20. In any case in which it shall appear to the said board that the institution of legal proceedings is requisite or desirable with respect to any charity, or the estates, funds, property, or affairs thereof (b), and that under the circumstances thereof it is desirable that such proceedings should be instituted by the Attorney-General (c), it shall be lawful for the said board, if they so think fit, to certify such case, in writing under the hand of the secretary of the said board, to her Majesty's Attorney-General, together with such statements and particulars (if any) as in the opinion of the said board may be requisite or proper for the explanation of such case (d); and thereupon the said Attorney-General, if upon consideration of the circumstances he think fit, shall institute and prosecute such legal proceedings as he shall consider requisite or proper under the circumstances of such case, by information or petition in the Court of Chancery, or by application to a judge thereof at chambers (e), or to a district court of bankruptcy, or county court (f) under the jurisdiction given by this Act (g).

Power for Board to certify certain cases to the Attorney-General.

(a) See s. 15, which does not preclude inquiries as to adverse claims.

(b) As to *recover* the property thereof, withheld by persons claiming adversely.

(c) As in *Philpott* v. *St. George's Hospital*, 28 L. J., Ch. 657, where it turned out that through the interests of the charity not having been duly represented, there had been a decree against it.

(d) Not its proof. The "statements" would afford or suggest the *means* of proof; and the "case" would be of course nothing without them.

(e) See s. 28.

(f) See s. 32.

(g) So now by the Act of 1860, s. 2, certain direct administrative powers vested in the commissioners in such cases as they might certify to the Attorney-General under this clause.

Power of Board to sanction compromises.

Board may sanction compromise of claims on behalf of charity.

23. (*a*) If in any case it appear to the trustees or persons acting in the administration of any charity that any claim or demand or cause of suit (*b*) against any person in relation to such charity (*c*) may, with advantage to the charity, or should, under the special circumstances of the case, be compromised or adjusted without taking or without continuing any proceedings at law or in equity, such trustees or persons may, or the person against whom such claim, demand, or cause of suit exists or is alleged to exist (*d*), may, with the consent of the trustees or persons acting in the administration of such charity, submit to the said board a statement and proposal for such compromise or adjustment; and if it appear to the said board after such inquiry in relation thereto by one of their inspectors, as they may deem requisite, or otherwise, that such proposal, either with or without any modification, is fit and proper, and for the benefit of the charity, it shall be lawful for the said board to make such order for and in relation to such compromise or adjustment as they may think fit; and upon the due performance of the terms and conditions of such compromise or adjustment as aforesaid, such agreement shall be a final bar to all actions (*e*), suits, claims, and demands by or on behalf of the charity concerned therein,

---

(*a*) This section is transposed into what seems its proper place. So of the two next sections.

(*b*) At law or equity, see the word "actions" post (*e*). This shows that the scope of the action comprises claims against strangers, for claims against trustees would be in *equity*.

(*c*) Either a co-trustee who has committed a breach of trust or a party holding property adversely to the charity. The Amending Act (s. 31) provides—"The twenty-third section of the principal Act shall extend to authorise a compromise or adjustment of any claim, demand, or cause of suit *against* any charity, or the trustees or administrators thereof, and the order of the board in relation thereto, shall have the like effect as in the case of any compromise or adjustment for which provision is made by the said section,"—which plainly shows that the provision of the above section in the principal Act comprises adverse claims.

(*d*) This again shows that the scope of the action embraces adverse claims.

(*e*) At law, which would be by trustees against strangers holding property adversely.

in respect to the cause of action, suit, or matter in respect to which such compromise or adjustment shall have been made.

Power of Board to sanction dismissals of officers.

22. (*a*) It shall be lawful for the board, upon proof to their satisfaction that any schoolmaster or schoolmistress (*b*) or other officer (*c*) of any charity (*d*) has been negligent in performing his or her duties, or that he or she is unfit or incompetent to discharge them properly, either from immoral conduct, age, or any other cause whatsoever (*e*), to empower the trustees of such charity to remove such schoolmaster or mistress or other officer (*f*), and to charge the salary of his or her successors, or any other portion of the revenues of the charity, with such retiring pension or allowance, if any, in favour of the person so removed, and generally to impose such conditions as to the said board shall appear proper : Provided always, that where there shall be any special visitor of the charity, the consent of such visitor, in writing under his hand, shall be necessary in order to such removal (*g*). {Commissioners to authorise trustees to remove officers.}

[The Act of 1860, s. 13, adds a power for magistrates on the certificate of the board, and complaint of the trustees, to give summary provisions of school buildings and property held over by schoolmasters or officers of charities. See the Grammar Schools Act, 3 & 4 Vict. c. 77, containing similar provision.]

(*a*) These sections (21 and 22) are transposed, so as to put them in what appears their proper order with reference to subject matter.

(*b*) *Vide ante*, p. 88.

(*c*) This includes any officer of a charity other than a preacher or minister of a chapel; chapels and colleges being excepted. It would include the master of a hospital.

(*d*) See the interpretation clauses and the exceptions, s. 62.

(*e*) Which would justify dismissal in most cases, *vide ante*, p. 88.

(*f*) They may do so—on their own risk—without this authority, the object of which is to save them from responsibility.

(*g*) See *Whiston* v. *the Dean of Rochester*, 7 Hare, 532, as to the power of the visitor.—The Act of 1860, s. 14 makes a further provision for the removal of schoolmasters and mistresses. See also the Grammar Schools Act, 3 & 4 Vict. c. 77.

Power of Board to sanction leases.

Board may sanction building leases, working mines, doing repairs and improvements;

21. (*a*) If in any case it appear to the trustees or persons for the time being acting in the administration or management of any charity (*b*), or the estates or property thereof, that any part of the charity lands or estates may be beneficially let on building, repairing, improving, or other leases, or on leases for working any mine, or that the digging for or raising of stone, clay, gravel, or other minerals, or the cutting of timber, would be for the benefit of the charity, or that it would be for the benefit of such charity that any new road or street should be formed or laid out, or any drains or sewers made through any part of the charity estates, or that any new building should be erected, or that any existing building should be repaired, altered, rebuilt, or wholly removed, or that any other improvements or alterations in the state or condition of the lands or estates of such charity should be made (*c*), it shall be lawful for such trustees or persons to lay before the said board a statement and proposal in relation to any of the matters aforesaid (*d*); and it shall be lawful for the said board, if they think that the leases or acts to which the statement and proposal relate (with or without modifications or alterations) would be beneficial to the charity, to make such order under their seal for and in relation to the granting of such leases, or the doing of any other such acts as aforesaid, and any circumstances connected therewith, as they may think fit (*e*), although such leases or acts respectively shall not be authorised or permitted by the trust; and the said board, by any such order, may authorise the application of any monies or funds belonging to the charity for any of the purposes or acts aforesaid, and, if necessary, may authorise the trustees to raise any sum of money by mortgage of all or

and may authorise the applica-

(*a*) Transposed with s. 23 to put it in its proper place, with reference to the following clauses, *in pari materiâ*.
(*b*) See s. 48.
(*c*) *Vide ante*, p. 103.
(*d*) See in the Act of 1855 a provision for new schemes as to letting.
(*e*) And by the Act of 1860, s. 15 the power is to extend to the application of any like monies to any other purpose or object, which the board shall consider to be beneficial to the charity or the estate or the objects thereof, and which shall not be inconsistent with the trusts or intentions of the founders.

any part of the charity estates; [provided that compulsory provisions be reserved in every such mortgage for the payment of the principal money borrowed by annual instalments, and for the redemption and reconveyance of the mortgaged estates, within the period of not more than thirty years.] (*a*).

tion of the charity funds or the raising of money on mortgage for those purposes.

Power of Board to authorise sales or exchanges, &c.

24. Upon application to the said board by the trustees or persons acting in the administration of any charity, representing to the said board that, under the special circumstances of any land belonging to the charity, a sale or exchange of such land can be effected on such terms as to increase the income of the charity, or would otherwise be advantageous to the charity, such board may, if they think fit, inquire into such circumstances (*b*), and if after inquiry they are satisfied that the proposed sale or exchange will be advantageous to the charity, may authorise the sale or exchange, and give such directions in relation thereto, and for securing the due investment of the money arising from any such sale, or by way of equality of exchange for the benefit of the charity, as they may think fit (*c*).

Board, under special circumstances, may authorise sale or exchange of charity lands.

(*a*) The Act of 1855 provides (s. 30)—"So much of section twenty-one of the principal Act as requires a compulsory provision to be inserted in every mortgage for the payment of the principal money borrowed by annual instalments, and for the redemption and reconveyance of the mortgaged estates within the period of not more than thirty years, is hereby repealed; but the board authorising any mortgage to be made of any charity estate shall make such provisions, by the same or any other order, as to them may seem necessary, for directing the trustees or persons administering the charity to discharge the principal debt or any part thereof by such yearly or other instalments within thirty years from the date of the security, as to the said board may seem fit, or to form an accumulation or sinking fund out of the income of the charity for discharging the principal debt or any portion thereof within the same period, and shall give directions as to the investment and accumulation of such fund, and the trustees for the time being, or persons administering the charity, shall carry such order into effect.

(*b*) By an inspector, if convenient.
(*c*) See the Act of 1855.

Application of Trust Property.—Testator devised a house to trustees in trust for, and appointed the same to the use of, a female charity school. The premises became in lapse of time ruinous, and not suited for the purpose of a female school, but

Leases, sales, &c. authorised by the Board to be valid.

26. The leases, sales, exchanges, and other transactions authorised by such board under the powers of this Act shall have the like effect and validity as if they had been authorised or directed by the express terms of the trust affecting the charity.

Board may authorise the redemption of rentcharges.

25. The said board shall have authority, upon such application as aforesaid (a) to authorise the sale to the owners of the land charged therewith of any rentcharge, annuity, or other periodical payment charged upon land and payable to or for the benefit of any charity, or applicable to charitable purposes, upon such terms and conditions as they may deem beneficial to the charity, and to give such directions for securing the due investment of the money arising from such sale for the benefit of the charity, or for securing the due application thereof to such charitable purposes, as they may think fit; and in like manner the trustees of any charity, with the consent of the board, may purchase any rentcharge or other yearly payment to which the charity estate is or shall be liable.

Power of Board to sanction purchases of land.

Trustees of charities enabled to purchase sites for building from owners, under

27. Where any land shall be required for the erection or construction of any house or building with or without garden, playground, or other appurtenances, for the purposes of any charity, [and the trustees of the charity shall be legally authorised to purchase and hold such land (b)], but by reason of the disability of any person having an estate or interest in such land, or of any

---

were valuable for commercial purposes. There was no fund for repairing the house. Upon a petition presented by the trustees, under the 52 Geo. III. c. 101, the court refused to refer it to the master to inquire whether it would be for the benefit of the charity to sell the house, but granted a reference whether it would be for its benefit to let the house, and apply the rent in procuring a suitable place for carrying on the school.—*Re the Suir Island Female Charity School*, 3 J. & L. 171.

(a) See s. 24.

(b) Under their trust. There is no disability in law except as to corporations. See the Act of Geo. II., which excepts *purchases* for charitable uses. Therefore in the Amending Act these words are to be omitted, and it is enacted that "incorporated trustees of any charity shall be competent to purchase and hold lands for the purposes mentioned in the same section without licence in Mortmain," alluding to the statute of 7 & 8 Will. III. c. 37.

defect in title thereto (*a*), a valid and perfect assurance disability, of the same land cannot be made to the trustees of the &c., according to the sanction of the said board (*b*) (such ing to the sanction to be certified under the hand of their secre- provisions tary), to take and purchase such land according to the of Lands provisions of "The Lands Clauses Consolidation Act, Clauses 1845" (*c*); and for that purpose all the clauses and Consolidation Act, provisions of the last-mentioned Act with respect to the 1845. purchase of lands by agreement (*d*), and with respect to the purchase money or compensation coming to parties having limited interests (*e*), or prevented from treat-

---

(*a*) Such as would prevent a court of equity from forcing the estate on an unwilling purchaser. *Pell* v. *De Winter*, 27 L. J., Ch. 230; *Ashton* v. *Wood*, 3 Smale & Giff. 436.

(*b*) Such sanction is not necessary to the purchase in the class of cases supposed; but this clause provides farther facilities than by law were before afforded to remove difficulties and cure defects of title; and when this clause is to be applied, the sanction of the board is necessary.

(*c*) See *Lord Grosvenor* v. *Hampstead Junction Railway Company*, 1 De Gex & J. 446; purchase of land by a charity to build upon. See as to taking lands of a rectory, *Ex parte Rector of Bredicot*, 17 L. J., Ch. 414; *In re Leeds Railway Company*, 19 L. J., Ch. 329. As to purchase from a dean and chapter, see *Ex parte Dean of Gloster*, 19 L. J., Ch. 400; *Ex parte Ward*, 17 L. J., Ch. 249; 2 De Gex v. Smale, 10. As to purchase of estate of lunatic, see *In re Taylor*, 1 Mac., V. 320. As to purchase from a vicar, see *Ex parte Vicar of E. Derham*, 21 L. J., Ch. 477.

(*d*) The purchase not being compulsory, as in the case of a railway company, of course there is no necessity for the power of arbitration and assessment of compensation. See *In re Perk's Estate*, 1 Sm. & Gif. 5. Neither is it necessary to resort to the Court of Chancery, as to the investment of the proceeds in the case of purchase from a *charity*, which can be authorised by the commissioners under other powers and provisions of the Act by analogy to the jurisdiction of Chancery in authorising sales of trust estates. *In re Carron Estate*, 19 L. J., Ch. 376.

(*e*) As to the practice under the Act in cases of purchases from tenants for life, see *Ex parte Hollick*, 16 L. J., Ch. 71; *In re Lancashire Railway Company*, 19 L. J., Ch. 56. It should seem, however, that it would be within the power of the commissioners to accept such title as they think sufficient and satisfactory, coupled with s. 16, as to their power of restraining any application to Chancery, so far as the interests of the charity are alone concerned, and in *that* view the above provision is in their *aid*, and enables them to have recourse to the machinery

ing (*a*), or not making a title, and also with respect to conveyances of lands (*b*), so far as the same clauses and provisions respectively are applicable to the cases contemplated by this provision (*c*), shall be incorporated in this Act; and in all cases contemplated by this provision, the expression "the Special Act," used in the said clauses and provisions of the said "Lands Clauses Consolidation Act" shall be construed to mean this Act; and the expression "the promoters of the undertaking," used in the same clauses and provisions, shall be construed to mean the trustees of the charity in question.

Jurisdiction in Chancery in cases above thirty pounds.

In cases of charities, the incomes of which exceed 30*l*., 28. Where the appointment or removal of any trustee (*d*), or any other relief, order, or direction relating to any charity (*e*) of which the gross annual income for the time being exceeds thirty pounds (*f*), shall be con-

---

of the Land Clauses Act in cases which they deem subject to doubt and difficulty. The enactment is not compulsory. The Commissioners of Charities, however, are in a different position from that of a railway company, only as regards the interests of the charity; and the scope of the provisions of the Lands Clauses Act bear reference to the protection of the interests of the parties entitled to the estate purchased by the charity. The course in such cases is payment of the purchase money into the bank, where it awaits the order of the court on the petition of the parties interested. *Ex parte Thurston,* 17 L. J., Ch. 167; *Jones* v. *Lewis,* 19 L. J., Ch. 163; 2 Mac. & G. 163; *Ex parte Harborough,* 23 L. J., Ch. 210.

(*a*) *Vide* p. 139, n. (*a*).
(*b*) *Vide* p. 139, n. (*b*).
(*c*) *Vide* p. 139, n. (*d*).
(*d*) See the Trustees Acts 1850 and 1855, *vide ante.* There is no express provision in the Charitable Trusts Act as to appointment of trustees; the subject is left to the jurisdiction of the Court of Chancery, in general, or under those Acts, controlled by the provision empowering the Charity Board to restrain application to the court (s. 17), and to give advice and direction, and by this clause.

(*e*) These are the most general words which could be adopted (see Romilly's Act); they comprise every possible case, and include making of new schemes (s. 36); and in all those cases in which by s. 17 no application can be made to the court without the sanction of the board. There is by this clause a special jurisdiction created in cases above £30, viz., a jurisdiction *at chambers* in Chancery.

(*f*) To be determined by the board for that purpose, *vide*

sidered desirable (*a*), and such appointment, removal, or other relief, order, or direction might now be made or given by the Court of Chancery, in respect either of its ordinary or its special or statutory jurisdiction, or by the Lord Chancellor intrusted with the care and commitment of the custody of lunatics, it shall be lawful for any person authorised in this behalf by the order or certificate of the said board (*b*), or for the Attorney-General (*c*), to make application (without any information, bill, or petition,) to the Master of the Rolls or one of the Vice-Chancellors sitting at chambers, for such order, direction, or relief as the nature of the case may require (*d*); and the Master of the Rolls or the Vice-Chancellor, to whom any such order shall be made, shall and may proceed upon and dispose of such application in chambers, save where he may think fit otherwise to direct (*e*), and shall and may have and exercise thereupon all such jurisdiction, power, and authority, and make such orders and give such directions in relation to the matter of such application, as might now be exercised, made, or given by the Court of Chancery or by the Lord Chancellor intrusted as aforesaid, in a suit regularly instituted, or upon petition, as the case may require; and the Master of the Rolls and Vice-Chancellors respectively shall, in relation to such applications as aforesaid, and the proceeding thereon (subject to any rules which may be made by the Lord Chancellor, with the advice and consent of them or any two of them,) have all such powers of directing matters to be heard in open court, and of ordering what matters shall be heard and investigated by themselves and their chief clerks respectively, and such other powers and authorities as by the

Master of Rolls and Vice-Chancellors, upon applications to them at Chambers, to have the same jurisdiction as the Court of Chancery or Lord Chancellor now has upon information, &c.

Act of 1860, s. 2 and s. 11, making the limit to £50, and giving the commissioners power to make orders.

(*a*) By the trustees and the board. If the board do not think so, they will not give a certificate.

(*b*) See s. 17.

(*c*) *Without* such order, s. 19.

(*d*) Which no doubt practically will be indicated by the board, or their opinion on which will appear to the judge by the circumstances of the application. The board are supposed to have considered the matter, and formed an opinion that certain relief, order, or direction is desirable. *Vide supra.*

(*e*) As that it shall be heard in court, *or referred* to the chief clerk for inquiry. But see Act of 1860, s. 2, giving the commissioners direct powers of making orders in such cases.

15 & 16 Vict. c. 80. Act of the last session of Parliament, chapter eighty (*a*), are vested in or authorised to be exercised by them at chambers, and the provisions of the said Act applicable to orders made by the Master of the Rolls or any of the Vice-Chancellors at chambers (*b*) shall extend to all orders so made under this Act: Provided always, that, save as may be otherwise provided by any rules to be made by the Lord Chancellor, with such advice and consent as aforesaid (*c*), the determinations of the Master of the Rolls and Vice-Chancellors respectively upon and in relation to such applications as aforesaid shall not be subject to appeal in any case where the gross annual income of the charity does not exceed one hundred pounds (*d*): Provided also, that it shall be lawful for the Master of the Rolls or any Vice-Chancellor, where, under the circumstances of any application as aforesaid, he may so see fit, to direct that for obtaining the relief, order or direction sought for by such application, an information, bill, or petition, as the case may require (*e*), shall be filed or presented and prosecuted as now by law required, and to abstain from further proceeding on such application.

Provision as to charities within the jurisdiction of the Court of Chancery of the County Palatine of Lancaster.

29. The jurisdiction created and given by this Act to the Master of the Rolls and the Vice-Chancellors sitting in chambers, upon any application to them respectively as aforesaid (*f*), shall extend concurrently to and may be exercised by the Chancellor of the Duchy and county Palatine of *Lancaster*, and the Vice-Chancellor of the same county Palatine respectively for the time being (*g*), as to every charity within the jurisdiction of the Court of Chancery of the said county palatine, whose gross

---

(*a*) The Chancery Procedure Amendment Act.

(*b*) Including provision as to *appeal;* as to which see the next proviso.

(*c*) *Vide* Appendix.

(*d*) See Act of 1860 as to orders of commissioners in such cases, and appeal thereupon.

(*e*) The jurisdiction under Romilly's Act is discretionary. *Ex parte Rees*, 3 Vesey & Beames, 11, and only extends to clear cases of mere breach of trust. So, under the Trustees' Act or Turner's Act. To declare a trust, or a right adverse thereto, there must be a bill or information; *Hutchinson* v. *Stephens*, 5 Sim. 498; *Walton* v. *Nerry*, 6 Simon, 328.

(*f*) By the preceding section, 28.

(*g*) Who may obtain the direction and advice of the court by special case under Sir G. Turner's Act, *vide ante*. See *Temple* v. *The Eccl. Com.*, 23 L. J., Ch. 673; 3 De Gex M. & G. 418.

annual income for the time being exceeds thirty pounds (a), upon application being made to such Chancellor or Vice-Chancellor respectively; and it shall be lawful for the Chancellor of the said duchy and county palatine, with the concurrence of the Vice-Chancellor of the same county palatine, from time to time to make and issue any rules and orders for regulating the modes of proceeding, and the fees to be taken in respect of proceedings under this Act.

30. Provided always, That the provisions of this Act applicable to any charity the gross annual income whereof exceeds thirty pounds shall extend to any charity established or administered or applicable to or for objects or purposes within the City of *London*, the gross annual income whereof does not exceed thirty pounds, in like manner as if such income exceeded that amount.

Provisions as to charities exceeding 30l. per annum to extend to charities in London not exceeding 30l.

31. It shall be lawful for the Lord Chancellor, with the advice and consent of the Master of the Rolls and Vice-Chancellors, or any two of them, to make and issue general rules and orders (b), for regulating the mode and form of applications at the chambers of the Master of the Rolls and Vice-Chancellors respectively under this Act, and the proceedings thereon, and for determining in what cases and under what conditions and restrictions the determinations of the Master of the Rolls and Vice-Chancellors respectively upon or in relation to such applications shall be subject to appeal, and the fees and allowances to solicitors of the Court of Chancery, and the fees to be payable in money or by stamps to the officers of the said court in respect of such applications and proceedings thereon; and such rules and orders may from time to time be varied by the like authority, and all such rules and orders shall be deemed general orders of the said court.

Lord Chancellor, with the advice of Master of the Rolls and Vice-Chancellors, or two of them, to make general orders.

Jurisdiction in cases not above thirty pounds.

32. Where any charity of which the gross annual income for the time being does not exceed thirty pounds (c) shall be established or administered or be applicable

District courts of bankruptcy and county

(a) *Fifty.* See Act of 1860, s. 2.
(b) *Vide* Appendix, *post.*
(c) Fifty. See Act of 1860, s. 2, giving the board power to make orders in such cases. The amount is to be determined by the board for this purpose.

courts to have jurisdiction in cases of charities the incomes of which do not exceed 30l. [now 50l.]

wholly or partially (*a*) to or for objects or purposes within the district, or any (*b*) two or more of the districts of any (*c*) district court of bankruptcy or of any county court or courts holden under the Act of the session holden in the ninth and tenth years of the reign of Her Majesty, chapter ninety-five, and the appointment or removal of any trustee, or any other relief, order, or direction whatsoever concerning such charity (*d*) shall be considered desirable (*e*), and such appointment or removal, or other relief, order, or direction, (*f*), might now be made or given by the Court of Chancery in respect either of its ordinary or its special or statutory jurisdiction (*g*) or by the Lord Chancellor intrusted with the care and commitment of the custody of lunatics, it shall be lawful for any person authorised in this behalf by the order or certificate of the said board (*h*), or for the Attorney-General, to make application to such district or county court, or, as the case may be, to any one of such district or county courts, for such order, direction, or relief as the nature of the case may require (*i*); and such district or county court shall entertain such application, and shall hear the

---

(*a*) The charity, &c., or the persons entitled to the benefits of it, may, as in parochial charities, be partly in one district and partly in another.

(*b*) The county courts have jurisdiction in cases of legacies or bequests of residues. *Pears* v. *Wilson*, 6 Exch. 833, 20 L. J., Ex. 381 : so that in cases under £50 the county court judge may adjudge a legacy to a charity, and also administer it.

(*c*) *Vide* same words, s. 28. They include the making of new schemes, s. 30.

(*d*) The same words as in Romilly's Act, as to which *vide* Treatise, p. 104.

(*e*) In the opinion of the board, who otherwise will not allow of an application, see s. 17 and the subsequent part of this clause. Under Romilly's Act, Turner's Act, the Trustees' Act, or by bill or information. But if the money is *in court* under the Trustee Relief Act, there may be an application to Chancery *without* the sanction of the board. *Vide ante* p. 116.

(*f*) *Vide* s. 17. If necessary, the board may direct an application to the Court of Chancery, s. 35. These sections are enabling, not restraining.

(*g*) *Without* such sanction. See s. 18.

(*h*) The nature of which will be indicated by the board. See s. 28. It is not said that the order is to be conclusive, or with what power of appeal. See s. 36.

(*i*) Accordingly, in the West Moulsey charities, the county court of Surrey appointed the rector and churchwardens trus-

matter in open court, and shall give such relief, and make such orders and directions in relation to the matter of such application, as might now be made or given by the Court of Chancery or by the Lord-Chancellor, intrusted as aforesaid, in a suit regularly instituted, or upon petition, as the case may require (*a*); and the clerk of such county court shall transmit a copy of such order or direction to the office in London of the registrar of county courts judgments, to be there enrolled: Provided always, that no judge of any district or county court shall be authorised to vary any decree, order, or direction of the Court of Chancery, or of any judge thereof, or to make or give any order or direction inconsistent or conflicting with any such decree, order, or direction: provided also, that where two or more district or county courts shall have concurrent jurisdiction with respect to any charity under this Act, no application in respect of such charity shall be made to or entertained by more than one of such district or county courts at the same time.

33. The jurisdiction hereby created and conferred on the county courts with respect to any charity shall not be exercised by any deputy or other person who may for the time being be appointed to sit and shall be sitting for any such judge. *Deputy sitting for county court judge not to exercise jurisdiction.*

34. Where two or more district courts of bankruptcy or county courts shall concurrently have jurisdiction under this Act with respect to any charity, it shall be lawful for the said board (*b*) to order to which of such courts any application with respect to such charity shall be made; and every such order shall be conclusive as to the jurisdiction with respect to the application referred to in such order. *Where two or more courts have concurrent jurisdiction, Board to direct to which court applications shall be made.*

---

tees. The jurisdiction of the county courts under this clause is especially suited to parochial charities, or in cases of almshouses or other charities for the relief of the poor, sick or aged, requiring *speedy* relief, as in the case of the Rugby charity trustees, 9 D. & R. 214, where aged claimants on an almshouse fund at an advanced age applied for increased payments, and the most summary application to Chancery would have been too tardy.

(*a*) *Vide* Treatise, *ante*, p. 104.
(*b*) On any application by letter under s. 17 for advice and direction, or by letter from any person claiming the benefit of the charity, *vide* p. 112.

146   Act of 1853.

Board may direct cases within the jurisdiction of a district or county court to be taken before a judge of the Court of Chancery in the first instance.

35. It shall be lawful for the said board (*a*) to direct that any application as to any charity within the jurisdiction of any district court of bankruptcy or county court (*b*) shall be made before a judge of the Court of Chancery, or as to any charity within the jurisdiction of the Court of Chancery of the county palatine of Lancaster, either before the Chancellor or the Vice-Chancellor of the same county palatine, or before a judge of the High Court of Chancery, according to the provisions herein contained applicable to a charity the gross annual income whereof exceeds thirty pounds (*c*), and in such case such application shall be made and may be heard and determined accordingly, in like manner as if the gross annual income of such charity exceeded thirty pounds (*d*); and upon the production of the order or certificate containing such directions or of a copy thereof (*e*), the application with respect to which such order or certificate shall have been made shall not be entertained or proceeded with by such district or county court.

No order of district or county court for the appointment or removal of

36. Whenever any order or decision is made by any district court of bankruptcy or county court for the appointment or removal of any trustee of any charity, or approving of any scheme for regulating or directing the administration of any charity, or the estate, funds, property, or income thereof (*f*), a copy of every such

---

(*a*) On any application for advice or direction under s. 17.

(*b*) S. 32. The limit is now £50, Act of 1860 s. 11. By s. 2 of that Act the board may determine such cases themselves, on the application only of certain persons mentioned in s. 43 of this Act.

(*c*) Fifty. Act of 1860 s. 11, 12.

(*d*) Fifty, *vide supra*. See now Act of 1860 s. 2, power for the board to determine such cases themselves.

(*e*) Before judgment, or after; for proceedings after judgment would be upon the application, and the judgment cannot be proceeded upon until confirmed. See next section.

(*f*) Only in those two classes of cases. Therefore in all others there is no direct provision that the order must be confirmed by the board. But see s. 35. And the board have a general power to direct applications to the Court of Chancery, and that court could of course reverse the order, under its supreme general jurisdiction. It is not said that the order of the county court judges is ever to be conclusive (s. 32); nor on the other hand is there (save under the clause) any appeal to the *board*, though the board under s. 35 may remit an order for reconsideration. See s. 38. But see s. 39, that there is to an appeal.

order or decision shall immediately upon the making trustees or thereof be delivered or transmitted by the deputy regis- approval of trar of such district court, or by the clerk of the county a scheme to court, as the case may be, together with all requisite be valid particulars, to the said board, for the purpose of being unless considered by them; and no such order or decision shall firmed by be valid or effectual until the same shall have been Board. approved by the said board, such approval to be testified by a certificate in writing, signed by the secretary of the said board, and no such approval shall issue from the said board until one calendar month shall have elapsed after the receipt by the board of such copy and particulars.

37. In case any such order or decision as last afore- Board, if said (a) of any district court of bankruptcy or county dissatisfied court shall not be approved by the said board, it shall with the be lawful for such board to remit the same for recon- order of sideration and decision by such district or county court, district or with such remarks and recommendations thereon (if any) county as shall seem fit and expedient to such board (b), or, in court may the discretion of the board, to order and direct that the remit the subject matter to which such order or decision relates, re-conside- together with such order or decision, shall be submit- ration, or ted to the consideration and decision of a judge of the may trans- Court of Chancery (c), and in such last-mentioned fer the case (d) no further proceedings shall be had or taken in matter to a the district or county court with respect to the matter judge of the in question; and in case the order or decision of the Court of district or county court, on the reconsideration of any Chancery. order or decision so remitted for reconsideration, be disapproved as aforesaid by the said board, such board shall refer such orders and decisions, and the subject matter thereof, to a judge of the Court of Chancery (e), or as to any charity within the jurisdiction of the court of Chancery of the county palatine of Lancaster, either

---

(a) See s. 36. That is only as to the matters there mentioned, *vide suprà*.

(b) The county court judge must thereupon alter his judgment. See end of clause.

(c) This they might do without the power of this clause, which was required and intended to give the *alternative*.

(d) Or if the parties authorised to apply under s. 43 shall apply to the board to determine the matter, they can now do so under the Act of 1860 s. 2.

(e) At chambers. See s. 28.

to the Chancellor or the Vice-Chancellor of the same county palatine, or to a judge of the High Court of Chancery ; and where any order or decision is referred to a judge of the Court of Chancery, or of the Court of Chancery of the said county palatine of Lancaster, under this provision, such judge shall have and exercise all such jurisdiction, power, and authority in relation thereto (*a*) as in the case of a charity the gross annual income whereof exceeds thirty pounds (*b*), and may make such order in relation to the matter of such order or decision as to him may seem proper.

How orders of district or county court under this Act to be enforced.

38. Subject to any orders to be made by the Lord Chancellor as herein-after mentioned (*c*), and to the other provisions of this Act, all proceedings to be taken in any district court of bankruptcy or county court, and all orders and directions to be made or given by any such district court or county court by virtue of the jurisdiction hereby created and conferred on such court (*d*), shall respectively be subject to the same rules and regulations (*e*), and have the same effect, and be registered, enforced, and executed in the same manner, as the other proceedings, orders, judgments, and directions of the same court under its ordinary jurisdiction (*f*), and it shall be lawful for any such district court, or for

---

(*a*) That is at chambers, s. 28.
(*b*) Fifty. See Act of 1860, s. 10.
(*c*) See s. 45.
(*d*) To frame schemes, remove trustees, or any relief, order, and direction, as under Romilly's Act, *vide ante* s. 32, and Treatise, p. 104.
(*e*) As to appeal and otherwise. As to appeals, however, see s. 79, County Courts Act. It is difficult to apply this provision so as to give an appeal to the Court of Chancery in cases; reading that clause and this in connection with s. 20, giving the board a general power to direct applications to Chancery, and s. 16 enabling them to restrain any application.
(*f*) The orders of the county court under its ordinary jurisdiction are either for payment of money or delivery of possession of premises ; the former are enforced by execution as judgments in the superior courts, 9 & 10 Vict. c. 95 s. 94, which the clerk must issue on requisition ; and if he does not, the judge himself will order. *Davis* v. *Rugby,* 15 Jur. 1159. A verbal order for payment of money suffices. *Egg* v. *Moule,* 5 Ex. 918. The order for delivery of possession of premises the bailiff executes (s. 122) : but when parties have obtained unsatisfied judgments (s. 98), they may apply for a summons ; and if the

any county court, with the consent of the board (a), to rescind or vary any order which shall have been previously made by such court, without prejudice to any Act or matter in the meantime done under such order; and for executing and putting in force any order to be made by any county court under this Act, every judge of any such court shall and may have and exercise all such powers as by the Act of the session holden in the ninth and tenth years of Her Majesty, chapter ninety-five, are given for enforcing the payment of any debts, damages, or costs under the said Act.

39. Where any person authorised to make any application under this Act (b), (other than Her Majesty's Attorney-General acting *ex officio*,) (c) or any other person who may have been made a party to any proceeding upon any application under this Act (d), is aggrieved by or dissatisfied with any order made by any district court of bankruptcy or county court upon any such application, or any proceeding thereon, he may, within one calendar month after the making of such order, give notice in writing to the said court, and also to the said board (e), that he is desirous to appeal against the same; and if the said board think it reasonable and proper that such appeal should be entertained, and give a certificate to that effect (f), such district or county court shall suspend any proceedings upon the order appealed against during such time as the circumstances may require (g) ; and the said board, if they so think fit, may require the person giving any such notice of appeal to become bound with two

Appeal.

---

party summoned shall not attend, and shall not allege a sufficient excuse for not attending, or shall, if attending, refuse to be sworn, or to disclose his means of satisfying, &c., or shall not make answer to the satisfaction of the judge, he may be committed for forty days (s. 99 *Ex parte Weal* 10 Com. B. 57). And this provision appears applicable to every case that may arise.

(a) S. 37.
(b) See s. 32.
(c) S. 20.
(d) That is either as the party against whom it was made, or for whose supposed *benefit* it was made, as one of the parties entitled to share the benefits of the charity.
(e) S. 17.
(f) S. 17, and see note (a), p. 150.
(g) To enable the party to complete the securities required by the next provision in the clause.

sufficient sureties (a), to be approved by the deputy registrar of such district court, or by the clerk of the county court, as the case may be, to the treasurers of the said courts respectively, or such other person as the said board may see fit, in such sum as to the said board shall seem reasonable, to pay such costs of the proceedings on the appeal as shall be ordered to be paid by such appellant, and also (if the said board so think fit) to indemnify the charity against the costs and expenses of or attending such appeal; and every bond executed under this provision shall be exempt from stamp duty: Provided always, that it shall be lawful for Her Majesty's Attorney General (acting *ex officio*), at any time within three calendar months after the making of any order by a district court or county court under this Act, to lodge and commence and prosecute an appeal against such order, without giving any such notice or becoming bound as aforesaid, and every such last-mentioned appeal shall thereupon be allowed by the order of such district or county court, and shall have such other effect as any other appeal under this Act (b).

Jurisdiction in cases not above 50l. Appeal.

Proceedings on appeal.

40. Where any order allowing an appeal has been made as aforesaid (c), the person thereby allowed to appeal shall within three calendar months (d) present a petition to the Court of Chancery, setting forth the order appealed against, and the order allowing such appeal, and praying such relief as the case may require; and upon the hearing of such petition the court may confirm, vary, or reverse the order appealed against, or may remit such order to the district Court of Bankruptcy or County Court by which the same was made, with or without any declaration or directions of the Court of Chancery in relation thereto, or may proceed in relation to the charity to which such order relates as in the case of an application under this Act (e)

(a) The board will direct *in what time*. And they may make the bond or condition precedent to their order allowing an appeal.
(b) In suspending execution, &c.
(c) See the previous section.
(d) From the *order*, which may be made conditional upon the security, varying the scheme, altering the apportionment, &c.
(e) That is, may hear it at chambers, s. 28.

Special Jurisdictions: Provisions as to.

to a judge of the Court of Chancery at Chambers (*a*), and any judge of such court sitting at chambers or in open court may make or give any such orders or directions in relation to the matter of such order as he may see fit, or the court may make such other order in relation to the matter of any such appeal as to the court may seem just (*b*), and as might be made in the case of a suit regularly instituted, or a petition, as the case may require; and in case the party allowed to appeal do not within such three calendar months present such petition of appeal, the order against which such appeal was allowed shall be final; and in case any costs adjudged on any such appeal to be paid by the party allowed to appeal be not paid, such bond as aforesaid may be put in suit, and the money to be recovered on every such bond shall be applied to indemnify the charity estate or the person damnified, or otherwise in such manner as the justice of the case may require, and the court or judge by whom such appeal may have been heard shall think fit.

Bond to prosecute appeal may be put in suit.

Special Jurisdictions : Provision as to Adverse Claims.

41. Provided always, That no judge of the Court of Chancery (*c*), nor any district court of bankruptcy, or county court (*d*), shall upon any proceedings under this Act (*e*) have jurisdiction to try or determine the title at

No chancery judge, or district or county

(*a*) That is, not merely reversing the order made, but itself making such order, giving such relief or direction, as it thinks just.
(*b*) As in the first sentence of the clause mentioned.
(*c*) At chambers under s. 28.
(*d*) Under s. 32.
(*e*) The provision as to the jurisdiction of Chancery only refers to jurisdiction at chambers, under s. 28. It does not mean that on any proceeding directed by the board (under s. 17), the court shall not have jurisdiction over adverse claims; for such could not be a proceeding "under the Act," seeing that *without* such direction the court has *jurisdiction ;* whereas it has *not*, but for this Act, jurisdiction in all charity matters at *chambers*. Therefore, the board may direct suits to try the title, at law or in equity, to any real or personal property, as between any charity and a person holding or claiming it adversely to the charity—*i.e.* for his own benefit—or to try any exception as to the existence or extent of a charge or trust. But it would not be within the scope of the jurisdiction of the board to direct such suit, when the result would probably be to dis-

152   Act of 1853.

court, in proceedings under this Act to try titles, &c.
law or in equity to any real or personal property, or any term or interest therein, as between any charity or the trustee thereof, and any person holding or claiming such real or personal property, terms or interest adversely to such charity (a), or to try or determine any question as to the existence or extent of any charge or trust.

Special Jurisdiction: Provisions as to.

Notice to be published of application for schemes or appointment or removal of trustees under this Act.
42. Before any application shall be made to any judge of the Court of Chancery (b), or to any district court of bankruptcy or county court (c), under any of the provisions herein contained (d), for the establishment or alteration of a scheme, or the appointment or removal of any trustees or trustee (e), notice in writing of such intended application shall be given (f) in such form and manner as the said board shall have directed (g); and if the order be that such notice be affixed to or near the door of any parish or district church, the incumbent and churchwardens of such parish or district are hereby respectively required to allow such notice to be affixed and to remain so affixed during such period, not less than fifteen days, as the

close a secret trust illegal, or an invalid title to the charity property, or a trust not disclosed, and on the failure of which the property would result to the heir or next of kin; should they do so, not fully aware of the circumstances, they must be duly informed by an application under s. 17 for their advice and direction.

(a) That is *bonâ fide* and really claiming, and not colourably and for the mere purpose of excluding the jurisdiction of the county courts. *Lloyd* v. *Jones*, 6 Com. Bench. Rep. 81; *Lilly* v. *Harvey*, 5 Dowl. & Lowndes, 648. Nor is the jurisdiction of the Court excluded by the mere claim; the court must still determine whether it is *real*, and whether title or trust really does come in question. *Latham* v. *Spedding*, 20 L. J., C. P., 302; *Ingham* v. *Thompson*, 19 L. J., Q. B. 189. Though the decision of the judge is not conclusive on the question, which may be raised by prohibition on application for committal of the party for contempt, or for execution.

(b) S. 28.
(c) S. 32.
(d) S. 35.
(e) S. 36.
(f) To the parties or inhabitants of the place intrusted.
(g) By ss. 17, 28, and 32 they are to give an order or certificate before any proceeding can be instituted.

said board shall have ordered; and in any case in which the order shall be that such notice shall be affixed to any place, evidence that the same has been so affixed shall be deemed and taken as *primâ facie* evidence that it has remained affixed during the period prescribed by the board.

43. Every application to any judge or court under the jurisdiction created or conferred by any of the provisions of this Act (*a*), may be made by Her Majesty's Attorney General (*b*), or, subject to the provisions aforesaid (*c*), by all or any one or more of the trustees or persons administering or claiming to administer, or interested in (*d*), the charity which shall be the subject of such application (*e*), or any two or more inhabitants of any parish or place within which the charity is administered or applicable (*f*); and it shall be lawful for Her Majesty's Attorney-General for the time being, acting *ex officio*, to make application by petition to the Court of Chancery with respect to any charity (*g*) under the provisions of the Act passed in the fifty-second year of King George the Third, chapter one hundred and one (*h*), or under the provisions of any Act or Acts passed (*i*) or to be passed, authorising the application to the same court by petition according to the provisions of the said Act. {By whom applications may be made. Attorney-General may petition under 52 G. 3. c. 101.}

(*a*) S. 28 and s. 38.

(*b*) Without the sanction of the board, s. 8.

(*c*) The provisions of ss. 17, 28, and 32, requiring the sanction of the board.

(*d*) As recipients, or possible recipients, as where the selection is to be from the poor inhabitants of a place all would be "interested." *At.-G.* v. *Vivian*, 1 Russ. 226. See *Hall* v. *M'Farlane*, 3 Jur., N. S., 1262.

(*e*) Excluding (by the interpretation clause) registered chapels, but *not* excluding cathedral schools nor grammar schools, though special provisions made by the grammar school, are 4 & 5 Vict. c. 77 s.

(*f*) Whether "interested" or not, *vide* former sentence.

(*g*) That is in any of the cases in which application may be made under this Act; the words of which—"relief, order, and direction"—are the same as in Romilly's Act, *vide ante* p. 104.

(*h*) Sir S. Romilly's Act, *vide ante*, p. 104.

(*i*) The Trustees Relief Act, 10 & 11 Vict. c. 96, or the Trustees' Acts of 1850 and 1855.

Special Jurisdictions: how determined.

Statement in certificate of board of the amount of income of any charity to be sufficient evidence for determining the jurisdiction or proceedings under this Act.

44. For the purposes of determining the jurisdiction under this Act with respect to any charity (*a*), or the right to appeal from the determination of a judge of the Court of Chancery (*b*), it shall be lawful for the said board to declare, according to such judgment as they may be able to form upon the returns or statements before them in relation to any charity (*c*), whether the gross annual income for the time being of such charity does or does not exceed thirty pounds (*d*) or one hundred pounds (as the case may require), and a statement in any certificate or order of the said board (*e*) that according to such judgment as aforesaid the gross yearly income of any charity does or does not exceed thirty pounds or one hundred pounds shall be sufficient evidence of the amount of the gross annual income of such charity, for the purpose of determining such jurisdiction or right to appeal as aforesaid (*f*); and any certificate or order made by the said board under this Act, authorising any proceeding or application concerning any charity to be taken or made to any district court of bankruptcy or county court (*g*) or to the Court of Chancery or any judge thereof (*h*), shall state that the gross annual income for the time being of such charity does not exceed thirty pounds (*i*), or does exceed thirty

Proviso as to particular endowments.

pounds (as the case may be): Provided always (*k*), that where any charity, or the trustees thereof, in addition to the principal endowment for its general objects and purposes, shall be possessed of or entitled to any other endowment for any particular or special object or purpose arising out of or in its nature or application connected with the general objects or purposes of such

---

(*a*) Ss. 28, 39.
(*b*) S. 39.
(*c*) S. 10.
(*d*) Fifty. Act of 1860 s. 2.
(*e*) As required by the ss. 28 and 32 referred to.
(*f*) S. 28.
(*g*) S. 32.
(*h*) S. 28. But now fifty. See Act of 1860 s. 2.
(*i*) S. 32.
(*k*) See as to societies partly supported by voluntary contributions, but having such special endowments for special purposes, s. 62.

Special Jurisdiction : Regulation of. 155

charity (a), it shall be lawful for the said board, having regard to the circumstances of each such case, and to the object and extent of the proposed application and litigation, to determine whether such endowment for such particular or special object or purpose should, for the purposes of jurisdiction and proceedings under this Act (b), be considered and treated as forming part of the general endowment of the charity, or as a separate or independent charity, and such board shall frame their certificate or order accordingly.

Special Jurisdiction : regulation of.

45. The Lord Chancellor shall make such orders for regulating proceedings by and before the judges of district courts of bankruptcy and county courts under this Act (c), and for fixing and determining the fees to be taken in respect of such proceedings, as he may see fit; and, subject to such orders, such judges may regulate the proceedings before them respectively so as to render them as summary and inexpensive as conveniently may be. Lord Chancellor to make orders for regulating proceedings before district and County Courts. Judges to regulate proceedings.

46. Nothing herein contained (d) shall diminish or detract from any right or privilege which by any rule or practice of the Court of Chancery, or by the construction of law, now subsists for the preference or the exclusive or special benefit of the Church of England, or the members of the same church (e), in settling any scheme for the regulation of any charity, Reservation of rights and privileges of Church of England with re-

---

(a) *Vide ante*, 154, n. (k).
(b) Only for that purpose. To blend the funds would be in effect to alter the charity, and that would require the sanction of the court for a new scheme.
(c) S. 38.
(d) That is in s. 17 as to advice or direction (the only power in *this Act* given to the board, and that indirectly, to settle schemes); or in s. 28 and 32 as to jurisdiction of judges under this Act, in settling schemes, &c.
(e) See *At.-G.* v. *Pearson*, 7 Sim. 201; *At.-G.* v. *Callum*, 1 Y. & C. (N. S.) 411; *In re Norwich Charities*, 2 Myl. & N., 275; *the Chelmsford Grammar School case*, 24 L. J., Ch. 742; *Re Ilminster School*, 4 Jur., N. S., 444; *Sherborne Grammar School case*, 18 Beavan 256. The rule is that where there is nothing to show what the religion is, it is to be presumed that it is to be that of the Church of England, and that when this is so, the trustees ought to be of that church. See the Endowed Schools Act of 1860, which that rule leaves intact while pro-

Act of 1853.

spect to charities.
or in the appointment or removal of trustees, or generally in the application or management of any charity.

Vesting Charity Property in official Trustee.

Secretary to be treasurer of charities; such treasurer to be a corporation.
47. The secretary for the time being of the said board shall by virtue of his appointment be the treasurer of public charities (*a*); and such treasurer shall, for the purposes of taking (*b*), holding, conveying, assigning, transferring, and transmitting real property (*c*), including leaseholds for lives or years (*d*), be a corporation sole by the name of "The Treasurer of Public Charities" (*e*), and by that name shall have perpetual succession, and plead and be impleaded before all courts, justices, and others.

Vesting Charity Property : realty.

Land holden upon trust for a charity, subject to jurisdiction of Court of Chancery and of judge, may be vested in treasurer.
48. Where any land, or any term or estate therein, holden upon trust for any charity, shall be vested in any persons other than the persons acting in the administration and application of the rents (*f*); or where there shall be no trustees thereof, or the trustees, or any of them, shall be unwilling to act, or it shall be uncertain in whom such land, term or estate, shall be vested, or all or any of the persons in whom such land, term or estate, shall be vested, cannot be found, or shall be under age, lunatic, or of unsound mind (whether found such by inquisition or not), or otherwise incapable of acting, or shall be out of the jurisdiction or not amenable to the process of the Court of Chancery, or where by reason of the reduced number of trustees or other causes (*g*) a valid appointment of new trustees

---

viding for the admission of dissenters' children into Church of England schools.

(*a*) See Act of 1855 s. 17. Other official trustees may be joined.

(*b*) Therefore there may be bequests and devises to him for any charity.

(*c*) As to stock, &c., see Act of 1855 s. 18-19.

(*d*) By the Act of 1855 s. 115, the name is to be "official trustee."

(*e*) So that he or trustees in his name may sue for the rents or dividends of charity property vested in him.

(*f*) So that the trustees of the *charity* have no control over the *property*.

(*g*) This makes the scope of this clause as large as that of

cannot be made, or where by reason of the expenses incident to the appointment of new trustees, and the conveyance or assignment of such land, term or estate, to such new trustees, it shall appear to the Court of Chancery (*a*), or to any judge of such court (*b*) or of any court (*c*) having jurisdiction with respect to such charity under this Act, desirable so to do, such court or judge may order that such land, term or estate, be vested in such treasurer (*d*), and thereupon the same shall vest in such treasurer and his successors for all the estate and interest holden in trust for the charity as aforesaid, without any conveyance or assurance thereof (*e*), but no such vesting order as aforesaid shall be made in respect of any land, or term or estate as aforesaid, holden in trust as aforesaid, vested in a corporation, without the consent of the corporation; and no such vesting order shall take effect in respect of any copyhold land without the consent of the lord of the manor; and the Court of Chancery, or such judge, may direct such periodical or other payment, as such court or judge may think fit, to be made to the lord of the manor, in compensation for fines or other profits which would have become due upon death or admittance of tenants. *Proviso.*

65. The legal estate in all lands which at the time of the passing of the Act of the Session holden in the fifth and sixth years of King William the Fourth, chapter seventy-six, was vested in the body corporate of any borough which became subject to the provisions of the said Act, or in any one or more of the members of such body corporate, in his or their corporate capacity, solely or together with any person or persons elected solely by such body corporate, or solely by any particular number, class, or description of members of such *Legal estate of lands now vested in municipal corporations on charitable trusts to be vested in trustees. 5 & 6 W. 4. c. 76.*

---

the Trustees Acts of 1850 and 1855, and seems to include every possible case; but under these Acts the Court of Chancery can appoint new trustees. See the Acts, *et vide ante,* p. 62.

(*a*) Under the Trustees Acts, *vide ante*, p. 62.
(*b*) S. 28.
(*c*) S. 32.
(*d*) S. 47.
(*e*) For purposes of security, pending any application for the appointment of new trustees, see next section. He is to be a " bare trustee," *i.e.* only of the legal estate, s. 50.

body corporate, in whole or in part in trust or for the benefit of any charitable uses or trusts whatsoever (*a*), and which legal estate shall not have been since duly conveyed or assured to and vested in the trustees appointed by the Lord High Chancellor under the provisions of the said Act, or such of them as shall be surviving and continuing trustees, or otherwise lawfully conveyed, aliened, or disposed of by such body corporate or member or members thereof (*b*), shall, from and immediately after the passing of this Act, and without any actual conveyance, assignment, or other assurance thereof, be vested in the Trustees so appointed, or such of them as shall be surviving and continuing trustees under such appointment as aforesaid, according to the respective estates and interests therein, and subject to such and the same charges and incumbrances and upon such and the same trusts as the same were respectively subject to previously to such vesting (*c*); and in every case, upon the death, resignation, or removal of any of the trustees, and upon any appointment of any new trustee or trustees respectively (*d*), the legal estate in the same lands, and in all other lands subject to any such charitable uses or trusts which may for the time being be vested in the trustees or any of them, or in any persons or the heirs or devisees of any person who may have died, resigned, or been removed, shall vest in the persons who after such death, resignation, or removal, and such appointment of such new trustee or trustees respectively, shall continue to be the trustees for the time being, without any conveyance or assurance whatsoever.

Orders may be made revesting
49. It shall be lawful for any court or judge by whom respectively any such vesting order may have been made (*e*), or for any other court or judge having juris-

---

(*a*) There was a doubt whether the clause on the Municipal Corporation Act applied to the legal estates in the lands or only to the rights and powers of the trustees in the charitable trusts; and whether it applied in cases where the municipal corporation was also another corporation for charity purposes, or were trustees jointly with others, &c. See Doe d. *Governors of Bristol Hospital* v. *Norton*, 11 M. & W. 913, *et vide ante*, pp. 11, 12, 13; and other cases cited *ante*, p. 12.

(*b*) Therefore on the passing of the Act in all such cases the legal estate in the charity lands became vested in the trustees.

(*c*) Under the Trustees Act, *vide ante*, p. 62.
(*d*) S. 28.
(*e*) S. 48.

diction in the matter (*a*), if it shall so seem fit to such lands, &c. court or judge, from time to time to order that all or any in the part of the land, term, or estate, which shall for the time trustees of being be vested in the said treasurer by virtue of any the charity. such vesting order as aforesaid, shall be devested (*b*), and that the same shall be vested in the acting trustees or trustee for the time being of the charity; and such last-mentioned order shall operate to vest such land, term, and estate, in the trustees or trustee therein named without any conveyance or assurance.

50. Subject to the orders and directions of the Court Treasurer of Chancery or of any such judge (*c*), such treasurer to be a bare shall be deemed a bare trustee (*d*), and shall permit the trustee. persons acting in the administration of the charity to have the possession, management, and control of the trust estates (*e*), and the application of the income thereof (*f*), as if the same had been vested in them.

Vesting Property: Personalty.

51. The secretary for the time being of the said Judge may board (*g*), and such other public officer or officers as the order trustees, &c. Lord Chancellor shall appoint (*h*), shall be official trustees tees, &c. of charitable funds (*i*), and where trustees or other persons holding having in their names, or in the name of any deceased stock, &c. person of whom they are representatives, in the books of belonging the Bank of England, or of the East India, or South Sea subject to company, or of any other public company, or annuities, his juris- stock, or shares, or holding any Government or Parlia- diction to

---

(*a*) Ss. 28 and 32.
(*b*) On the appointment of new trustees, *vide ante*, p. 158.
(*c*) By whom such vestry order may have been made, s. 49, or under s. 48; the judge of the Court of Chancery at chambers, s. 28; or the county court judge, s. 32.
(*d*) Merely to take care of the legal estate or property.
(*e*) But still, the legal estate being in the official trustee, they would have to use his name in suing for rents, dividends, &c.
(*f*) When they have received or recovered it, *vide suprà* (*e*). It is implied that they may *receive* and *recover* in his name. See s. 52, as to stock, and see subsequent clause as to their power of letting, which is to be the same as if they were legal owners. That would not be necessary to enable them to recover trusts of charity property which they *had* let: for *cestui que* tenant in possession may recover rent from persons he has let into possession. *Churchward v. Ford*, 26 L. J., Ch. 354.
(*g*) S. 47, and Act of 1855 s. 15.
(*h*) Act of 1855, s. 17.
(*i*) *Ibid* s. 48.

transfer same to official trustees.

mentary or other securities in trust for any charity, shall be desirous to transfer or deposit the same to or with the said official trustees in trust for such charity (*a*), or where any person (*b*) shall be desirous of transferring or depositing as aforesaid any annuities, stocks, shares, or securities for discharging any legacy or charge (*c*) given or made to or for the benefit of any charity (*d*), or where it shall appear to the Court of Chancery (*e*), or to any judge of such court (*f*), or of any district court of bankruptcy, or county court having jurisdiction under this Act (*g*), that any annuities, stock, shares, or securities held in trust for any charity ought, for the purpose of security or convenient administration, to be transferred or deposited as aforesaid, it shall be lawful for such court or judge to order the transfer or deposit of such annuities, stock, shares, or securities to or with such official trustees (*h*).

Secretary to keep separate accounts of funds of each charity.

52. The secretary of the said board shall keep separate accounts of the annuities, stock, shares, and securities belonging to each separate charity, and the said official trustees (*i*) shall pay the dividends or interest or income thereof to the trustees or persons acting in the administration of such charity (*k*), or otherwise dispose thereof, and transfer such annuities, stock, shares, or securities (when occasion shall require), as the Court of Chancery (*l*), or any judge of such court (*m*), or of any district court of bankruptcy, or county court (*n*) having

---

(*a*) A proper course to preserve the property, and relieve themselves or the charity from risk of responsibility for acts of co-trustees.

(*b*) Executors, administrators, or devisees.

(*c*) Legacy out of personalty or charge upon realty. A charge on land for benefit of charity may be a mere liability, not a trust estate.

(*d*) It cannot legally be so by *will*, nor otherwise than by deed under statute 9 Geo. II. c. 36, *vide ante* p. 52, which extends to any charge on land for the benefit of a charity.

(*e*) Under its own general jurisdiction or under the Trustees Act, or under this Act.

(*f*) S. 28.
(*g*) S. 32.
(*h*) See further, on this subject, the Act of 1855, s. 22.
(*i*) While they hold the property, and until divested under s. 49.
(*k*) *Vide* ss. 16 and 48.
(*l*) Under its own jurisdiction.
(*m*) S. 28.
(*n*) S. 32.

jurisdiction under this Act, or other lawful authority, shall direct.

53. It shall be lawful for any trustees or other persons having the custody of any deeds or muniments of or relating to such charity to deposit the same for security in a repository which may be provided by the said board (*a*), subject to any regulations to be made by the said board under this Act. *Trustees may deposit deeds, &c. for security in a repository provided by the board.*

Application to Parliament for New Schemes.

54. Where upon the application of any trustees or other persons concerned in the management or administration of any charity (*b*), or interested in the benefits thereof (*c*), (and after such examination or inquiry as the board may think necessary in relation thereto), or upon any report of an inspector (*d*), or information otherwise obtained by the said board under this Act, with relation to any charity, it shall appear to the said board to be desirable to have a new scheme for the application or management of the charity (*e*), and such new scheme as contemplated or considered desirable by the board cannot be, or it shall in the opinion of the board be doubtful whether it can be carried into complete effect by the Court of Chancery (*f*), or by any district or county court under the jurisdiction created by this Act, or otherwise than by the authority of Parliament, it shall be lawful for the said board in every such case provisionally to approve and certify such new scheme (*g*) in the manner and subject to the regulations herein-after mentioned. *Power to board to frame schemes for the appropriation of charitable property to varied trusts.*

55. One month at least before any such new scheme shall be so provisionally approved, notice thereof shall be given in such manner as the board may in each case consider proper or expedient for ensuring due publi- *Notice to be given before approval of*

(*a*) See in the Act of 1860 a *compulsory* provision on the same subject, enabling the board to *require* and *retain* charity deeds.
(*b*) S. 48.
(*c*) S. 43.
(*d*) See s. 9.
(*e*) Application of the funds or benefits and internal management of the charity.
(*f*) See recital of Grammar Schools Act, *ante* p. 10.
(*g*) After a month's notice, &c., as in next clause.

Act of 1853.

schemes, and objections may be submitted for the consideration of the board.

city (*a*), and every such notice shall contain such particulars of the proposed scheme as the said board think fit, and as shall be deemed by the said board sufficient to show the nature of such scheme, and where the nature thereof cannot conveniently be shown in the said notice(*b*), such notice shall refer to some convenient place within the parish or district, and to the office in London of the Board(*c*) [Registrar of County Courts Judgments](*d*) where a copy of the proposed scheme shall be deposited and may be inspected, and every such notice shall require any objections to such scheme to be stated or transmitted to the said board or their secretary within one month from the time when the notice shall have been given.

Board may alter or modify or approve of schemes.

56. If after such notice as aforesaid any objections or suggestions shall be made, the board shall consider the same, and may thereupon, if to them it shall seem fit, alter or modify the scheme according to any such objections or suggestions; and after all such objections and suggestions, if any, have been disposed of, or if no such objections or suggestions have been made, the board, in case they shall not think fit to refer such scheme to an inspector under the provision next herein-after contained, may proceed to approve such scheme, and to certify the same in manner herein-after mentioned.

The matter of schemes may be referred to an inspector for local inquiry.

57. Upon the requisition of any person interested (*e*) in the charity in question (in case the said report, after due consideration, shall be of opinion that there are sufficient grounds for complying with such requisition), or in any other case, if the said board shall consider it desirable, the matter of any scheme in question may be referred by the said board to one of their inspectors, and such inspector shall thereupon proceed to make a local inquiry and examination into the matter of the scheme in question, and for the purposes of such inquiry, such inspector may hold a sitting or sittings in some convenient place in the parish or one of the parishes of the district to or in which respectively the charity in question is wholly or partially situated or is administered, and may take and receive any evidence and information, and

---

(*a*) Publication in the local newspapers will be the only effectual means.
(*b*) As it *can* be, fully and easily, if published in the newspapers.
(*c*) The Act of 1855, s. 49, substitutes here the *office of the board*.
(*d*) Act of 1855, s. 43.
(*e*) See s. 48.

hear and inquire into any objections or questions relating to the scheme or charity in question (*a*), and may from time to time adjourn any such sitting; and public notice shall be given by such inspector of every such sitting (except an adjourned sitting) fourteen days at the least before the holding thereof, in such other mode as in the judgment of the said board shall be sufficient to ensure publicity (*b*).

58. Every inspector to whom any such matter shall be referred shall report in writing to the said board the result of his inquiry, and whether in his opinion the scheme in question should be approved with or without any alteration or modification thereof, and such report shall specify or indicate the alterations (if any) which such inspector shall consider desirable with the reasons for the same and also the nature of the objections (if any) which shall have been made to the scheme, and the opinion of the said inspector thereon, and the said board shall consider such report, and if, as the result of such report or after further inquiry, they shall be satisfied therewith, they may proceed to approve the scheme in question either with or without any alteration, and to certify the same in manner herein-after mentioned. *Inspectors to report the result of inquiry to the board.*

59. Every scheme to be approved by the said board shall be certified by them, and for that purpose shall be embodied in a certificate to be made by the said board, and sealed with their seal; and in every case a copy of such certificate shall be deposited in some convenient place within the parish or one of the parishes or the district in which the charity in question shall wholly or partially be situated or administered, and at the office of the board (*c*), and a notice shall also be given, in such manner as the board shall direct (*d*), which notice shall refer to the certificate so deposited, and shall state the intention of the board to proceed with the scheme thereby certified. *Schemes when approved to be certified by the board. Copy of such certificate to be deposited in the parish or district, and notice given.*

Accounts of Trustees.

60. The said board shall in the month of *February* in every year make a report to Her Majesty of all their *Annual report to be*

(*a*) As the master under the old system in Chancery, or the chief clerk now, in settling new schemes.
(*b*) Publication in the local newspapers.
(*c*) Act of 1855, s. 43.
(*d*) Publication in the local papers.

Act of 1853.

laid before Parliament, which shall set forth all the schemes approved.
proceedings during the preceding year up to the thirty-first day of December then last, and such report shall, within fourteen days after the making thereof, be laid before both Houses of Parliament, if Parliament be then sitting, or otherwise within fourteen days after the meeting thereof; and in such report the said board shall specially distinguish and set forth in full all the schemes (if any) approved by them under the provisions lastly herein-before contained, together with the grounds of such their approval, and the objections (if any) which have been made thereto, and all proceedings had in respect of such objections, and the grounds on which any such objections have been over-ruled; and in case it shall be enacted by any Act of Parliament (*a*) that any such scheme or schemes so certified shall be confirmed and take effect, either with or without any alterations or modifications thereof respectively, every such Act shall be deemed a Public General Act.

Accounts of trustees of charities to be regularly kept (see s. 44 of Act of 1855).
61. The trustees or persons acting in the administration of any charity shall, in books to be kept by them for that purpose, regularly enter or cause to be entered full and true accounts of all money received and paid respectively on account of such charity (*b*).

[The rest of the clauses repealed. See substituted clause, Amending Act, s. 44.]

Exemptions.

Exemptions from the operation of Act.
62. This Act shall not extend to the Universities of Oxford, Cambridge, London, or Durham, or any college in the said Universities of Oxford, Cambridge, and Durham, or to any cathedral or collegiate church (*c*), or *to any building registered as a place of meeting for religi-*

(*a*) See several such schemes so confirmed, 1856-7-8.

(*b*) The remainder of this clause is repealed by the Act of 1855, s. 44, which is substituted for it, and explains the accounts required. The enactment applies to trusts in which the trustees have a discretionary power as to the selection of objects and distribution of the funds; for they are bound to apply the *whole* fund to the purposes for which it is given, and the commissioners have jurisdiction to see that this is done, and therefore to require accounts to be rendered which shall show whether it has been done or not.

(*c*) The cathedral or collegiate schools are *not* exempted. See end of clause. Endowed chapels of the Church of England are not exempted, nor augmentations of vicarages, &c., see p. 3.

Exemptions. 165

ous *worship* with the registrar-general of births, deaths, or marriages in England and Wales (*a*), and *bonâ fide used as a place of meeting for religious worship* (*b*); nor of Queen Anne's bounty, or to the British Museum, nor shall this Act for the period of two years from the passing thereof extend or be in any manner applied to charities or institutions, the funds or incomes of which are applicable exclusively for the benefit of persons of the Roman Catholic persuasion, and which are under the superintendence or control of persons of that persuasion, nor shall this Act extend or be applied to the commissioners of any friendly or benefit society, or savings bank (*c*), or any institution, establishment, or society for religious or other charitable purposes, or to the auxiliary or branch associations connected therewith, wholly maintained by voluntary contribution (*d*), or any bookselling or publishing business carried on by or under the direction of any society wholly or partially exempted from this Act, so far as such business is or shall be carried on by means of voluntary contributions only, or the capital or stock of such business; and where any charity is maintained partly by voluntary subscriptions and partly by income arising from any endowment (*e*), the powers and provisions of the Act shall, with respect to such charity, extend and apply to the income from endowment only (*f*), to the exclusion of voluntary subscriptions, and the application thereof; and no donation or bequest unto or in trust for any such charity as last aforesaid, of which no special application or appropriation shall be directed

Provisions as to charities supported partly by voluntary subscriptions.

(*a*) Under 15 & 16 Vict. c. 70; 18 & 19 Vict. c. 86.

(*b*) This exemption does not extend to the endowments for their support,—at all events, not to the endowments for the support of preachers or ministers, nor of public worship in such places. See now the Roman Catholic Charities Act, 1860, *post*.

(*c*) Self-supporting; therefore not supported by *gifts*, and so not charities.

(*d*) So not coming within the *definition;* see the interpretation clause, s. 66 "Endowment." The distinction is, that voluntary contributions given are generally placed at the absolute control of the governing body of the society for its general purposes; whereas endowment presupposes some special application or appropriation.

(*e*) In which case it will appear from the statement of account, *vide* s. 10, how much is endowment.

(*f*) Except, it is presumed, as to statement of account, s. 10.

or declared by the donor or testator (*a*), and which may legally be applied by the governing or managing body of such charity as income in aid of the voluntary subscriptions (*b*), shall be subject to the jurisdiction or control of the said board, or the powers or provisions of this Act (*c*); and no portion of any such donation or bequest as last aforesaid (*d*), or of any voluntary subscription, which is now or shall or may from time to time be set apart or appropriated and invested by the governing or managing body of the charity, for the purpose of being held and applied or expended for or to some defined and specific object or purpose connected with such charity, in pursuance of any rule or resolution made or adopted by the governing or managing body of such charity, or of any donation or bequest in aid of any fund so (*e*) set apart or appropriated for any such object or purpose as aforesaid, shall be subject to the jurisdiction or control of the said board or the powers or provisions of this Act; and nothing in this Act shall subject the funds or property of any missionary or other similar society, or the missionaries, teachers, or officers of such society, or of any branch thereof, which funds or property shall not be within the limits of England or Wales (*f*), to the jurisdiction of the said board : provided always, that the said exemption shall not extend to any cathedral, collegiate, chapter, or other schools (*g*).

Exempted charities may petition com-

63. It shall be lawful for any of the charities exempted from the operation of this Act, by order or resolution duly made in conformity with the constitu-

---

(*a*) Which will in effect constitute a trust.
(*b*) At their absolute disposal for *general* purposes.
(*c*) Save as to accounts, s. 10. See on this subject Wellbeloved, 1 S. & S. 41, *et vide ante*, p. 16.
(*d*) That is, *not* specially applied by the donor.
(*e*) That is, by rule or resolution only, and *not* by any donor. Special funds of this kind are often established, and then donations and bequests are made to it; these are by this clause exempted.
(*f*) Which implies that so far as the funds and property are within the jurisdiction, such societies are within the operation of the Act, that is as regards their endowments, *vide suprà*.
(*g*) Which therefore *may* be, but are not necessarily, within the operation of the Act, and are only so if the relation of trustee and *cestui que* trust exists between the chapter or college and the school. See *At.-G.* v. *Magdalen College;* 10 Beav. 402; *Whiston* v. *the Dean of Rochester*, 7 Hare, 532.

tion or rules of such charity (and which in that case only shall be binding), to apply by petition to the commissioners to have the benefit of this Act (*a*) either generally or as to any of the provisions herein contained (*b*); and such petition shall be under the seal of such charity if incorporated, and if not, then under the hands of the major part of the trustees and governing body of such charity (*c*); and in such case it shall be lawful for the commissioners, if they shall think fit, to make an order in conformity with such application, and such charity shall thenceforth be entitled to and be bound by all the provisions of this Act, if admitted generally thereto, or by such of the enactments thereof as shall be mentioned and specified in such order of the commissioners, but in either case in the same manner as if such charity had not been exempted from this Act, or such exemption had not extended to the enactments specified in such order. *[missioners to have benefit of Act.]*

64. Provided also, That if any question or dispute shall arise among the members of any charity (*d*), Act of 1855, s. 46, &c. (*e*), in relation to any office, or the fitness or disqualification of any trustee or officer (*f*), or his election or removal, or generally in relation to the management of the charity, it shall be lawful for two-thirds of the members present at any special meeting, duly convened by notice for the purpose in the same manner in which meetings of such charity are by the *[Disputes among members of exempted charities may be referred to arbitration of commissioners.]*

(*a*) And the Acts of 1855 and 1860, which are to be deemed together with this as *one* Act.

(*b*) As the provisions with respect to sales, leases, or exchanges of charity funds; or dismissal of masters or officers, or appointment of new trustees, or framing of new schemes, especially by the board, under the Act of 1860, s. 2.

(*c*) Who will still retain the internal management of the charity.

(*d*) This clause applies as well to exempted charities as to others; *i. e.* to chapels as well as to schools; to friendly societies and institutions, established by voluntary grants and assessments, *vide ante*, p. 15.

(*e*) Act of 1855, s. 46: "The Sixty-fourth section of the principal Act shall apply as well to members of any charity within the operation of that Act as to members of any charity exempted from the operation thereof."

(*f*) See clause 22 as to the power of the board to sanction removal of *any* officer. The Grammar Schools Act, 3 & 4 Vict. c. 77, empowers the *court* to authorise dismissal of any master of a grammar school, *vide ante*, p. 10, *et vide* Act of 1860.

rules thereof appointed to be held and convened, to refer such question or dispute to the arbitration of the commissioners, who shall accept such reference and act therein as arbitrators, and their award shall be final, and may be made a rule of Her Majesty's High Court of Chancery.

Interpretation Clause.

Interpretation of terms.
66 (*a*). In the construction of this Act, except where the context or other provisions of the Act may require a different construction, the expression "Court of Chancery" shall mean and include the Master of the Rolls and every judge of the Court of Chancery in England; the expression "Lord Chancellor" shall mean and include the Lord Chancellor of Great Britain and the Lord Keeper and Commissioners of the Great Seal of Great Britain for the time being; the expressions "District Court of Bankruptcy" and "District Court" shall mean and include every District Court of Bankruptcy established or to be established under the Act of the fifth and sixth years of the reign of Her present Majesty, chapter twenty-two, or under any other Act or Acts passed or to be passed for the alteration or amendment or the extension of the same Act, or for the establishment of any District Court or Courts of Bankruptcy in England or Wales, and every commissioner or judge of every such District Court; the expression "County Court" shall mean and include every County Court holden or established or to be holden or established under the Act of the ninth and tenth years of Her Majesty, chapter ninety-five, or any Act or Acts passed or to be passed (*b*) for the alteration or extension of the same Act, and every judge of any such court; the expression "Charity" shall mean every endowed foundation and institution taking or to take effect in England or Wales (*c*), and coming within the meaning,

---

(*a*) S. 65 is transposed into its proper place, *vide ante*, p. 157.
(*b*) 13 & 14 Vict. c. 61 ; 19 & 20 Vict. c. 108.
(*c*) There is a distinction between the endowed foundation or institution and the donations or bequests to it, though there may be a donation or bequest for the *purpose* of establishing one. And there may be donations or bequests for such institutions already endowed and established, not by way of endowment, but in *addition* to its income, as in either case the commissioners have jurisdiction ; for instance, they are to have accounts of all

purview, or interpretation of the statute of the forty-third year of Queen Elizabeth, chapter four (*a*), or (*b*) as to which, or the administration of the revenues or property whereof, the Court of Chancery has or may exercise jurisdiction; the expression "Trustee" of any charity shall mean and include every person and corporation seised or possessed of or entitled to any real or personal estate, or any interest therein, in trust for or for the benefit of such charity, or all or any of the objects or purposes thereof, and every member of any such corporation (*c*); and the expression "the Board" shall mean the said Charity Commissioners sitting as a board under this Act (*d*); and the expression "Endowment" shall mean and include all lands and real estate whatsoever, of any tenure (*e*), and any charge thereon (*f*), or interest therein (*g*), and all stocks, funds, monies, securities, investments, and personal estate whatsoever, which shall for the time being belong to (*h*) or be held in trust for (*i*) any charity (*k*), or for all or any of the objects or purposes thereof (*l*); and

---

income, and every gift must be stated in such accounts, see s. 44 of Act of 1855. The provision of the Act (s. 10) is not only any *charities*, but the estates, income, and property thereof.

(*a*) *Vide ante*, p. 19.

(*b*) This "or" is probably to be read conjunctively, introducing a synonymous definition, for the court has *not* charitable jurisdiction except in cases coming within that Act.

(*c*) So that, where a municipal or ecclesiastical corporation are trustees of a charity, the members are all equally amenable to the jurisdiction of the commissioners, in so far as the powers and provisions of the Act are applicable; for example, as to summoning them to be examined. But precepts to produce corporation books should be directed to the corporation or its head in the first instance.

(*d*) *Vide ante*, p. 124.

(*e*) Freehold or copyhold, or customary tenure.

(*f*) A charge not necessarily making the estate a trust estate, see *Dormayt* v. *Borrodaile*, 12 Beavan, 263. *Hunt* v. *Bateman*, 11 Irish Eq. Rep. 10.

(*g*) Leasehold, or a mortgage.

(*h*) That is, if legally vested in the trustees.

(*i*) As either by legal title or by declaration of trust, which is a title in equity, if valid.

(*k*) That is, already established, or to be established.

(*l*) Including gifts either for the general purposes or for some special purposes, except as to societies or institutions partly supported by voluntary subscriptions (as to which *vide ante*, 15);

I

the expression "Land" shall extend to and include manors, messuages, buildings, tenements, and hereditaments, corporeal and incorporeal, of every tenure and description.

Extent of Act.
67. This Act shall not extend to Scotland or Ireland.

Short title.
68. This Act may be cited as "The Charitable Trusts Act, 1853" (a).

---

the Act does not apply to special funds, unless *donations* for special purposes.

(a) While this sheet is passing through the press, a case has been reported (*Daugars* v. *Rivaz*, 29 L. J., Ch., 685), in which the Master of the Rolls restrained the Elders of a French Protestant church from removing their pastor. At first sight this might appear inconsistent with the doctrine laid down and the cases cited *ante*, p. 91 ; but if it were, those cases being established on the highest authority, and not having been cited nor considered, the decision referred to could not be considered satisfactory. The real ground on which it rested, however, was, that there was in truth no removal at all, but a mere abuse of power; the Elders being themselves mere lay trustees; and having, in their own favour, in a dispute to which they were parties, assumed an absolute authority *which, by the constitution of their church, they did not possess*. In this view, the case is *not* inconsistent with the doctrine above laid down, and it is conceived that in that view alone it can be supported; on any other view it would be contrary to the recent decision of Vice-Chancellor Kindersley in *Perry* v. *Shipway*, 28 L. J., Ch., 660.

The Charitable Trusts Act, 1855.
(18 & 19 Vict. c. 124.)

1. THE Charitable Trusts Act, 1853, hereinafter called "the Principal Act," and this Act shall be construed together as one Act (*a*); and any provisions of the principal Act inconsistent with this Act are hereby repealed. *16 & 17 Vict. c. 187, and this Act to be construed together.*

2. [Not necessary to be inserted]. *Provision as to the salary of one of the commissioners repealed.*

3. [Not necessary to be inserted]. *Power to appoint additional inspectors.*

4. Every act of the board may be sufficiently authenticated by the seal of the commissioners, and the signature of their secretary, or in his absence of the chief clerk. *The acts of the board, how to be authenticated.*

5. All orders, certificates, schemes, and other documents issued under the seal of the board shall be deemed and taken to be the originals, and copies thereof shall be entered in the books of the board, and all such entries may be sufficiently certified by the signature of the secretary, or in his absence of the chief clerk: Every order, certificate, scheme, and other document purporting to be sealed with the seal of the board shall be received in evidence without further proof (*b*); and any writing purporting to be a copy extracted from the said books, and to be certified as aforesaid, shall be received in evidence in like manner. *Entries in and extracts from the books of the board, how to be authenticated.*

(*a*) This is very important, and has a double application. It applies to the enactments of *this* Act any of the powers and provisions of the *principal* Act (capable of such application), and it applies to the enactments of the *principal* Act any of the applicable powers and provisions of *this* Act. And as there is a *similar* provision in the Act of 1860, *vide post*, the effect is that all three Acts are to be construed as one; and hence any of the powers and provisions in any one of them applicable or capable of being applied in aid of any of the enactments in any of the other Acts are to be so applied. For example, see s. 9 of this Act.

(*b*) *Vide* principal Act, s. 8; and *vide* 14 & 15 Vict. c. 99.

Accounts and Statements of Charities.

The powers of the commissioners and inspectors to inquire into charities extended.

6. The board (*a*), or any commissioner or inspector, such inspector acting under the authority of the board, may (*b*) require written accounts and statements (*c*) and answers to inquiries relating to any charity (*d*), or the property or income thereof, to be rendered or made to them respectively by all or any of the following persons; that is to say,

 Trustees or persons acting or concerned in (*e*) the administration of the charity, its property or income, or in the receipt or payment of any monies thereof:
 Agents of any such trustees or persons (*f*):
 Depositories of any funds or monies of the charity (*g*):
 Persons in the beneficial receipt of any funds thereof or of any income or stipend therefrom (*h*):
 Persons having the possession or control of any documents concerning the charity or any property thereof (*i*):

And the board or the commissioner or inspector may require the persons rendering or making any such account, statement, or answer to verify the same by oath or otherwise, and may administer such oath: Provided always, that nothing herein contained shall extend to give to the said board or their inspectors any power of requiring from any person (*k*) holding or

---

(*a*) See Act of 1853, ss. 9 and 10.

(*b*) Of their own motion, or on any information.

(*c*) As to *annual* accounts, see s. 44, to be read with this clause.

(*d*) As to what is a charity, see the interpretation clause, Act of 1853. The board in each case must judge; and they have jurisdiction to determine the preliminary question. Supposing them to err, and to meddle in a charity without jurisdiction, there might probably be an injunction or prohibition to restrain; or, on refusal of parties to attend, the question will be raised by application for process of contempt; s. 9.

(*e*) This includes any persons claiming to be entitled to be recipients of the benefits.

(*f*) As to attorneys, see *Russell* v. *Jackson*, 21 L. J. (N. S.) Ch. 146. *Semble* an attorney may be examined; at all events, unless his client really claims adversely.

(*g*) As bankers, or other bailees.

(*h*) As for receipt, *not* beneficial; see the first part of the clause.

(*i*) See Act of 1853, s. 61, and see Act of 1860.

(*k*) This provision does not prevent them from obtaining the

Accounts and Inquiries. 173

claiming to hold any property whatsoever adversely to any charity, or free or discharged from any charitable trust or charge (*a*), any information, or the production of any deed or document whatever, in relation to the property so held or claimed adversely, or any charitable trust or charge alleged to affect the same.

Accounts and Inquiries.

7. The board, or any commissioner or inspector acting as aforesaid, may require all or any such trustees and persons as aforesaid to attend before them respectively at such times and places as may be reasonably appointed (*b*), for the purpose of being examined in relation to the charity (*c*), and to answer such questions as may be proposed to them, and to produce upon such examination any documents in their custody or power relating to the charity or the property thereof (*d*), and may examine upon oath or otherwise all such persons (*e*) and all persons voluntarily attending (*f*), and may administer such oath: Provided always, that no person shall be obliged to travel in obedience to any such requisition more than ten miles from his place of abode. Power to require trustees and others to attend and be examined.

8. All requisitions made under the foregoing authorities shall be made respectively by the order of the board, or by precept, under the hand of the commissioner or inspector making the same. Precepts or orders for the preceding purposes, how to be made.

9. Any person refusing or wilfully neglecting to comply with any such requisition (*g*), or with any order Persons not complying

---

information from any one else, except perhaps the attorney of the party, *Russell* v. *Jackson*, 21 L. J. (N. S.) Ch. 146.

(*a*) As for his own benefit; but the claim must be *real*, and whether it is so or not is for the commissioners to decide.

(*b*) By board, commissioners, or inspector, respectively, as the case may be, and the board must judge of the reasonableness, whether as to time allowed for appearance, mode of service, &c., *Re Williams*, 21 L. J., M. C. 46. See next section, as to form of precept.

(*c*) That is, the charity spoken of in the preceding section, under which it is presumed accounts have (or have not) been delivered, or if delivered are not satisfactory, or require further explanation.

(*d*) The language used in affidavits as to discovery, see Common Law Procedure Act, 1854, ss. 50 and 51.

(*e*) As have been summoned to attend, *vide supra*.

(*f*) As informants, relators, or witnesses, interested or not in the charity, provided their testimony is likely to be useful.

(*g*) As to not answering questions duly or satisfactorily, that

with requisitions, &c., to be deemed guilty of a contempt of the Court of Chancery.
of the board, made under the provisions of this Act or the principal Act, or destroying or withholding any document required to be produced or transmitted by him, shall be taken to be guilty of a contempt of the High Court of Chancery, and shall be liable to be attached and committed by such court, on summary application by the commissioners to the same court or to any judge thereof, and shall pay such costs attending such contempt as the said court or judge shall direct: Provided always, that the court may at any time discharge, on such terms as it may deem just, any person attached or committed on any such application, or on any application made under section fourteen of the principal Act.

Apportionment of Charities.

Power to apportion parochial charities after division of parishes.
10. Where any parish or ecclesiastical district entitled to the benefit of a charity (*a*) has or shall have been divided into separate parishes or ecclesiastical districts (*b*), and no apportionment of charities originally applicable to the parish or district so divided shall have been made by Parliament or other competent authority (*c*), the board, in respect of all charities the gross annual income whereof does not for the time being exceed thirty pounds (*d*), may apportion the benefit of the charity between each new parish or district, or any portion thereof taken from the parish or district originally entitled to the whole benefit, and the remainder of such last-mentioned parish or district (*e*), in such manner and such proportions as upon a consideration of the purposes of the charity, the population of each parish or district, and other circumstances, they

---

would not be a contempt within this clause, unless it really amounted to a refusal or evasion of any *real* answer at all; and as to what would amount to such evasion and substantial refusal of a real answer, the cases of committals by commissioners of bankrupts for not answering will afford obvious analogies. See *Re Bradbury*, 23 L. J., C. P. 25.

(*a*) As to parochial charities, see p. 11, and p. 102.
(*b*) Under Church Building Acts, &c.
(*c*) As under 8 & 9 Vict. c. 70, *vide ante*, p. 71.
(*d*) *Fifty*, see Act of 1860, s. 40. As to other charities the board may give directions and advice under s. 17, or authorise an application to the court.
(*e*) See cases cited *ante*, p. 72.

may think fit, and may also apportion the principal endowments between such parishes or districts, if it be thought fit, and may appoint separate trustees of any part of the endowments.

Additional Vesting Clauses.

15. The secretary for the time being of the board (*a*) shall be a corporation sole by the name of "The Official Trustee of Charity Lands," for taking and holding charity lands, and by that name (instead of the name of "Treasurer of Public Charities") shall have perpetual succession; and all land, or estates or interests in land, now vested in the "Treasurer of Public Charities" by that name shall become, upon the passing of this Act, and by virtue thereof, vested in like manner and upon the same trusts in "The Official Trustee of Charity Lands," and all provisions of the principal Act (*b*) which have reference to the treasurer of public charities shall operate as if the name of the "Official Trustee of Charity Lands" had been used therein instead of the name of "Treasurer of Public Charities." *The official trustee of charity lands constituted.*

16. The acting trustees of every charity, or the majority of them, provided that such majority do not consist of less than three persons, shall have at law and in equity power to grant all such leases or tenancies of land belonging thereto, and vested in the official trustee of charity lands (*c*), as they would have power to grant in the due administration of the charity if the same land were legally vested in themselves (*d*); and all covenants, conditions, and remedies contained in or incident to any lease or tenancy so granted (*e*) shall be enforceable by and against the trustees or persons acting in the administration of the charity for the time being, and their alienees or assigns, in like manner as if such lands had been legally vested in the trustees granting *Power to acting trustees to grant leases.*

(*a*) Act of 1853, s. 47.
(*b*) Sect. 48.
(*c*) It had already been enacted that the official trustee was to be a bare trustee.
(*d*) That is, as *trustee*, of course.
(*e*) Incident to, of course includes distress for rent, or action for use and occupation; even apart from this clause the trustees, if allowed by the official trustee to let persons into possession, might sue them for use and occupation, *Churchward* v. *Ford*, 26 L. J., Ex. 354.

such lease or tenancy at the time of the execution thereof (*a*), and had legally remained in or had devolved to such trustees or administrators for the time being, their alienees or assigns, subject to the same lease or tenancy.

Appointments of official trustees of charitable funds regulated.

17. The Lord Chancellor may from time to time by writing under his hand appoint any persons to be, jointly with the secretary for the time being of the said board, the official trustees of charitable funds, and remove any such trustees, and every such appointment or removal shall be published in the *London Gazette*.

Such trustees to have perpetual succession, and may hold funds in that name.

18. The present official trustees of charitable funds, and their successors, to be so appointed, shall have perpetual succession by the name of "The Official Trustees of Charitable Funds," and may hold by that name stock in the public funds, and stock and shares of any public company, securities, and monies (*b*), which shall respectively devolve to their successors, the official trustees of charitable funds for the time being, without transfer or assignment.

Funds to vest in the official trustees for the time being.

19. All stock in the public funds vested in the joint names of Henry Morgan Vane, Thomas Hare, and Walker Skirrow, Esquires, the present official trustees of charitable funds, shall upon the passing of this Act be transferred by the Governor and Company of the Bank of England from their names to the account of the official trustees of charitable funds.

The official trustees to keep banking account.

20. The official trustees of charitable funds shall, for the purposes of their trust, keep a banking account in their official name in the books of the Governor and Company of the Bank of England (*c*), and the secretary of the board shall keep separate accounts of the monies held upon such account, and belonging to each separate charity.

Mode of drawing on the banking account.

21. All orders for payment of any money held upon such banking account shall be signed by one at least of the official trustees of charitable funds, not being

---

(*a*) As in the case of leases under a power, *Greenaway* v. *Hart*, 23 L. J., C. P. 115.

(*b*) Transferred to them under any order of the court or commissioners, under s. 15 ; or voluntarily by the trustees themselves, under s. 22.

(*c*) That is, one entire account comprises *all* the charities, the secretary keeping the *separate* accounts.

the secretary of the board, and also by the secretary, and shall be countersigned by one of the commissioners, or shall be otherwise signed or authenticated in such manner as the Lord Chancellor shall from time to time by order under his hand direct; and such orders shall be a sufficient authority to the bank paying the same for all such payments.

22. Any trustee or other person (*a*) may, on obtaining an order of the board for the purpose (*b*), transfer any stock or pay any money to the official trustees of charitable funds in trust for any charity. Trustees may transfer stock to official trustees.

23. All principal monies belonging to any charity directed to be paid to the official trustees of charitable funds shall be paid to their account at the bank, and, subject to any order of the court or judge or of the board by which respectively the payment shall have been authorised, shall be forthwith invested in the public funds (*c*), in the names of the official trustees of charitable funds for the benefit of the charity to which they shall belong. As to disposal of principal monies paid to them.

24. The dividends arising from all stock in the public funds standing in the name of the official trustees of charitable funds shall from time to time be received by the Governor and Company of the Bank of England, under the authority of this Act, for the credit of the said official trustees, and shall be placed to their banking account accordingly (*d*); and all dividends and interest arising from any other stock, shares, or securities standing in the name of or held by the official trustees of charitable funds shall be paid only to the Governor and Company of the Bank of England for the account of the same trustees; and the said trustees shall from time to time execute to the said governor and company all such powers as shall be found necessary for enabling them to receive and give effectual discharges for the last-mentioned dividends and interest. All dividends and interest due to the official trustees of charitable funds to be placed to their banking account.

25. No transfer of any stock, shares, or securities shall be made to the official trustees of charitable funds, nor shall any money, other than the dividends or interest of any such stock, shares, or securities as aforesaid, be For the Regulation of transfers and pay-

---

(*a*) As an executor or administrator under a will leaving stock or money to a charity.
(*b*) As to investment, *vide ante*, p. 100.
(*c*) This is essential, see s. 25.
(*d*) Under s. 20.

ments to or by the official trustees. paid to their account, except in pursuance of an order of the Court of Chancery, or of some judge thereof, or of a district court of bankruptcy or county court, or of the board (a); and no transfer of any such stock, shares, or securities shall be made by the official trustees, except under the order of such court or judge, or under the order of the board signed by two commissioners, or authenticated in such manner as the Lord Chancellor from time to time by any order under his hand direct; and no transfer to or by the official trustees shall be permitted by the Governor and Company of the Bank of England or any other company contrary to this provision.

Copies of orders affecting the account of the official trustees to be sent to the board. 26. Copies of all orders made by any court or judge for any transfer, deposit, or payment of stock, shares, securities, or monies to or by the official trustees of charitable funds (b) shall be forthwith transmitted to the board by the parties obtaining such orders.

Indemnity to the bank and others. 27. Every order made under the principal Act or this Act, requiring or authorising the transfer, payment, or deposit of any stock, shares, securities, or monies to or with the trustees of any charity or the official trustees of charitable funds, or conferring a right to call for or to make such transfer, shall be a complete indemnity to the Governor and Company of the Bank of England and all companies and persons for any Act done pursuant to such order; and the said governor and company and other companies and persons shall be required to give effect or to conform to every such order, and it shall not be necessary for them to inquire concerning the propriety of such order, or the jurisdiction of the court or judge or the board to make the same.

Dividends on stock in name of official fund trustees to be carried to account free from income tax. 28. All dividends arising from any stock in the public funds standing in the name of the official trustees of charitable funds, and which shall be certified by the board to the Governor and Company of the Bank of England to be exempt from the property or income tax, shall be paid or carried to the banking account of the official trustees without any deduction of such tax; and all dividends arising from any stock in the public funds standing in any other names or name, and which the board shall certify to the Governor and Company of the Bank of England to be subject only to charitable trusts,

---

(a) See s. 22.   (b) s. 22.

Additional Powers as to Sales, &c.

and to be exempt from such tax, shall be paid without any deduction thereof.

29. It shall not be lawful for the trustees or persons acting in the administration of any charity (*a*) to make or grant otherwise than with the express authority of Parliament, under any Act already passed (*b*), or which may hereafter be passed (*c*), or of a court or judge of competent jurisdiction (*d*), or according to a scheme legally established (*e*), or with the approval of the board (*f*), any sale, mortgage (*g*), or charge, of the charity estate, or any lease thereof in reversion after more than three years of any existing term, or for any term of life, or in consideration wholly or in part of any fine, or for any term of years exceeding twenty-one years. *Restrictions of charges and leases of charity estates.*

30. [Inserted in Act of 1853, s. 21.] *Sinking fund to be provided for paying off mortgages in lieu of provision in mortgage deeds.*

31. [Inserted in Act of 1853, s.23.] *Extension of power of board as to compromise of claims.*

32. The board may authorise the application of any funds belonging to any charity in payments for equality of exchange or partition, or in payment of any expenses incident thereto, or may authorise the trustees to raise any money for such purposes by mortgage of any land acquired on such exchange or partition, or belonging to the charity. *Board may authorise payment for equality of exchange or partition.*

Additional Powers as to Sales, Charges, and Exchanges.

33. Where there shall be uncertainty as to the specific part of any lands out of which any rent, annuity, or *Power to ascertain*

(*a*) Governors, &c., or trustees of charities of which the estates are vested in the official trustees as *bare trustees*, *vide ante*, p. 175.

(*b*) As of the Acts of 13 Eliz. c. 10, or the other Acts enabling governors of hospitals to lease; see those mentioned, s. 38.

(*c*) Sect. 38.

(*d*) On an application otherwise than for a scheme, under the general jurisdiction of the court if under the special jurisdiction of a judge at chambers created under the Act of 1853, s. 28; or the County Court Act, s. 32.

(*e*) Under an application to Chancery.

(*f*) By way of direction, under s. 17 of the Act of 1853; or of direct authority, under s. 39; or Act of 1853, s. 21; or by order under Act of 1860, s. 2.

(*g*) See *Minn* v. *Stant*, 20 L. J., Ch. 614.

lands charged with rents to charities.
other periodical payment, not exceeding the yearly sum of ten pounds, charged upon some part of the same lands, for the benefit of a charity (*a*), shall be payable, it shall be lawful for the board, upon the application of the trustees or persons acting in the administration of the charity, and with the consent of the persons interested, according to the aforesaid definition of "persons interested," in the same lands (*b*), to determine by their order the land charged with such rent, annuity, or other periodical payment (*c*), which shall thenceforth stand charged with such rent, annuity, or periodical payment, accordingly, to the exoneration of the residue of such lands therefrom.

Expenses of exchanges and partitions, and determining application of charges.
34. The expenses incident to the application for and procuring of any such order of exchange or partition, or order determining the land charged with any rent, annuity, or periodical payment, shall be paid by the trustees or administrators of the charity, or by the other parties to such transactions, or by both, as the board may direct.

Incorporated charities and trustees for
35. Any incorporated charity, or the trustees of any charity, whether incorporated or not, may, with the consent of the board, invest money arising from any sale of land belonging to the charity (*d*), or received by way of

---

(*a*) As under a devise or conveyance of lands severally subject to certain charges, including one or more for the benefit of a charity. A mere *charge* of that kind does not make the estate a trust estate in the lands of the devisee or grantee beneficially interested so that he cannot alienate it; but the charge passes with the estate into the hands of each successive owner of the *whole* estate, so that no conveyance of any part of it could be made, but for this clause, except subject to *all* the charges. The object is to meet this difficulty.

(*b*) By some mistake no such definition is inserted, but it is easy to see who are the parties interested, viz., the parties entitled to all the charges on the lands, and the owners of all the lands affected thereby.

(*c*) Of course, in the case of lands subject to *several* charges, *all* must be included, for there must be an apportionment; *vide supra*.

(*d*) That is, *legally* belonging; the clause would not extend to sanction sale of lands under a devise to a charity invalid by the mortmain law, not *directed* to be sold by the will. But if the trustees had been in possession for twenty years they would have a title.

equality of exchange or partition, in the purchase of · charities
land, and may hold such land, or any land acquired by · may re-in-
way of exchange or partition, for the benefit of such · vest in
charity, without any licence in mortmain. · land.

36. All orders of the board for the investment of · Order of
money coming to any charity (a), or the trustees thereof · board for
on any sale, exchange, or partition shall be carried into · invest-
effect by the trustees or persons administering the charity; · ments to be
and all monies which the board shall order to be provided · carried into
out of any income or property of a charity, for the pay- · effect, and
ment of the costs of any such transaction, shall be pro- · costs to be
vided or raised by the trustees or administrators of the · raised.
charity, and applied accordingly.

37. It shall be lawful for the board to authorise or · Board may
order and direct the official trustee of charity lands and · direct offi-
the official trustees of charitable funds respectively to · cial trus-
convey lands, and to assign, transfer, and pay over · tees to con-
stocks, funds, monies, and securities, as the board shall · vey lands,
think expedient. · &c.

38. All leases, sales, exchanges, partitions, and trans- · Leases, &c.,
actions authorised by the board under the principal · to be valid,
Act (b) or this Act (c), shall be valid and effectual, · notwith-
notwithstanding the Act of the thirteenth year of the · standing
reign of Queen Elizabeth, chapter ten, the Acts of the · disabling
fourteenth year of the same Queen, chapters eleven and · Acts.
fourteen, the Acts of the same Queen, chapters six and
eleven, the Act of the thirty-ninth year of the same
Queen, chapter five, and the Act of the twenty-first year
of the reign of King James the First, chapter one, or any
disabling Act applicable to the charity the estates
whereof shall be the subject of any such transaction (d).

39. It shall be lawful for the board to prepare, and · Board may
under their seal to approve of, any scheme for the let- · approve
ting of the property or any part of the property of any · schemes for
charity (e), and all leases granted by any trustees or · letting
persons acting in the management of any charity,

(a) *Vide* s. 35.
(b) Sect. 21.
(c) Sect. 29.
(d) See *Pennington* v. *Cardale*, 27 L. J., Ex. 438.
(e) Generally "schemes" are for the administration of charity funds, not for the management of charity property; this clause is to provide a general system of letting. All leases above seven years must, by 8 & 9 Vict. c. 106, be by deed; and if both parties execute (as *lessors must*, *Swatman* v. *Ambler*,

Charitable Trusts Act, 1855.

charitable property. pursuant to or in conformity with such scheme, shall be valid.

Taxation of Costs—Copies of Deeds.

Power to refer bills of costs in charity matters to taxation. 40. The board may order the bill of costs or charges claimed by any attorney or solicitor on account of business conducted or transacted by him on behalf of any charity (a), or the trustees thereof (b), to be examined and taxed by the taxing masters of the Court of Chancery, or by the proper taxing officers of any of the superior courts at Westminster, who shall proceed to examine and tax the same bill accordingly; and if the same shall be reduced upon such taxation by the amount of one sixth part or more of the amount thereof, the costs of the taxation shall be paid by such attorney or solicitor, but otherwise out of the funds of the charity by the trustees thereof; and the board may, after being satisfied as to any bill that it contains exorbitant charges, order any such bill to be so taxed, notwithstanding that the same may have been paid by the trustees of the charity at any period not more than six calendar months previously to such order; and any amount taxed off any such paid bill shall be a debt due from the attorney or solicitor to the trustees of the charity, and shall be forthwith paid by him to such trustees accordingly.

Construction of sect. 27 of 16 & 17 Vict. c. 137. 41. Section twenty-seven of "The Charitable Trusts Act, 1853," shall be construed and operate as if the words "and the trustees of the charity shall be legally authorised to purchase and hold such land" had been omitted therefrom, &c. [Inserted in Act of 1853.]

---

22 L. J., Ex. 81) there will be estoppel as between the parties and their assignees. This clause, therefore, is chiefly to guarantee the trustees or their lessees as against the *charity* in equity, and to do so without the expense of successive applications on each occasion.

(a) As to costs *against* a charity in any *adverse* suit, no enactment is necessary; they will be taxed in the ordinary course of practice. This clause refers to costs charged for business transacted in and about the affairs of the charity, in preparing leases, carrying out exchanges, recovering rents, &c., whether costs of suits in which the charity (through no default or neglect) has failed, or extra costs of suits in which it has *succeeded.*

(b) That is, of course, *as* trustees. *Vide* s. 36.

Accounts of Charities.

42. Any deed, will, or document relating to any charity may be enrolled by the board in books to be provided and kept by them for that purpose at their office, and a copy of any such deed, will, or document made from such books, and certified under the hand of the secretary or one of the commissioners, shall be received as evidence of the contents of the same deed, will, or document.

Deeds, &c., relating to charities may be enrolled at the office, and copies to be evidence.

43. [Inserted in Act of 1853.]

Construction of sects. 55 and 59 of 16 & 17 Vict. c. 137.

Accounts of Charities.

44. (*a*) Section sixty-one of "The Charitable Trusts Act, 1853," except so much thereof as enacts that the trustees or persons acting in the administration of every charity (*b*) shall, in books to be kept by them for that purpose, regularly enter or cause to be entered full and true accounts of all money received and paid respectively on account of such charity, shall be repealed as to all accounts which such trustees or administrators shall not have been bound to render before the passing this Act (*c*); and the trustees or administrators of every charity shall, on or before the twenty-fifth day of March, One thousand eight hundred and fifty-six, prepare and make out and transmit to the board an account (*d*) of the endowments then belonging to the charity (*e*), showing, in the case of realty not in hand, the manner in which the same is let or occupied, and in the case of personalty the existing investment or employment thereof, and in what names such investments are made (*f*); and such trustees or administrators shall also, on or before the twenty-fifth

Amendment of sect. 61 of 16 & 17 Vict. c. 137.

(*a*) This clause is to be read with s. 6.
(*b*) *Vide* interpretation clause of Act of 1853, p. 168.
(*c*) *Vide* (*b*).
(*d*) These are to be regular accounts, or accounts without requisition. The accounts and statements in the previous clause, s. 6, are to be special, and on the requisition of the board, &c.
(*e*) The parties giving the accounts are in the first instance to state what *they* deem to belong to a charity; but they may be examined thereupon, and on oath, under the previous provisions, and may be called upon to produce deeds and other documents showing what the disposition of the property was.
(*f*) The persons in whose names such investments are made may be summoned and examined, under s. 6.

day of March next, after the acquisition of any endowment not included in the foregoing account, prepare and make out in like manner, and transmit to the board, a similar account of such last-mentioned endowment, and in case of any alienation, or charge, or transfer of any real or personal estate of the charity, shall, on or before the twenty-fifth day of March then next following, transmit to the board an account of such alienation, charge, or transfer, and such trustees or administrators shall also, on or before the twenty-fifth day of March in every year, or such other day as may be fixed for that purpose by the board, or as may have been already fixed, for rendering the accounts thereof required by the principal Act, prepare and make out the following accounts in relation thereto : (that is to say)—

(1.) An account of the gross income arising from the endowment, or which ought to have arisen therefrom (*a*), during the year ending on the thirty-first day of December then last, or on such other day as may have been appointed for this purpose by the board:

(2.) An account of all balances in hand at the commencement of the year, and of all monies received during the same year on account of the charity (*b*):

(3.) An account for the same period of all payments (*c*):

(4.) An account of all monies owing to or from the charity, so far as conveniently may be:

which accounts shall be certified under the hand of one or more of the said trustees or administrators, and shall be audited by the auditor of the charity, if any (*d*) ; and

---

(*a*) *Vide* s. 6.
(*b*) *Vide supra* (*a*).
(*c*) This will apply even to charities of which the funds are to be distributed or applied at the discretion of the trustees, that the commissioners may see whether the whole of the funds *have* been so applied, *vide ante*, p. 51. Trustees are allowed to charge for all necessary expenses in carrying out their trust, and in certain cases *remuneration ;* and where they are themselves to perform services in carrying out the charity, they may retain a remunerative stipend or reward ; but *retainer* is payment, and must be stated and accounted for as such.
(*d*) If there are not, there is no provision for auditing, *vide* next note.

the said trustees or administrators shall, within fourteen days after the day appointed for making out such accounts, deliver or transmit a copy thereof to the commissioners at their office in London (*a*), and in the case of parochial charities shall deliver another copy thereof to the churchwarden or churchwardens of the parish, or parishes with which the objects of such charities are identified (*b*), who shall present the same at the next general meeting of the vestry of such parishes, and insert a copy thereof in the minutes of the vestry book; and every such copy shall be open to the inspection of all persons at all seasonable hours, subject to such regulations as to the said board may seem fit; and any person may require a copy of every such account or of any part thereof, on paying therefor after the rate of twopence for every seventy-two words or figures.

45. The board may from time to time make such orders as they may think fit in relation to the delivery or transmission of the said accounts, and the forms of such accounts, and such orders shall be executed by all trustees and persons from whom the accounts to which they may relate are required. Board may make orders as to delivery and publication of accounts by trustees, &c.

46. [As to this, see the Act of 1853, s. 64.] Application of sect. 64 of 16 & 17 Vict. c. 137.

(*a*) There is no express provision for the auditing of the accounts by the board (in case there are no auditors of the charity), but under the next clause, and s. 10 of the principal Act, the board have power to summon trustees to be examined on oath; and under ss. 17, 22, and 32, have power to direct proceedings in Chancery, &c., and would of course exercise that power in case of any gross or wilful defalcations or misapplications of charity monies.

(*b*) *Vide*, as to parochial charities, Treatise, p. 11, and p. 102. And see Hobhouse's Act, 1 & 2 Will. 4, c. 60, by which the vestry of every parish adopting the Act, must make out, once a year, a list of all charitable foundations and bequests belonging to the parish, and under the control of the vestry, *with the names of the trustees, and of the persons partaking of the benefits*, and to leave the lists open for the inspection of the ratepayers. This remains in force.

The Charitable Trusts Act of 1860.
(23 & 24 Vict. c. 136.)

WHEREAS it is expedient to provide increased and inexpensive facilities for the administration of endowed charities: Be it enacted by the Queen's Most Excellent Majesty, by and with the advice and consent of the Lords spiritual and temporal, and Commons, in this present Parliament assembled, and by the authority of the same, as follows:—

The Charitable Trusts Acts to be construed with this Act.
1. "The Charitable Trusts Act, 1853," and "The Charitable Trusts Amendment Act, 1855," and this Act shall be construed together as one Act (*a*), and any provisions of the said former Acts inconsistent with this Act are hereby repealed.

Certain administrative powers to be exercisable by the Charity Commissioners.
2. The Board of Charity Commissioners for England and Wales, subject to the restrictions (*b*) and rights of appeal (*c*) herein-after provided, shall have power from time to time, upon the application of any person or persons, who, under the forty-third section of "The Charitable Trusts Act, 1853" (*d*), might be authorised to apply to any judge or court for the like purposes, to make such effectual orders (*e*) as may now be made by any judge of

---

(*a*) This applies all the provisions of the former Acts applicable to this; for example, it applies to the orders of the board under the next section, the provision as to enforcing orders of the board contained in s. 9 of the Act of 1855.
(*b*) Sect. 4—7.
(*c*) Sect. 8.
(*d*) Any one or more of the trustees or persons administering, or claiming to administer, or interested in the charity, or any two or more inhabitants of the place within which it is administered or applicable. But if the income is above 50*l.*, the application must be by the trustees, or a majority, s. 4.
(*e*) This probably is intended to mean "orders as *effectual*," *i. e.*, orders having *de jure* as much effect as the orders of the county court judges, or of judges in chancery at chambers, under the jurisdiction created by the Act of 1853, s. 28, and nothing is here said as to the mode of *enforcing* the orders of the board. The Act of 1855, however, s. 9, provides a remedy for any disobedience to an order of the board under that Act or

the Court of Chancery sitting at Chambers (*a*), or by any county court or district court of bankruptcy, for the appointment or removal of trustees of any charity (*b*), or for the removal of any school master or mistress or other officer thereof (*c*), or for or relating to the assurance, transfer, payment, or vesting of any real or personal estate belonging thereto (*d*), or entitling the official trustees of charitable funds, or any other trustees, to call for a transfer of and to transfer any stock belonging to such estate (*e*), or for the establishment of any scheme for the administration of any such charity (*f*).

Powers of the Board to make Orders.

3. The said board, previously to making any order under the jurisdiction vested in them by this Act (*g*), shall notify to the trustees or administrators (if any) of the charity to be affected thereby their intention of exercising such jurisdiction by notice in writing, to be delivered to them, or sent to them by the post at their last-known place of abode in Great Britain or Ireland. *Board to notify to trustees of charity their intention of exercising, jurisdiction.*

4. The said board shall not make any order, under the jurisdiction vested in them by this Act, with respect to any charity of which the gross annual income, exclusively of the yearly value of any buildings or land used wholly for the purposes thereof, and not yielding any pecuniary income, shall amount to fifty pounds or upwards (*h*), except upon the application of the trustees or persons acting in the administration of the charity, or a majority of them, to be made to the said board in *The powers to be exercisable over no charities of which the gross income shall exceed 50l.,*

---

the principal Act, and the first section of the above Act makes it one Act with the former.

(*a*) Act of 1853, s. 28.
(*b*) Act of 1853, s. 32. For personal unfitness in facts *admitted*, as lunacy, infancy, bankruptcy, &c., as under the Trustees Act, 1855, not on matters controverted. See s. 4.
(*c*) See Act of 1853, s. 22.
(*d*) *Ibid.* s. 48.
(*e*) *Ibid.* s. 49.
(*f*) *Vide ante*, p. 64.
(*g*) Which they may be about to make on the application of only one of the trustees, or of some person other than a trustee. See s. 2.
(*h*) As estimated by the board on the accounts supplied to them, and the inquiries they may have made.

without application of trustees.

writing (*a*), under their hands if they shall be unincorporated, or under their common seal if they shall be incorporated, and the board shall not make any order removing any trustee on the ground only of his religious belief (*b*).

The board shall not exercise jurisdiction over contentious cases.

5. The said board also shall not exercise the jurisdiction hereby vested in them in any case which, by reason of its contentious character, or of any special questions of law or of fact (*c*) which it may involve (*d*), or for other reasons, they may consider more fit to be adjudicated on by any of the judicial courts.

Notices to be given of certain orders, and objections or suggestions to be received.

6. No order appointing or removing a trustee, or establishing a scheme for the administration of any charity, shall be made by the said board, before the expiration of one calendar month after public notice of the proposal to make such order shall have been given as they may consider most expedient and effectual for ensuring the publicity thereof (*e*), in each parish or district in which the charity, if of a local character, shall be applicable, or among all persons interested therein; and no order removing a trustee or school master or mistress or other officer of a charity who shall have any known place of residence in Great Britain or Ireland, and who shall not be consenting to be discharged, shall be made before the expiration of one calendar month

---

(*a*) Describing the nature of the order, relief, or direction required.

(*b*) That is, on the ground only that his religious belief unfits him for the office, having regard to the particular nature of the charity, religious or educational (*vide ante*, p. 90). So that the jurisdiction of the board under this clause as to trustees (especially coupled with the next clause), rather resembles that of the Court of Chancery on petitions under the Trustees Acts, in which it cannot determine disputed questions of fact, nor as to the unfitness of trustees with reference to the nature of a particular trust, but merely on some plain ground admitted as matter of fact; as where it is admitted that the trustee is a lunatic or infant. If that is *not* admitted, the court has no jurisdiction on petition.

(*c*) As, of *facts*, if the alleged reasons for the appointment of new trustees are disputed or denied.

(*d*) If of law, Sir G. Turner's Act, or Lord St. Leonards', may afford a convenient course; if of *fact*, there must be an application to the court in the ordinary way.

(*e*) By publication in the local newspapers would be obviously the only effectual mode.

after notice of the proposal to make such order shall have also been delivered to him or her, or sent by the post or otherwise to such his or her place of residence, and until after sufficient hearing of the matter before the said board, or some member thereof, or one of their inspectors (*a*), and every notice hereby required shall contain (so far as conveniently may be) sufficient particulars of the objects of the proposed order, and shall prescribe a reasonable time within which any objections thereto or suggestions thereon may be made or transmitted to the board (*b*); and the said board shall receive and consider all such objections and suggestions, and may withhold, suspend, or modify their proposed order, as they shall thereupon, or in the result of further inquiry, or otherwise, think expedient (*c*).

7. A copy of every such order when made shall, in the case of any local charity, be deposited for the space of one calendar month in some convenient place within the parish or one of the parishes or in the district in which the charity shall be applicable, and shall be open to public inspection there at all reasonable hours during the same period; and a copy also of every such order relating to any charity, whether local or general, shall be kept open to public inspection at all reasonable hours, at the office of the commissioners, during a like period of one calendar month; and in each case effectual publicity shall be given to the making of the order by such means as the board shall consider most expedient for that purpose (*d*). *Publication of definitive orders.*

Power of Appeal against Orders of Board.

8. The Attorney-General, or any person authorised by him or by the said board, in the case of any charity, whatever may be the yearly income of its endowments, and any trustee or person acting in the administration of or interested in any charity of which the gross yearly income to be calculated in manner aforesaid (*e*) shall ex- *Power to appeal against orders of board.*

(*a*) *Vide ante*, p. 127.
(*b*) To be sent by post; see the Charitable Notices Act.
(*c*) And must give notice to the trustees before they exercise their jurisdiction, s. 3.
(*d*) Publication in the local newspapers will be by far the most effectual.
(*e*) *Vide ante*, p. 154.

ceed fifty pounds (*a*), or any two inhabitants of any parish or district in which the same shall be specially applicable (*b*), may, within three calendar months next after the definitive publication of any order of the said Board(*c*) appointing or removing a trustee or trustees, or for or relating to the assurance, transfer, payment, or vesting of any real or personal estate, or establishing a scheme for the administration of the charity (*d*), present a petition to the High Court of Chancery in a summary way (*e*), appealing against such order, and praying such relief as the case may require; and any schoolmaster or schoolmistress or other officer removed by the order of the board, without the concurrence of the trustees or persons acting in the administration of the charity, or a majority of them (*f*), and without the approval of a special visitor, if any, of the charity, may, within two calendar months (next after his or her removal), appeal in like manner against the order of removal; and the court, upon or before the hearing of any such petition of appeal as aforesaid or at any stage of the proceedings, may require, if it shall think fit, from the said board, their reasons for making the order appealed against, or for any part of such order, and may remit the same to the board for reconsideration, with or without any declaration in relation thereto, or may make any substitutive or other order in relation to the matter of the appeal, as it shall think just; and the court may make any order respecting the costs, charges, or expenses incident to the appeal, and may also, before hearing or proceeding with the same, require from any appellant, other than the Attorney-General, proper security for such costs, charges, and expenses, as may be eventually payable by him; but no such petition of appeal shall be presented by any person other than the Attorney-General, before the expiration of twenty one days after written notice, under the hand of such appellant, of his or her intention to present such petition, shall have been delivered to the said board at their office.

Who may   9. The Attorney-General, if he shall think fit, or any

---

(*a*) *Without* such sanction of the board or Attorney-General.
(*b*) *Without* any sanction.
(*c*) Sect. 7.
(*d*) Sect. 6.
(*e*) As under Romilly's Act, *vide ante*, p. 104.
(*f*) Sections 2 and 3.

person authorised by him or by the said board, may be the respondent upon any such appeal, and the spondent court may make any order respecting the costs, charges, on appeals. and expenses of the Attorney-General or other defendant. Powers to

10. The jurisdiction vested by this Act in the said be applicable to board shall be exercisable with reference to charities charities vested in any corporation sole or aggregate (*a*), who, vested in either solely or jointly with any other person or persons, corporations, &c. shall also be the recipients of the benefit thereof.

11. The jurisdiction vested by the Charitable Trusts Jurisdiction of the Act, 1853 (*b*), in the district courts of bankruptcy and district county courts, over charities not possessing a larger gross courts of yearly income than thirty pounds, shall be exercisable bankruptcy by the said courts respectively for the like purposes and and county under the like provisions over charities of which the gross courts enlarged. yearly income for the time being, to be calculated in manner aforesaid, shall not exceed fifty pounds (*c*), in the same manner as if the last-mentioned limit to the jurisdiction of the said courts had been fixed by the said former Act.

12. Any court or judge, or the said board, having Official jurisdiction to authorise the official trustees of charitable trustees of funds to call for a transfer of and to transfer any annui- charitable ties, stock, or securities (*d*), may empower them also to funds may receive and recover (*e*), in trust for the charity to which be empowered to the same shall belong, all dividends, interest, and income receive accrued from any such annuities, stock, or securities arrears of respectively, and which shall for the time being be in dividends. arrear.

Powers as to Dismissal of Officers, &c.

13. Where any school master or mistress or other Power for officer (*f*), or any recipient of the benefit of a charity, magistrates being in possession by virtue of his or her office, or as such to give possession of recipient, of any house, buildings, land, or property of the charity (*g*), shall have been removed from or shall school

---

(*a*) Ecclesiastical persons, or deans and chapters, *vide ante*.
(*b*) Sect. 32.
(*c*) Estimated by the board, *vide ante*, p. 154.
(*d*) Act of 1853, s. 51.
(*e*) That is, sue for, at law or in equity; either from the trustees of the charity, if the stock, &c., is re-vested in them, or from the persons bound to pay the interest, &c.
(*f*) As to dismissal of whom, *vide* Act of 1853, s. 22; and ss. 2—6 of this Act.
(*g*) As in cases of hospitals, *vide ante*, p. 6, and p. 88.

buildings and property held over by officers or recipients of charities.
cease to hold such his or her office, or his or her place as such recipient (*a*), but he or she, or any person claiming under him or her, shall refuse or neglect to relinquish the possession of such house, buildings, land, or property within one calendar month next thereafter, to his or her successor, or to the trustees or persons acting in the administration of the charity, or as they shall direct, it shall be lawful for any two or more justices of the peace acting for the district, division, or place in which such house, buildings, land, or property shall be situate, in petty sessions assembled, and they are hereby required, on the complaint of the said trustees or administrators, and on the production of an order of the said board certifying such school master or mistress or other officer or recipient to have been duly removed from or to have ceased to hold his or her office or place (*b*), which order under the seal of the said commissioners shall be conclusive evidence of the facts thereby certified, and of the jurisdiction of the said commissioners to make such order for all the purposes of this enactment, and shall afford a complete indemnity to all persons acting thereunder, to issue a warrant under the hands and seals of such justices to any constables or peace officers of the same district, division, or place, commanding them, within a period to be thereby appointed, not being less than ten or more than twenty-one clear days thereafter, to enter into the premises, and deliver possession thereof to the said trustees or administrators, or their nominee or agent, and to remove therefrom such former school master or mistress, or other officer or recipient, and all persons claiming in his or her right, as fully and effectually, and subject to the same provisions, as nearly as the case will permit, as justices of the peace are empowered to give possession of any properties to the landlord or his agent upon the determination of the tenancy thereof, under an Act passed in the first and second years of the reign of Her Majesty, chapter seventy-four, for facilitating the recovery of possession of tenements after the determination of the tenancy.

(*a*) The board have no express power as to removal of recipients, unless it is comprised in the power given in s. 2 ; but *vide post.*

(*b*) As to which, if the removal have not been upon their own order, they must first hear evidence, *R.* v. *Smith,* 5 Q. B. 614, as the trustees themselves must.

Removal of Masters.

14. Every school master and mistress appointed after the date of this Act (*a*) shall be removable from his or her office (*b*), after reasonable notice by the trustees or persons acting in the administration of the charity (*c*), as they shall think expedient in the interests thereof (*d*), so nevertheless that the removal by virtue only of this provision of a master or mistress who would be otherwise irremovable from his or her office (*e*) shall be determined on by all or a majority of such trustees or administrators (*f*) assembled at a meeting convened by due notice, delivered or sent by the post to all such trustees or administrators who shall have any known place of residence in Great Britain or Ireland, by the space of not less than twenty-eight days previously, for the special purpose of considering and determining on the question of such removal, and of which intended meeting a notice shall also be delivered or sent in like manner to the master or mistress by the same previous space, and so also that the resolution of the meeting for the removal of any such last-mentioned master or mistress shall be forthwith certified under the hands of the trustees or persons acting as aforesaid who shall have concurred therein, or under the hand of the chairman of the meeting, and shall within seven days next thereafter be transmitted to the said board for their approval, and the same shall not take effect unless or until the same shall have been approved by the said

Masters and mistresses of endowed schools to be removable.

(*a*) As to others, *vide ante*, pp. 88 and 133.

(*b*) See Act of 1853, s. 22; this clause provides for dismissal on the ground of incapacity, &c.

(*c*) What is "reasonable notice" may be matter of question; it would probably be, in the case of a master of a free grammar school, not less than six months, ending with the current year; as to others it would depend on the terms of the engagement; but if paid by yearly salary, it could not be less than a quarter's notice; but the question is practically to be determined by the board; see the end of the clause.

(*d*) The trustees are to judge in the first instance, and the clause in the principal Act, s. 17, as to advice and direction of the trustees, would not apply here as an indemnity (the rights of third parties being involved), but may be useful for guidance, see s. 13, and the subsequent proviso, as to approval.

(*e*) That is, not removable for misconduct, &c., see s. 13.

(*f*) That is, a majority, not of those present, but of the whole number, otherwise the sentence would have read "a majority of the trustees assembled," &c.

K

board, who may also, if they so think fit, fix the time or any reasonable conditions at or under which the same shall come into operation (*a*); if also there shall be any special visitor of the charity who shall be resident in Great Britain or Ireland, and free from incapacity, no removal of any such last-mentioned master or mistress shall be made under the authority only of the preceding provision without the written consent of such visitor (*b*): provided always, that this section shall not apply to any endowed grammar school (*c*).

Power as to Investment, Leasing, &c.

Sect. 21 of 16 & 17 Vict. c. 137, extended.

15. The power vested in the said board by the twenty-first section of "The Charitable Trusts Act, 1853," of authorising the application of monies belonging to any charity, or to be raised on the security of the properties thereof, to the improvement of such properties, shall extend to authorise the application of any like monies to any other purpose or object which the board shall consider to be beneficial to the charity or the estate or objects thereof, and which shall not (*d*) be inconsistent with the trusts or intentions of the foundation.

A majority of trustees to have legal power of dealing with the charity estates.

16. A majority of two-thirds of the trustees of any charity assembled at a meeting of their body duly constituted, and having power (*e*) to determine on any sale, exchange, partition, mortgage, lease, or other disposition of any property of the charity (*f*), shall also have a legal power, on behalf of themselves and their co-trustees (*g*), and also of the official trustee of charity lands (*h*), where his concurrence would be otherwise

---

(*a*) As to the duration of the "reasonable notice" required, *vide* p. 193, n. (*c*).

(*b*) See *Whiston* v. *Bishop of Rochester*, 7 Hare, 532.

(*c*) See 3 & 4 Vict. c. 77, the Endowed Grammar Schools Act, which contains a similar provision.

(*d*) That is, in the opinion of board. For by s. 17 of the principal Act, no application to the Court of Chancery can be made without their sanction, except by the Attorney-General.

(*e*) That is, by the terms of their trust, or with the sanction of the board, under s. 29 of Act of 1855.

(*f*) Where they have *not* such power, the *board* can sanction such dispositions; *vide* (*e*).

(*g*) Dissenting.

(*h*) *Vide* Act of 1855, s. 16.

required (a), to do, enter into, and execute all such acts, deeds, contracts, and assurances as shall be requisite for carrying any such sale, exchange, partition, mortgage, lease, or disposition into legal effect, and all such acts, deeds, contracts, or assurances shall have the same legal effect as if the same were respectively done, entered into, or executed by all the acting trustees for the time being, and by the said official trustee.

17. No official trustee of charitable funds, appointed under or in pursuance of the first (b) or secondly recited Act (c), shall be chargeable with or accountable for any loss or misapplication of the said charitable funds, or the dividends, interest, or income thereof, unless the same shall have been occasioned by or through his own wilful neglect or default (d).

<small>Official trustee not to be accountable for loss unless occasioned by his own neglect.</small>

18. The official trustees of charitable funds shall lay before Parliament annually, on or before the fourteenth day of February, or as soon as practicable after Parliament shall be sitting, an account of the total amount of the capital stock, shares, and securities transferred to them in the year ending the thirty-first day of December preceding, and of the total amount of monies, other than dividends or interest, paid to them or to their account during the same period, and of the investment thereof, and of the capital stock, shares, and securities sold or re-transferred by them during the same period, and of the aggregate amount of the capital stock, shares, funds, and securities, and the balance of cash, held by them on such preceding thirty-first day of December.

<small>Accounts to be laid before Parliament.</small>

19. The board may require any person having the custody or control of any deed or document in which any charity or charities shall be solely interested (e) to transmis-

<small>Power to require the transmis-</small>

(a) The reason of his having the legal estate vested in him. The gist of the enactment is to carry out the principle that he is to be a bare trustee (*vide ante*, p. 175), and to give the majority the same powers of acting with out his concurrenceas if *they* had the legal estate, and also to do away with questions as to non-concurrence of co-trustees. See the end of the clause.

(b) Act of 1853, s. 47.
(c) Act of 1855, s. 15.
(d) See Lord St. Leonards' Act, 22 & 23 Vict. c. 35, s. 31.
(e) This stringent enactment, therefore, does not apply where there are dispositions in the deed or will for the personal or

sion of documents belonging to charities.

transmit the same to the office of the said commissioners for examination (a); and where such deed or document shall not be held by any person entitled as a trustee or otherwise (b) to the custody thereof, the board may either retain the same, for the security thereof, in the repository provided by them under the sixty-third section of "The Charitable Trusts Act, 1853," or, as they may think most advantageous to the charity, may thereupon, or at any time thereafter, return or issue the same to the trustees or persons acting in the administration of the charity, for the purposes thereof.

Orders, how enforced and obeyed.

Orders to be enforceable as under former Acts.

20. All orders made by the said board under the provisions of this Act shall be enforceable by the same means, and shall be subject to the same provisions, as are applicable, under the Charitable Trusts Act, 1853 (c), and the Charitable Trusts Amendment Act, 1855 (d), respectively, to any orders of the said board made thereunder.

Board to make minutes.

21. The said board shall from time to time make such minutes as shall be required relative to the institution and conduct of their proceedings under the jurisdiction created by this Act (e).

Indemnity to the Bank of England and others.

23. Every order made under this Act under which any stock, shares, securities, or monies shall be transferred or paid to or deposited with the trustees of any charity, or the official trustees of charitable funds, shall afford a complete indemnity to the Governor and Company of the Bank of England, and to all companies and persons by whom respectively any such transfer, payment, or deposit shall be permitted or made, for per-

---

absolute benefit of any party. The board may *ascertain* whether this is so by calling for its *production* under the powers of the principal Act. See the Act of 1853, s. 12.

(a) Which must mean more than mere *production;* for the board had already been empowered to call for the production of *any* deed; see Act of 1853, s. 12, and Act of 1855, s. 7. It probably includes the power of taking copies for more mature consideration than can be convenient in the case of an *original.*

(b) The enactment only applies to deeds or documents in which there are no dispositions but in trust for a charity, *vide supra,* p. 195 (e).

(c) See s. 14, and s. 20.
(d) See s. 9.
(e) See the minutes in Appendix, *post,* 211.

mitting or making the same, and the said governor and company and other companies and persons shall be required to give effect or conform to such order, and it shall not be necessary for them to inquire concerning the propriety of the same order, or the jurisdiction under which the same shall purport to be made.

24. Every commissioner, secretary, and inspector acting under or employed for the purposes of the said Acts shall be exempt from serving on juries while he shall be so acting or employed. *Commissioners, &c., exempted from serving on juries.*

25. This Act may he cited for all purposes by the short title of "The Charitable Trusts Act, 1860" (a). *Short title.*

(a) *Vide ante,* p. 186.

Roman Catholic Charities Act.
(23 & 24 Vict. c. 134.)

Charities for lawful purposes not to be invalidated by the addition of unlawful trust, but the property may be apportioned, and

1. No existing or future gift or disposition of real or personal estate upon any lawful charitable trust for the exclusive benefit of persons professing the Roman Catholic religion (*a*) shall be invalidated by reason only the same estate has been or shall be also (*b*) subjected (*c*) to any trust or provision deemed to be superstitious (*d*), or otherwise prohibited by the laws affecting persons professing the same religion (*e*), but in every such case it shall be lawful for the High Court of Chancery, or any judge thereof sitting at chambers, in exercise of the jurisdiction created by the Charitable Trusts Act, 1853, upon the application of Her Majesty's Attor-

---

(*a*) That is, for Roman Catholic chapels, or clergymen as such, or the Roman Catholic worship or schools, under 2 & 3 Will. 4, c. 115. *Vide ante*, p. 30.

(*b*) That is, the *same* gift or disposition—one entire gift for the lawful and the unlawful uses. If the gifts are separate, and are deemed superstitious, the clause as to the lawful gift is not needed, and as to the other will not apply. In point of fact there are no gifts for the uses deemed superstitious, except connected with some gifts to individuals, lay or ecclesiastical; if to ecclesiastics, gifts for their support are lawful charitable trusts, *vide supra*; or if to laymen, other charitable purposes are usually added; but if not, probably the gift for the uses deemed "superstitious" might, as it would be impossible to give effect without aiding the support of a priest, be itself deemed in part for a lawful charitable trust. It is implied, by the fifth section, that there may be such dispositions without any deed or document declaring the trusts, as to which see that clause; whence it results that, if the application has not for twenty years been partly to the uses deemed superstitious, the commissioners must frame a scheme.

(*c*) By express terms of the deed; or disposition and *request* will be sufficient, *vide ante*, p. 50; or by usage, according to s. 5.

(*d*) That is, for divine services to be offered for the benefit of the soul of a particular person or his family. Trusts for the celebration of Roman Catholic divine services *generally* have never been deemed superstitious since the Act 2 & 3 Will. 4, although such services are always *pro defunctis; vide ante*, p. 30.

(*e*) As by the law against *male* religionists.

ney-General, or of any person (*a*) authorised for this purpose by the certificate of the Board of Charity Commissioners for England and Wales (*b*), or for the said board (*c*) upon the application of the person or persons acting in the administration of such real or personal estate, or of a majority of such persons (*d*), to apportion the same estate, or the annual income or benefit thereof, so that a proportion thereof, to be fixed by such court or judge, or by the said board, as the case may require (*e*), may be exclusively subject to the lawful charitable trusts declared by the donor or settlor (*f*), and that the residue thereof may become subject to such lawful charitable trusts, for the benefit of persons professing the Roman Catholic religion (*g*), to take effect in lieu of such superstitious or prohibited trusts, as the said court or judge (*h*), or the said board, may consider under the circumstances to be most just (*i*); and also that it shall be lawful for the court or judge, or board, making any such apportionment by the same or any other order or orders to establish any scheme for giving effect thereto (*k*), and to appoint trustees for the administration of the several portions of such real and personal estate (*l*), according to the

the whole applied to lawful purposes.

(*a*) Trustee or other person, under s. 17, but in some way connected with or concerned in the charity.

(*b*) Sect. 17. The board can only *act* on the application of the trustees, but they may authorise any other person at all events interested in the charity to apply.

(*c*) See the Charitable Trusts Act of 1860, s. 2, last line.

(*d*) *Vide supra.*

(*e*) Implying that the gift is one entire gift of a fund, as an estate for uses partly lawful, partly not so; as to which, *vide supra*, p. 198 (*b*).

(*f*) *Vide supra*, p. 198.   (*g*) *Vide supra* (*b*).

(*h*) Consulting, as usual in framing schemes for religious schemes, not only the trustees and parties interested, but the ecclesiastical authorities, as to the proper mode of giving effect to the trusts, according to the discipline of the Roman Catholic Church; *vide ante*, p. 96.

(*i*) As in case of a gift of a gross sum or fund to an ecclesiastic, with a general request for the benefit of divine services. This would authorise the court or commissioners to allot to the individual ecclesiastic a reasonable stipend, and allot the rest to other ecclesiastics or the ecclesiastics of various chapels.

(*k*) See Charitable Trusts Act of 1860, s. 2.

(*l*) As in the case of allotment of a gift as above, the inter-

trusts established of the same proportions respectively; and to vest the estate to be so apportioned in the trustees so to be appointed.

No proceedings to be instituted as to dealings with Roman Catholic charities prior to 2 & 3 Will. 4 c. 115.

2. No proceedings at law or in equity shall be brought or instituted (*a*) on account or in respect of any dealings, transactions, matters, or things with or concerning any real or personal estate subject to any use, trust, gift, foundation, or disposition for any charity relating to or connected with the Roman Catholic religion which took place prior to the passing of the Act of the second and third years of the reign of King William the Fourth, chapter one hundred and fifteen (*b*): provided that nothing herein contained shall extend to sanction or exempt from such proceedings as aforesaid the fraudulent misapplication or (*c*) conversion of any such real or personal estate to any private use or purpose not being charitable (*d*).

Certain deeds for Roman

3. No deed nor other assurance for any charity relating to or connected with the Roman Catholic religion made subsequently to the passing of the Act 9 Geo. 2,

---

vention of trustees being necessary to secure the permanence or continuance of the endowments.

(*a*) This may, by its terms, either mean proceedings by any parties entitled to the *benefit* of the trust or foundation, or the heirs or legal representatives of the donors, claiming adversely to the charity, on the ground of the illegality or invalidity of the disposition. The proviso at the end rather tends to show that the former is the meaning, especially as, since the statute, the period of twenty years has run. Moreover, as to illegality, it is provided for by the first clause ; as to invalidity (under the Act of George 2, against alienations of land for charitable uses, except by deed enrolled), it is provided for in the next section. The scope of the clause, therefore, seems *breach of trust*. And as to breach of trust there is no limitation as between trustee and *cestui que trust ;* and any mis-application of such funds by the trustee, to his own benefit or otherwise, would be a breach of trust ; but (as the proviso at the end of the clause implies), there may be mis-application even to parties' own benefit without, yet not fraudulent, nor involving any restitution as to the *past*, although requiring rectification as to the future.

(*b*) The Act legalising gifts for support of the Roman Catholic religious worship and education, *vide ante*, p. 30.

(*c*) The word fraudulent is to be taken as if introduced here, clearly overriding both clauses of the sentence.

(*d*) That is, without any real or reasonable belief in a *right*. See the proviso to s. 6.

c. 36 (a), and before the passing of this Act (b), shall be void or voidable by reason of the same not having been made, perfected, or enrolled in the manner directed by the first-named Act or otherwise, under the provisions of the said Act (c), if such deed or assurance has been or shall be, within twelve months after the passing of this Act (d), enrolled in the High Court of Chancery: provided that every deed or assurance for any such charity as aforesaid coming within the provisions of the Act passed in the ninth year of the reign of King George the Fourth, intituled "An Act for remedying a Defect in the titles of Lands purchased for Charitable Purposes," shall have the benefit thereof notwithstanding anything herein contained (e).

Catholic charities not to be void if enrolled within twelve months from passing of Act. 9 Geo. 2, c. 36. 9 Geo. 4, c. 85.

4. The expense of the enrolment of any deed under the third section of this Act shall be defrayed out of the property subject to the charity to which the same may relate.

Expense of enrolment, how to be defrayed.

5. Where any (f) real or personal estate, subject to any use, trust, gift, foundation, or disposition for any charity relating to or connected with the Roman Catholic

The trusts of charities in the ab-

(a) Only such are within that Act. See p. 52.
(b) Passed, 28th August, 1860.
(c) It is only defects under that Act which are aided. If there is not a valid declaration of trust under the statute of Charles, the charity will not be aided: but see p. 57.
(d) That is, from the 28th day of August, 1860. No deed can safely be enrolled subject to a trust for uses deemed superstitious, nor if for any uses prohibited — as, for example, if the trusts are for a religious order of males. When a deed is now enrolled disclosing trusts for uses "deemed superstitious," the trustees or donees will have no alternative but to apply to the board or a judge at chambers to sanction a commutation of such trusts. There will be the alternative of risking the loss of the property in an adverse suit by the heir of donor, whose right, however, accruing on the entry of trustee or death of donor, will be barred by twenty years' possession of donee under the Statute of Limitations; as to which vide *Brassington* v. *Llewellyn,* 27 L. J., Ex., 297.
(e) 9 Geo. 4, c. 85, passed 25th July, 1828, *vide supra.* It provides for the enrolment of deeds executed before that time, conveying property to charitable uses for valuable consideration, omitting the enrolment, which it was supposed, erroneously, did not require enrolment.
(f) Any part of the property the subject of a disposition.

sence of settlements may be ascertained from the usage.

religion (*a*), shall have been applied upon any charitable trusts relating to or connected with the same religion (*b*) during any continuous period of twenty years, but the original trusts of such property shall not be ascertained by means of any written document (*c*), the consistent (*d*) usage of the last preceding twenty years (*e*), or of the last period of twenty years during which any consistent usage in the application of such property shall have prevailed, shall be deemed to afford conclusive evidence of the trusts on which the same property shall have been settled.

The Act not to prejudice past or pending proceedings or adverse possession.

6. Nothing in this Act contained shall extend to give effect to any use, trust, gift, foundation, or disposition heretofore made which has been already avoided in any proceeding at law or in equity, or to prejudice any suit at law or in equity commenced before the passing of this Act, or to affect (*f*) any property held or enjoyed beneficially by any person or persons at the time of the

---

(*a*) Whether "lawful" or "deemed to be superstitious," as mentioned in s. 1.

(*b*) Lawful, and not such as are "deemed to be superstitious," as in s. 1, for such are not charitable in the sense in which the courts use the word; *vide* Treatise, p. 36. And *quære*, what will be the effect of usage to apply the fund wholly or partly to such uses? In substance it can only have been applied to the support of the priest who celebrated the divine services, which would be a charitable use, if the donor had so declared it to be his object. If the clause does not apply to such a case, the only effect will be that the matter will be left as it would have been *without* the clause, *i.e.* usage will be *evidence*, but not *conclusive;* and supposing the commissioners satisfied that the trust was for uses "deemed superstitious," the first section will apply. Of course this clause does not refer to an application to the personal benefit of the donee; *vide* proviso in s. 6.

(*c*) If they are, then if *only* lawful, these clauses do not apply; if partly unlawful, the first clause applies.

(*d*) This seems superfluous: if the practice has not been consistent, it cannot have been a "usage,"—certainly not a usage of twenty years. If there is neither deed nor usage nor discretion in the donees or trustees, the court or commissioners must frame a scheme; *vide ante*, p. 49.

(*e*) If the usage has been to apply the funds wholly or in part in the offering of masses, then by virtue of this enactment the first clause will be applicable.

(*f*) "Nothing *in this Act* contained" (*i.e.* s. 1 or s. 5) "is to affect" such property, or the right to it, which remains where it did. The application of it, even for twenty years, for

passing of this Act adversely to any such use, trust, gift, foundation, or disposition.

7. Nothing in this Act contained shall be taken to repeal or in any way alter any provisions of an Act passed in the tenth year of His late Majesty King George the Fourth, intituled "An Act for the Relief of His Majesty's Roman Catholic Subjects," respecting the suppression or prohibition of the religious orders or societies of the Church of Rome bound by monastic or religious vows (a). {Nothing in this Act to repeal provisions of 10 G. 4, c. 7.}

8. In the construction of this Act, except where the context or other provisions of this Act shall require a different construction, the expression "Charity" herein contained shall be construed to mean and include the same matters and things as the like expression means and includes in the "Charitable Trusts Act, 1853" (b). {Interpretation of "Charity."}

---

donee's own use will not "affect" the right. Now s. 1 only applies in this way, that in substance a gift for uses "deemed superstitious" is a gift for the support of the priest, or priest who may celebrate the services; and that being so, such priest's enjoyment of the income cannot possibly be deemed "adverse," so as to bar the application of the Act; for it would be consistent with a secret trust for such uses or services, as in any view the priest would enjoy the fund for life under such trust. Then, as to the previous clause (5) it has—except in the view above suggested, viz., that of a gift in trust for the support of priests—no application to such a case; for it speaks only of a usage as to an application to any *charitable* trusts; and a bequest to a particular person or persons (as distinguished from a body or class) for their own personal benefit, is not a charity, but a private gift or legacy.; and if it be for a *succession* of persons, who are to exercise certain functions, it is a trust. *Vide ante*, p. 48.

(a) So that if any of the trusts are for the support of such houses or orders, they would have to be commuted under s. 1. And a usage so to apply a fund would not be evidence of a lawful charitable trust under s. 6.

(b) That definition includes chapels, and the exception of chapels in the Act of 1853 is not applied. But Roman Catholic chapels are always partly supported by voluntary offerings; so that even if endowed the Act applies only to the endowments. See Act of 1853, s. 62.

APPENDIX.

GENERAL ORDERS and RULES of the Court of Chancery, relating to Procedure under "The Charitable Trusts Act, 1853."

New Order of Court of Hilary Term, 1860, under the Charitable Trusts Act of 1853.

I, &c., in pursuance of an Act, &c., intituled "An Act for the better Administration of Charitable Trusts," direct:—

1. That any application to a judge at chambers, under "The Charitable Trusts Act, 1853," section twenty-eight(*a*), shall be made by summons, and such summons may be in the form set out in schedule [K. No. 1] annexed to the General Order (*b*), or as near thereto as the nature of the case may permit.

The fees payable on proceedings before the Master of the Rolls, or any of the Vice-Chancellors under the said Act, shall be the same as are payable according to the Orders XXXVIII. and XXXIX. (*c*), in respect of other pro-

---

(*a*) *Vide ante,* p.140.
(*b*) That is, "In Chancery.
　　　　In the matter of the [*the name of the charity*]
　　　　and of the Charitable Trusts Act, 1853
　　　　[*or* 1853 *and* 1855, *or* 1853-56 *and* 60,
　　　　as the case may be].

Let all parties concerned attend me at my chambers [*state where*] on, &c., on the hearing an application on the part of [*here state on whose behalf the application is made, and the precise object of the application*]. Dated, &c.

Note.—If you do not attend, either in person or by your solicitor, at the time and place above mentioned, such order will be made and such proceedings taken as the judge may think just and expedient.

See the new orders in Chancery, Order XXXV., as to proceedings in chambers; which embrace applications under the Trustees' Act.

(*c*) Goldsmith's *Practice of Equity,* Appendix, p. 69. There is

ceedings commencing by summons, and shall also be in all other respects regulated by those orders.

In all cases in which the Master of the Rolls, or any Vice-Chancellor, shall direct that any matter commenced by summons under the said Act shall be heard in open court, the same fees shall be payable, and the same costs shall be allowed, as would have been payable in respect of any other matter so heard.

No order made under the said Act by a judge in chambers shall be subject to appeal where the gross annual income of the charity has not been declared by the charity commissioners for England and Wales to exceed one hundred pounds, unless the judge by whom such order may have been made, shall certify that such appeal ought to be permitted, either absolutely or on such terms as the said judge may think fit to impose.

The Lord Chancellor's Orders as to the Jurisdiction exercised under the Charitable Trusts Act by the County Courts, 8th December, 1853.

ORDERS for regulating proceedings by and before the judges of county courts, under the Charitable Trusts Act, 1853, and for fixing and determining the fees to be taken in respect of such proceedings:

1. The clerk of every county court shall keep a book, in the form in the schedule hereunto annexed, to be called "The Charitable Trusts Book," in which a record shall be kept of all proceedings taken in that court in matters of charitable trusts.

2. When any person has obtained the required order or certificate from the charity commissioners, and he is desirous of taking proceedings in the county court, he shall produce such order or certificate to the clerk, who shall retain and file the same in numerical order in his office; and the party producing such order or certificate shall be deemed the plaintiff in such proceedings, and the person served with a *summons* under Order IV. shall be deemed the defendant.

3. When the Attorney-General shall propose to take

---

a provision in the Charitable Trusts Act, 1855, s. 40, for taxation of costs in charity cases; but, which is far more important, the Act of 1860 enables them in many cases to adjudicate *without* recourse to Chancery, which necessarily entails expense upon the charity.

proceedings in the county court, he shall cause to be delivered or transmitted to the clerk a written statement, showing the nature and object of the proposed proceedings, and the clerk shall retain and file such statement in numerical order in his office, and the Attorney-General shall in such proceedings be deemed the plaintiff, and the person served with a summons under Order IV. shall be deemed the defendant.

4. Upon the production of any order, certificate, or statement herein-before mentioned, the clerk shall, at the instance of the plaintiff, prepare a *summons* thereon, in the form set forth in the schedule hereunto annexed, in which shall be stated the substance of the order, certificate, or statement, and he shall make as many copies thereof as there are parties required by the plaintiff to be summoned, and two additional copies, the one to be filed in the clerk's office, and the other to be transmitted to the charity commissioners.

5. The clerk, if required by the plaintiff, shall prepare a *notice to attend proceedings*, in the form set forth in the said schedule, to be served on any persons indicated by the plaintiff, besides those summoned under the last preceding order, and the said clerk shall make as many copies thereof as there are persons to whom such notice is to be given, and two additional copies, one to be filed in his office, and the other to be transmitted to the charity commissioners.

6. The clerk shall forthwith transmit, by pre-paid post letter, a copy of the *summons* to each of the parties required to appear, and a copy of the *notice to attend proceedings* to each of the persons indicated by the plaintiff, and such transmission shall be sufficient service, unless the judge shall otherwise direct.

7. Where the plaintiff does not require any *summons* or *notice to attend proceedings* to be issued, the clerk shall prepare a *notice of hearing*, in the form set forth in the said schedule, and two additional copies thereof, one to be filed in his office, and the other to be transmitted to the charity commissioners, and shall either deliver such notice to the plaintiff, or cause it to be served on him by pre-paid post letter, unless the judge shall otherwise direct.

8. In all cases it shall be competent for the clerk, if required by the plaintiff, to *summon* some persons, and to serve others with either or both of the said *notices*, or to serve a *notice of hearing* on the plaintiff, and a *notice to attend proceedings* on any other person.

9. In all cases it shall be competent for the judge to

direct what persons, or additional persons, shall be served with a *summons* or *notice to attend proceedings* or *notice of hearing*.

10. Upon the requisition of the charity commissioners, a copy of the judge's note of the evidence taken at the hearing, or such part thereof as may be required by the commissioners, shall be transmitted by the judge to them at their office by post or otherwise.

11. Upon the requisition of the Attorney-General, in proceedings instituted by him, a copy of the judge's note of the evidence taken at the hearing, or such part thereof as may be required by the Attorney-General, shall be transmitted to him by post or otherwise.

12. A copy of the summons, notice to attend proceedings, notice to appear, together with a copy of the order made by the Court, shall in all cases be transmitted by the clerk, forthwith after the hearing, by post or otherwise, as the judge shall direct, to the office of the commissioners.

13. Where the annual income of the charity exceeds 10*l*. the court fees shall be payable as in cases within the ordinary jurisdiction of the Court, without prejudice to the privilege of the Attorney-General as to costs, and the charitable funds may be made liable to the payment thereof, at the discretion of the judge.

14. Where the annual income of the charity does not exceed the sum of 10*l*. no fees of court shall be payable out of the funds of the charity; nor shall any fees be paid by any party to the proceeding, unless the judge shall, in his discretion, order any of the parties to the proceeding before him to pay such fees of court as he shall think fit, without prejudice to the privilege of the Attorney-General as to costs.

15. Where court fees are payable, they shall be calculated according to the scale of fees applicable to proceedings for the recovery of tenements under the 9 & 10 Vict. c. 95, s. 122, the annual income of the charity, like the annual rent of the tenement, being treated as the basis of calculation.

16. The order or certificate of the commissioners, or statement of the Attorney-General, as to the amount of the annual income, shall be conclusive on the Court.

17. The enactments, Secretary of State's orders, practice, and forms in force and used in the county courts shall, subject to the foregoing orders, be adopted with reference to proceedings in matters of charitable trusts, so far as the same are applicable, *mutatis mutandis*.

18. The above orders shall be in force until further

orders shall be made, under the Charitable Trusts Act, 1853, for regulating proceedings in the county courts relating to charitable trusts.

SCHEDULE OF FORMS.

Summons.

In the County Court of ——, holden at ——.
(Seal).
    In the matter of (*title of charity*).
No. of charity.
 (*Name, description, and address of party to be summoned*). You are hereby summoned to appear at a county court, to be holden at ——, on the —— day of ——, 18—, at the hour of —— in the forenoon, upon the hearing of an application which has been made to the Court in the matter of the above charity, by which it is suggested (*here state substance of order, certificate, or statement*). And you are informed, that if you do not attend, pursuant to the requisition of this summons, the Court may proceed in the matter in your absence, and make such order as may appear just therein. And you are further informed, that if you do not obey such order, you will be liable to be imprisoned by order of the Court.

          A. B.,
          Clerk of the Court.
 Dated this —— day of ——, 18—.

Notice to attend Proceedings.

In the County Court of ——, holden at ——.
(Seal).
    (In the matter of (*title of charity*).
No. of charity.
 (*Name, description, and address of party to whom notice is to be given*). Take notice that the hearing of an application in the matter of the above charity, by which it is suggested (*here state substance of order, certificate, or statement*), will take place on the —— day of ——, 18—, at the above county court.
 The object of this notice is, that if you are desirous of attending the said hearing, you are at liberty to do so, and

you may be heard in support of any objection you may have to such proceedings in respect of the above charity.

But if you do not attend at the hearing, you will not be subject to any costs or penalty in respect of such non-attendance.

A. B.,
Clerk of the Court.

Dated this —— day of ——, 18—.

Notice of Hearing.

In the County Court of ——, holden at ——.
(Seal).
        In the matter of (*title of charity*).
No. of charity.
(*Name, description, and address of party to whom notice is to be given*). Take notice, that the hearing of the application in the matter of the above charity is appointed to take place at this court on the —— day of ——, 18— (*a*).

A. B.,
Clerk of the Court.

Dated this —— day of ——, 18—.

Form of Record.

Ashley, Lady, Charity of, In the matter of.
No. 1.

On the —— day of ——, 18—, an order ("certificate," or "statement," *as the case may be*) was produced by (*state the party producing or transmitting it*), and the same has been numbered 1, (*or as the case may be, according to the priority of production to the clerk*).

On the —— day of ——, 18—, a summons (*or other process, as the case may be*) was issued, and directed to be served by post (*or otherwise, as the case may be*) on (*state the parties*), requiring him ("her," or "them," *as the case may be*) to appear at this court on the —— day of ——, 18—.

At a court holden on the —— day of ——, 18—, appeared (*state parties appearing, or reasons for not appearing, and whether they appeared by counsel or otherwise. If any adjournment takes place, state the cause thereof, and adjourn-*

(*a*) This should be at the earliest convenient sitting of the Court.

ment, and until when adjourned; then, on the adjournment day, proceed in a similar manner as on the first day of hearing; and the same on every successive adjournment day. When the matter is finally disposed of, then proceed)—

The matter having been heard, the Court made the following order—(*Here state the order*. *If any other proceedings, whether before or after the final order, are taken in the matter, they must be recorded in a similar manner in their proper places. It will not be necessary to set forth on the record any of the evidence, as that will appear on the judge's notes; but any document produced, or any copy thereof, which the judge requires to be filed, should be filed along with the other papers relating to the matter*).

When the record of proceedings in any charity occupies more than one page, the record may be continued on the next blank page, and a reference should be made from such previous page to such next page, and from such next page to such previous page. The book in which the record is kept should be paged throughout, and have an alphabetical index at the end. The names of the charities should be arranged in the index alphabetically, and the numbers of the pages in which any proceedings are recorded should be given at the end of the names).

RULES OF THE CHARITY COMMISSIONERS.

No. 1.—General Minutes relating to the Proceedings of the Commissioners and their Inspectors;

No. 2.—Regulations and Instructions concerning Applications to the Board, with Forms of Application, &c.

No. 1.

General Minutes relating to the Proceedings of the Commissioners and their Inspectors.

1. The commissioners attending daily at their office for the despatch of business will sit as a board as often as occasion shall require, and, notwithstanding any ajournment, will resume their sittings when necessary.

2. All communications, papers, and documents addressed or sent to the commissioners or their secretary shall be forthwith registered, and laid before the board.

3. A separate register shall be kept of all deeds, muniments or documents relating to charities which may be deposited with the board.

4. Registers shall be kept of all letters, instruments, and documents sent from the office.

5. A summary or breviate shall be made, and kept in the office, of the proceedings in every matter brought under the consideration of the commissioners.

6. The seal of the commissioners shall not be affixed to any document except at a sitting of the board.

7. As a general rule, the board will require applications with reference to any charity to be made in writing, and signed by the applicants; but the board, without any precedent application to them, will institute inquiries and exercise their powers with respect to any charity where it shall appear to them expedient to do so.

8. As a general rule, applications will be proceeded with in the order in which they are received, except where the board shall (in

cases of urgency or for any special reason) think fit to depart from this rule.

9. All official correspondence shall be carried on in the name of the secretary.

10. Examinations and inquiries shall be conducted, as far as may be found practicable, by correspondence at the office of the commissioners, or by personal communications there made.

11. Every case in which local examination and inquiry shall be requisite shall be referred by the board to an inspector.

12. Upon every such reference a copy of the minute of the board relating thereto, signed by the secretary, shall be delivered to the inspector to whom the reference is made, and such copy shall be his authority for prosecuting the examination and inquiry thereby directed.

13. Every such examination and inquiry shall be made with such public and particular notices, and according to such general conditions as the board may prescribe, and, subject thereto, in such manner as the inspector, bearing in mind that the object is to insure the most just and beneficial application of the charity, shall think fit.

14. The general mode of conducting the examination and inquiry will be left to the judgment and discretion of the inspector, who shall be at liberty to avail himself of all such evidence and information as he may be able to obtain, and to exercise for that purpose all the available powers of the Act, except where the board shall have prescribed any particular limitation of the inquiry or of the exercise of such powers.

15. The inspector shall report to the board the result of every such examination and inquiry, and shall in his report mention the nature of the evidence and information obtained by him, and whether taken on oath or not.

(Signed) P. ERLE.
JAMES HILL.
RD. JONES.

No. 2.

Regulations and Instructions concerning Applications to the Board under " The Charitable Trusts Act, 1853" (16 & 17 Vict. c. 137).

I.—*Applications for Inquiry or Relief respecting any Charity.*

1. Any person or persons having reasonable grounds may apply to the board for inquiry or relief with respect to any charity.

2. The application should be in writing, addressed to the commissioners, and signed by the applicants, who should add their respective professions, occupations, or qualities, and residences.

3. No precise form is necessary; but the usual designation of the charity, and the name of the parish, township, or place for the benefit whereof the charity was founded, or in which it is administered, and the names, professions, or occupations and residences of the trustees or persons acting in the management or administration, should be stated in all cases. Such facts and circumstances as will sufficiently explain the nature and object of the application should also be stated.

4. A separate application should be made for each charity, except where several charities are administered together under one scheme or system of management.

5. On receipt of an application, the board will make such inquiries and adopt such proceedings as the case may require.

6. A form of initiatory application is subjoined. (See Appendix, No. 1.)

II.—*Inquiries to be instituted by the Board.*

1. When an examination and inquiry into any charity is considered necessary, the board will communicate with the trustees or other persons capable of giving the required information.

2. Forms of inquiry are subjoined. (See Appendix, Nos. 2, 3, 4, 5.)

III.—*Applications for the Opinion, Advice, or Direction of the Board.*

1. An application may be made by any trustee or other person having any concern in the management or administration of any charity, for the opinion, advice, or direction of the board, in the matter of the trust.

2. Every such application should contain concise statements, and, as far as conveniently may be, in numbered paragraphs, of all the

material facts and circumstances, upon which the opinion, advice, or direction of the board is desired.

3. It should be stated whether the application is made with the concurrence of all the trustees or persons concerned in the management or administration of the charity, or with the dissent of any and what proportion of them.

4. The application should be accompanied by any documentary evidence which will explain or substantiate the statements.

5. The board may require the statements to be explained and altered, in point of form, in such manner and as often as may be thought necessary.

6. The board may also, at any time, require the statements to be verified by the statutory declaration of the applicants or any of them.

7. On the application being approved, a duplicate will generally be required to be sent, which will be returned to the applicant with the opinion, advice, or direction of the board appended thereto, and the original application will be retained by the board and registered.

8. A form of application is subjoined. (See Appendix, No. 6.)

IV.—*Applications for an Order or Certificate of the Board authorising the Institution of any Suit or other Proceeding before any Court or Judge.*

1. Any person applying for an order or certificate of the board authorising the institution of any suit or other proceeding before any court or judge, should transmit to the board a notice and statement in writing, setting forth whether or not he is a trustee or person administering or claiming to administer, or interested in the charity, or an inhabitant of the parish or place within which the charity is administered or applied; the amount of the gross annual income of the charity; and all the other material facts and circumstances of the case; and explaining the nature and objects of the proposed suit or other proceeding.

2. The facts and circumstances should be stated in numbered paragraphs, as far as conveniently may be.

3. Where the object of the proposed proceeding is the removal of trustees, their names, descriptions, and residences, and the reasons for their proposed removal, should be stated.

4. The names, descriptions, and residences of the trustees proposed to be appointed should also be stated.

5. Where the object of the proposed proceeding is a new scheme, the notice and statement should contain information as to the past administration of the charity, and its results, and the nature and provisions of the proposed scheme.

6. In proposing schemes care should be taken to deviate as little as possible from the original purposes and intentions of the founder.

7. The board may require the statement to be explained and altered in point of form in such manner and as often as may be thought fit.

8. The board may also require the statement to be verified by statutory declaration or otherwise.

9. A form of application is subjoined. (See Appendix, No. 7.)

10. Where the proposed proceeding is to be taken under the special jurisdiction created by the Act, for the establishment or alteration of a scheme or the appointment or removal of any trustee, notice must be given in the mode which will be directed by the board.

11. Forms of notices, and supplementary forms for giving effect thereto, are subjoined. (See Appendix, Nos. 8, 9, 10, 11, 12, 13.)

12. When the board shall have been satisfied that the proposed proceeding is proper, and that any required notice has been duly given, the requisite order or certificate will be issued to the applicant, or to such other person as may be approved.

V.—*Applications for the Authority of the Board to grant building, repairing, improving, mining, or other Leases, or to cut Timber, or make Roads or other Improvements.*

1. Applications for the authority of the board to grant building, repairing, improving, mining, or other leases, or to cut timber or make roads or other improvements, can only be made by the trustees or persons acting in the administration or management of any charity or the estates or property thereof.

2. A form of application for authority to grant a lease is subjoined. (See Appendix, No. 14.)

VI.—*Applications for the Authority of the Board to effect Sales or Exchanges.*

1. Applications for the authority of the board to effect sales or exchanges can only be made by trustees or persons acting in the administration of any charity.

2. Forms for these purposes are subjoined. (See Appendix, Nos. 15 and 16.)

Appendix to Regulations and Instructions.

CONTENTS OF THE APPENDIX.*

No. 1.—Form of Initiatory Application 216
2.—Form of General Inquiry 217
3.—Form of Inquiry as to Rent Charges withheld . . 218
4.—Form of Inquiry as to Endowed Grammar Schools . 219
5.—Form of Inquiry as to Endowed National, British, Infant, and other Schools 222
6.—Form of Application for the Opinion, Advice, or Direction of the Board 224
7.—Form of Application for an Order or Certificate of the Board authorising any Suit or other Proceeding before any Court or Judge 225
8.—Form of Notice of Application for the Removal of Trustees, the Appointment of New Trustees, and the Establishment of a Scheme 226
9.—Form of Notice of Application for the Removal of Trustees and the Appointment of New Trustees . 227
10.—Form of Notice of Application for the Appointment of Trustees 227
11.—Form of Notice of Application for the Establishment of a Scheme 228
12.—Form of Requisition under Section 42 . . . 229
13.—Form of Certificate as to Publication of Notice . 229
14.—Form of Application for the Authority of the Board to grant a Lease 230
15.—Form of Application for the Authority of the Board for a Sale 231
16.—Form of Application for the Authority of the Board for an Exchange 233

No. 1.—*Form of Initiatory Application.*

To the Charity Commissioners for England and Wales.

* Insert the usual name or designation of the charity, and the name of the parish, township, or place for the benefit whereof the charity was founded, or in which it is administered.

In the matter of the Charity called *
   in the   of
   in the county of

The following statements are submitted for the consideration of the Board :—

The applicants should state here concisely and, as far as conveniently may be, in numbered paragraphs, the circumstances and the particular objects of the application.

1.

2.

3., &c.

I (or we) declare that the above statements are in all

---

* Any of the following Forms may be obtained separately on application at the office of the Commissioners in London.

Form of General Inquiry.

respects true according to my (or our) information and belief.

Dated this   day of   , 186 .

*

** The applicants should here sign their names, adding their professions or occupations and residences.

No. 2.—*Form of General Inquiry.*

Charity Commissioners for England and Wales.

In the matter of the Charity called†
in the   of
in the county of

Information is required by the Board upon the following points :—

† Insert the usual name or designation of the charity, and the name of the parish, township, or place for the benefit whereof the charity was founded, or in which it is administered.

1. The name of the founder of the charity and the date and description of the deed, will, or other instrument by which it was founded, and a short statement of the material contents.

2. Whether there has been any augmentation of the endowment, and, if so, by whom, and how made ? And whether there is any scheme of management or other modification of the original trusts ; and, if so, the date and particulars thereof?

3. In whose custody or possession, or under whose control, the deeds or instruments of foundation, and any other instruments affecting the charity, now are ?

4. The description, local situation, and other particulars of the endowments, property, and possessions of the charity, whether consisting of real or personal estate.

5. How the lands and real property (if any) belonging to the charity are let or occupied ; and the dates, reservations, and terms of the several leases or lettings ?

6. How, and in what names, the personal property (if any) is invested ?

7. The gross annual or other income of the charity from every source, distinguishing the several sources.

8. To what objects and in what manner the income of the charity is applied ?

9. The names, addresses and descriptions of the present trustees of the charity, or of the persons who act in the management or administration thereof.

L

10. How, and under what authority, and when the present trustees were appointed? Or, from what period the persons now acting in the management or administration of the charity have so acted?

11. Whether any conveyance or transfer of the charity property has been made to the present trustees, and, if so, the nature and date of such conveyance or transfer?

Any other statements or observations which may be necessary or proper for more fully explaining the circumstances of the charity should be added.

I declare that the above statements are in all respects true according to the best of my information and belief.

Dated this   day of   , 186 .

* The informant should here sign his name, adding his profession or occupation and residence.

No. 3—*Form of Inquiry as to Rent-charges withheld.*

Charity Commissioners for England and Wales.

† Insert the usual name or designation of the charity, and the name of the parish, township, or place for the benefit whereof the charity was founded, or in which it is administered.

In the matter of the Charity called †
in the   of
in the county of

Information is required by the Board upon the following points:—

1. The present trustees or other persons by whom the rent-charge should be received and distributed.

2. How the present trustees were appointed, and the dates of their several appointments?

3. Whether the rent-charge has been legally vested in the present trustees?

4. The date and other particulars of the deed, will, or other instrument by which the rent-charge was created, and of that by which it was devoted to the charity?

5. Whether the property subject to the rent-charge is described in the instrument creating it?—and, if so, in what manner?—or, what is the description of the property reputed to be now subject to the rent-charge?

6. Whether the deed or instrument creating the rent-charge and any other subsequent deeds or instruments relating thereto are in the pos-

session of the trustees? If not, what is known respecting them should be stated.

7. Whether the rent-charge was usually paid by the owner of any, and what, particular property during any, and what, period? And what proof can be given of such payment?

8. When, and by whom, was the last payment of the rent-charge made?

9. The name and address of the present owner of the particular property considered to be subject to the rent-charge; and whether he derives his title thereto from any person by whom the rent-charge is known to have been previously paid?

10. What reasons (if any) are assigned by the present owner for refusing payment of the rent-charge?

11. When the last demand for such payment was made?

12. Whether any, and what, proof of the identity of the property subject to the rent-charge can be obtained by reference to old maps or surveys, or parochial assessments, or other documentary evidence, or from the testimony of any of the inhabitants, or by any other means?

I declare that the foregoing statements are true according to the best of my information and belief.

Dated this   day of   , 186 .
*

* The informant should here sign his name, adding his profession or occupation and residence.

No. 4.—*Form of Inquiry as to Endowed Grammar Schools.*

Charity Commissioners for England and Wales.

In the matter of†   school
in the   of
in the county of

† Insert the usual name or designation of the school, and of the parish, township, or place in which it is situate.

Information is required by the Board upon the following points :—

1. The date and particulars of the foundation of the school.

2. The particulars of the estates and property forming the endowment.

3. The amount of the average gross annual income from every source, distinguishing each source.

4. The names, professions or occupations and residences of the governors, trustees, or managers of the school; how they were appointed, and the dates of their appointments.

5. The means of the renewal or continuance of the trust or management, upon the occurrence of any vacancy.

6. The name and residence of the visitor, if any.

7. Whether there are any statutes or regulations for the conduct or management of the school. (If so, a copy of the same should be sent, and it should be stated by what authority they were established and in whom any power of revision or alteration of them is vested.)

8. The names and ages of the masters, the dates of their appointments, and by whom and under what authority they were respectively appointed.

9. The particulars of the qualifications and duties of each master.

10. The particulars of the salary and emoluments of each master.

11. Whether a residence is provided for the masters.

12. Whether the masters are resident and devote their whole time to the duties of their offices. If not, state what other occupations they have, the time engaged, and the emoluments derived from them.

13. Whether the duties of the masters are performed to the satisfaction of the governors or trustees.

14. Whether any provision is made for the retirement of the masters on account of ill health, old age, or otherwise, or for their removal for any other reason.

15. The average number of boys attending the school for the last three years, distinguishing the free boys from the others.

16. The present number of boys attending the school—making the same distinction.

17. By whom the free boys are appointed.

18. The qualifications for appointment as to age, parentage, residence and condition in life, and up to what age boys are allowed to remain in the school.

19. The nature of the education afforded by the school.

20. Whether instruction in the catechism and doctrines of the Church of England is insisted upon in all cases, without reference to the religious tenets of the parents or guardians of the boys.

21. Whether any entrance fee or other charge is made for the boys termed "free boys." If so, the particulars and amount of each fee or annual or other charge for each boy.

22. How books and stationery are provided and paid for.

23. Whether the free boys derive any other benefit from the charity besides the instruction at the school. If so, state the nature and particulars of such benefit.

24. Whether there are any exhibitions or scholarships for the benefit of the school. If so, their number, and the value and duration and other particulars of each.

25. By whom such exhibitions or scholarships are awarded; the present number of exhibitioners or scholars; and the average number of such exhibitioners or scholars during the last three years.

26. Whether the exhibitioners or scholars are taken from the free and other boys indiscriminately, and whether they are appointed after any examination as to their respective merits; and in that case, by whom and in what manner such examination is conducted.

27. The nature and capabilities of the school-buildings and masters' residences, if any, and their condition as to repairs.

Any other information or particulars respecting the school with which the commissioners should be made acquainted, should be added.

I declare that the above statements are in all respects true, according to my information and belief.

Dated this   day of   , 186 .
*

* The informant should here sign his name, adding his profession or occupation and residence.

No. 5.—*Form of Inquiry as to Endowed National, British, Infant, and other Schools.*

Charity Commissioners for England and Wales.

* Insert the usual name or designation of the school, and of the parish, township, or place in which it is situate.

In the matter of*   school in the   of in the county of

Information is required by the Board upon the following points :—

1. The date and particulars of the foundation of the school.
2. The particulars of the estates and property forming the endowment.
3. The amount of the average gross annual income from every source, distinguishing each source.
4. The names, occupations or professions, and residences of the trustees or managers of the school, and of the visitor, treasurer, and secretary, if any.
5. The means for the renewal or continuance of the trust or management upon the occurrence of any vacancy.
6. Whether there are any rules or regulations for the conduct or management of the school. (If so, a copy of the same should be sent.)
7. The names and ages of the schoolmaster and schoolmistress, the dates of their appointments, and by whom or under what authority they were respectively appointed, and for what period the appointments are held.
8. Whether there is any provision for dismissing the schoolmaster or schoolmistress, and if so, in whom the power of dismissal rests.
9. The particulars of the qualifications and duties of the schoolmaster and schoolmistress.
10. The particulars of the salaries and emoluments of the schoolmaster and schoolmistress.
11. Whether residences are provided for them.
12. Whether the schoolmaster and schoolmistress are resident, and devote their whole time to the duties of their office. If not, state what other occupation they have, the

time engaged, and the emoluments derived therefrom.

13. Whether the duties of the schoolmaster and schoolmistress are performed to the satisfaction of the trustees or managers.

14. Whether there is any provision for the retirement of the schoolmaster or schoolmistress on account of ill health, old age or otherwise.

15. The average number of children attending the school for the last three years; distinguishing boys from girls.

16. The present number of children attending the school: making the same distinction.

17. The qualifications of children to be admitted to the school as to age, parentage, residence and condition in life; and to what age they are allowed to remain in the school.

18. The nature of the education afforded by the school.

19. Whether instruction in the catechism and doctrines of the Church of England is insisted upon in all cases, without reference to the religious tenets of the children's parents or guardians.

20. Whether any entrance fee or other charge is made for admission of children into the school, and, if so, the particulars and amount thereof.

21. How books and stationery are provided and paid for.

22. The nature and capabilities of the school buildings, and schoolmaster's and schoolmistress's residences (if any), and their condition as to repairs.

Any other information or particulars respecting the school with which the commissioners should be made acquainted should be added.

I declare that the above statements are in all respects true according to my information and belief.

Dated this   day of   , 186 .

*

* The informant should here sign his name, adding his profession or occupation and residence.

No. 6—*Form of Application for the Opinion, Advice, or Direction of the Board.*

To the Charity Commissioners for England and Wales.

* Insert the usual name or designation of the charity, and the name of the parish, township, or place for the benefit whereof the charity was founded, or in which it is administered.

In the matter of the Charity called*

in the   of

in the county of

† A trustee or person concerned in the management or administration of the charity.

The undersigned being†   .

submits the following statement :—

State here concisely and, as far as conveniently may be, in numbered paragraphs, the material facts and circumstances of the case.

1.

2.

3.

4., &c.

Opinion, advice, or direction.

Under the foregoing circumstances, the undersigned makes application to the board for their   on the following points ;

State here, as far as conveniently may be, in numbered paragraphs, the specific points upon which the opinion, advice, or direction is desired.

That is to say,

1st.

2nd.

I declare that the above statement is in all respects true according to my information and belief.

Dated this   day of   , 186 .

‡

‡ The applicant should here sign his name, adding his profession or occupation and residence.

Forms of Application.

No. 7.—*Form of Application for an Order or Certificate of the Board authorising any Suit or other Proceeding before any Court or Judge.*

To the Charity Commissioners for England and Wales.

In the matter of the Charity called *

    in the   of

    in the county of

The undersigned, being †

submits the following notice and statement :—

1. The gross annual income of the above-mentioned Charity amounts to

2.

3., &c.

Under the foregoing circumstances the undersigned is desirous of instituting proceedings for effecting the following objects ;
  That is to say,

    1st.

    2nd., &c.

The undersigned accordingly requests the board to issue an order or certificate authorising him to make an application to

for effecting the above objects.

I declare that the above statement is in all respects true according to my information and belief.

    Dated this   day of   , 186 .

        ‡

———

* Insert the usual name or designation of the charity, and the name of the parish, township, or place for the benefit whereof the charity was founded, or in which it is administered.

† The applicant should here state whether or not he is trustee or person administering or claiming to administer, or interested in the charity, or an inhabitant of the parish or place within which the charity is administered or applicable.

State here concisely and, as far as conveniently may be, in numbered paragraphs, all the material facts and circumstances of the case.

State here, as far as conveniently may be, in numbered paragraphs, the specific objects for which proceedings are proposed to be taken.

Describe the court and judge.

‡ The applicant should here sign his name, adding his profession or occupation and residence.

No. 8.—*Form of Notice of Application for the Removal of Trustees, the Appointment of new Trustees, and the Establishment of a Scheme.*

* Insert the usual name or designation of the charity, and the name of the parish, township, or place for the benefit whereof the charity was founded, or in which it is administered.

In the matter of the Charity called *

in the   of

in the county of

Notice is hereby given, that, with the sanction of the Charity Commissioners for England and Wales, application is intended to be made to

Describe the judge of the Court of Chancery, or the county or other court, as the case may be.

on or after the   day of   for the following objects; that is to say,

Insert the date, which must not be less than fifteen days after the affixing of the notice.

The removal of

Name or names of the trustee or trustees to be removed.

from being a trustee (*or* trustees) of the above-mentioned charity :

The appointment of new trustees of such charity :

And the establishment of a scheme for the regulation thereof.

Insert the names, descriptions, and residences of the proposed new trustees.

The following persons are intended to be proposed as new trustees of the said charity ; that is to say,

Describe the place within the above-mentioned parish or township where the scheme may be seen.

The proposed scheme may be inspected, without charge, on any day, excepting Sunday, during the next   days, between the hours of   and   in the forenoon and and   in the afternoon, at

and between the hours of   and   at the office of the said commissioners at   London.

Any person desirous of making objection to the removal of the said   or to the appointment of all or any of the proposed new trustees, or of proposing any other trustee or trustees, or of making objection to the proposed scheme, or of proposing any alteration thereof, will be at liberty to do so, and notice in writing of his intention in that behalf may be transmitted to the said commissioners, at their said office, within   days from the date hereof.

Insert the date.

Dated this   day of   , 186 .

† †Signatures, occupations, and residences of the persons intending to make the application.

Forms of Application. 227

No. 9.—*Form of Notice of Application for the Removal of Trustees and the Appointment of new Trustees.*

In the matter of the Charity called *
   in the   of
   in the county of

Notice is hereby given, that, with the sanction of the Charity Commissioners for England and Wales, application is intended to be made to

on or after the   day of   for the following objects; that is to say,

    The removal of

from being a trustee (*or* trustees) of the above-mentioned charity, and the appointment of new trustees of the same.

The following persons are intended to be proposed as such new trustees; that is to say,

Any person desirous of making objection to the removal of the said   or to the appointment of all or any of the proposed new trustees, or of proposing any other trustee or trustees, will be at liberty to do so, and notice in writing of his intention in that behalf may be transmitted to the said commissioners at their office at   London, within   days from the date hereof.

          Dated this   day of   , 186 .
          †

* Insert the usual name or designation of the charity, and the name of the parish, township, or place for the benefit whereof the charity was founded, or in which it is administered.

Describe the judge of the Court of Chancery, or the county or other court, as the case may be.

Insert the date, which must not be less than fifteen days after the affixing of the notice.

Name of the trustee or trustees to be removed.

Insert the names, residences, and descriptions of the proposed trustees.

Insert the date.

† Signatures, occupations, and residences of the persons intending to make the application.

No. 10.—*Form of Notice of Application for the Appointment of Trustees.*

In the matter of the Charity called ‡
   in the   of
   in the county of

Notice is hereby given, that, with the sanction of the Charity Commissioners for England and Wales, application is intended to be made to

‡ Insert the usual name or designation of the charity, and the name of the parish, township, or place for the benefit of which the charity is founded, or in which it is administered.

Describe the judge of the Court of Chancery, or the county or other court, as the case may be.

228 *Forms of Application.*

<small>Insert the date, which must not be less than fifteen days after the affixing of the notice.</small>

on the   day of   for the appointment of trustees of the above-mentioned charity.

<small>Insert the names, descriptions, and residences of the proposed trustees.</small>

The following persons are intended to be proposed as trustees thereof; that is to say,

Any person desirous of making objection to the appointment of all or any of the proposed trustees, or of proposing any other trustee or trustees, will be at liberty to do so, and notice in writing of his intention in that behalf may be transmitted to the said commissioners, at their office at London, within   days from the date hereof.

<small>Insert the date.</small>

Dated this   day of   , 186 .

<small>* Signatures, occupations, and residences of the persons intending to make the application.</small>

*

———

No. 11.—*Form of Notice of Application for the Establishment of a Scheme.*

<small>† Insert the usual name or designation of the charity, and the name of the parish, township, or place for the benefit whereof the charity was founded, or in which it is administered.</small>

In the matter of the Charity called †
   in the   of
   in the county of

Notice is hereby given, that, with the sanction of the Charity Commissioners for England and Wales, application is intended to be made to

<small>Describe the judge of the Court of Chancery, or the county or other court, as the case may be.</small>

on the   day of   for the establishment of a scheme for the regulation of the above-mentioned charity.

<small>Insert the date, which must not be less than fifteen days after the affixing of the notice.</small>

The proposed scheme may be inspected by any parishioner or person interested in the said charity, without charge, on any day, excepting Sunday, during the next   days, between the hours of   and   in the forenoon and   and   in the afternoon, at

<small>Describe the house or place within the above-mentioned parish or township where the scheme may be seen.</small>

and between the hours of   and   at the office of the said commissioners, at   , London.

Any person desirous of making objection to the proposed scheme, or of proposing any alteration thereof, will be at liberty to do so, and notice in writing of his intention in that behalf may be transmitted to the said commissioners, at their said office, within   days from the date hereof.

<small>Insert the date.</small>

Dated this   day of   , 186 .

<small>‡ Signatures, occupations, and residences of the persons intending to make the application.</small>

‡

———

Forms of Application.

No. 12.—*Form of Requisition, under Section 42.*

To the * of the of , in the county * Describe the persons to whom the requisition is to be addressed, and the church or chapel of the parish or place where the notice is to be published.
of

In the matter of the Charity called † † Insert the usual name or designation of the charity, and the name of the parish, township, or place for the benefit whereof the charity was founded, or in which it is administered.
    in the of *
    in the county of

Under the provisions of the 42nd section of "The Charitable Trusts Act, 1853," and in pursuance of an order of the Charity Commissioners for England and Wales, you are required to allow a notice of an application respecting the above charity, which is intended to be made to ‡ ‡ Describe the judge of the Court of Chancery, or the county or other court, as the case may be.

with the sanction of the said commissioners, to be affixed to or near the door of the and to remain so affixed for a period of fifteen days at the least.
              Dated this day of , 186 .
              §

§ Signatures, descriptions, and residences of the persons intending to make the application.

No. 13.—*Form of Certificate as to Publication of Notice.*

To the Charity Commissioners for England and Wales.

In the matter of the Charity called * * Insert the usual name or designation of the charity, and the name of the parish, township, or place for the benefit whereof the charity was founded, or in which it is administered.
    in the of
    in the county of

I

hereby certify that a notice in writing, in the form directed by the board, of an application intended to be made to †

Name, description, and residence of person certifying.

† Describe the judge of the Court of Chancery, or the county or other court, as the case may be.

for the

was in accordance with the directions of the said board duly affixed to the door of the of on the day of 186 .
              Dated this day of , 186 .
              ‡

State shortly here the purposes of the application.

‡ Signature, description, and residence of the person certifying.

No. 14.—*Form of Application for the Authority of the Board to grant a Lease.*

To the Charity Commissioners for England and Wales.

<small>* Insert the usual name or designation of the charity, and the name of the parish, township, or place for the benefit whereof the charity was founded, or in which it was administered.</small>

In the matter of the Charity called *

in the   of

in the county of

<small>Trustees or persons acting in the administration or management.</small>

The undersigned being the

of the above-mentioned charity, and being of opinion that the particular property hereinafter mentioned belonging to the same charity may be beneficially leased in the manner hereinafter mentioned, submit to the board the following statement and proposal in relation thereto, and they request the board to make such orders under their seal, for and in relation to the granting of a lease thereof, as they may think fit.

State,

1. The mode and date of the appointments of the existing trustees (if any) of the charity, and the number originally appointed.

2. Whether the charity property is legally vested in such trustees, and, if so, by what conveyance or assurance.

3. The name of the township, parish and county in which the particular property proposed to be leased is situate.

4. The nature, extent, and general description of the same property, and the interest of the charity therein, and whether forming the whole or part only of the property of the charity.

5. The manner in which it has been let or occupied for the last three years.

6. The amount of the gross rent or income arising therefrom during the last three years.

7. The amount and particulars of the outgoings or deductions in each of such years.

8. The present improved annual or rack-rent value of the particular property.

9. The object of the proposed lease, and whether for building, repairing, improving, mining or other purposes.

10. The reasons for supposing or believing that the grant of the proposed lease will be for the benefit of the charity.

11. The name, quality, profession or occupation, and residence of the proposed lessee.

12. The amount and particulars of the proposed rent and other reservations, if any.

13. The proposed term.

14. The nature of the special covenants or provisions (if any) intended to be inserted in the lease.

15. The name and address of any surveyor by whom the property has been or is proposed to be surveyed and valued on behalf of the charity, or to whom the terms and conditions of the proposed lease have been or are proposed to be submitted for approval.

Note.—If any report or valuation, or any map or plan, of the property has been made, the same or a copy of each should be sent herewith. The commissioners will, if they think fit, require the property to be surveyed and valued, and the proposed lease to be reported on or approved by a surveyor appointed by themselves.

We declare that the foregoing statement is in all respects true according to our information and belief.

Dated this   day of   , 186 .

*

* Signatures, professions, or occupations, and residences of applicants.

No. 15.—*Form of Application for the Authority of the Board for a Sale.*

To the Charity Commissioners for England and Wales.

In the matter of the Charity called†

in the   of

in the county of

† Insert the usual name or designation of the charity, and the name of the parish, township, or place for the benefit whereof the charity was founded, or in which it is administered.

The undersigned, being the‡   of the above-named charity, and being of opinion that under the special circumstances hereinafter mentioned a sale of the particular property hereinafter also mentioned can be effected on such

‡ Trustees or persons acting in the administration.

terms as to increase the income of the charity, or would otherwise be advantageous to the charity, hereby request the board to inquire into such circumstances, and, if after inquiry the board are satisfied that the proposed sale will be advantageous to the charity, to authorise the said sale, and give such directions in relation thereto, and for securing the due investment of the money arising from such sale, as the board may think fit.

State,

1. The mode and date of the appointments of the existing trustees (if any) of the charity, and the number originally appointed.

2. Whether the charity property is legally vested in such trustees, and, if so, by what conveyance or assurance.

3. The name of the township, parish, and county in which the particular property proposed to be sold is situate.

4. The nature, extent, and general description of the same property, and whether forming the whole or part only of the property of the charity.

5. The estate and interest of the charity therein.

6. The manner in which the particular property has been let or occupied for the last three years.

7. The amount of the gross rent or income arising therefrom during the last three years.

8. The amount and particulars of the outgoings or deductions in each of such years.

9. The present improved annual or rack-rent value of the particular property.

10. The special circumstances under which the sale is proposed, and the advantages likely to result to the charity therefrom.

11. Whether the sale is proposed to be made by public auction or private contract, and whether any offer for the purchase thereof has been received, and the terms of such offer.

12. The name, quality, profession or occupation and residence of the person by whom any such offer has been made.

13. The manner in which it is proposed that the purchase money should be invested, and how any such investment thereof is proposed to be secured.

14. The name and address of any surveyor by whom the property has been or is proposed

Forms of Application. 233

to be surveyed and valued on behalf of the charity.

Note.—If there is any report or valuation, or any map or plan of the property, the same or a copy of each should be sent herewith. The commissioners will, if they think fit, require the property to be surveyed and valued, and the proposed sale to be reported on or approved by a surveyor appointed by themselves.

We declare that the foregoing statement is in all respects true according to our information and belief.

Dated this   day of   , 186 .

*
———

* Signatures, professions or occupations, and residences of applicants.

No. 16.—*Form of Application for the Authority of the Board for an Exchange.*

To the Charity Commissioners for England and Wales.

In the matter of the Charity called†

in the   of

in the county of

† Insert the usual name or designation of the charity, and the name of the parish, township, or place for the benefit whereof the charity was founded, or in which it is administered.

The undersigned being the‡ of the above-named charity, and being of opinion that, under the special circumstances mentioned in the subjoined statement, an exchange of the particular property therein also mentioned and belonging to the charity can be effected on such terms as to increase the income thereof, or to be otherwise advantageous to the charity, hereby request the board to inquire into such circumstances, and, if after inquiry the board are satisfied that the proposed exchange will be advantageous to the charity, to authorise such exchange, and to give such directions in relation thereto, and for securing the due investment of the money to be paid by way of equality of exchange (if any) for the benefit of the charity, as the board may think fit.

‡ Trustees or persons acting in the administration.

State,

1. The mode and date of the appointments of the existing trustees (if any) of the charity, and the number originally appointed.

2. Whether the charity property is legally vested in such trustees, and, if so, by what conveyance or assurance.

3. The estate and interest of the charity in the property proposed to be exchanged.

STATEMENT—*continued.*

The particular property hereinbefore referred to and belonging to the said charity, and proposed to be exchanged, is situate in the township of   in the parish of   in the county of   and is described as follows :

Description.	Extent.	How let or occupied.	Present Gross Annual Value.	Deductions.

STATEMENT—*continued.*

The property proposed to be exchanged for the lands and hereditaments hereinbefore described is situate in the township of   in the parish of   in the county of   and is described as follows :

Description.	Extent.	How let or occupied.	Present Gross Annual Value.	Deductions.

STATEMENT—*continued.*

State,

4. Whether the charity is possessed of property in addition to that proposed to be exchanged.

5. The special circumstances under which the exchange is proposed, and the advantages likely to result to the charity therefrom.

6. The name, quality, profession or occupation, and address of the person with whom the exchange is proposed to be made.

7. The estate or interest of such person in the property to be given by him in exchange.

8. The manner in which the property to be given in exchange and the property to be received in exchange by the charity have respectively been let or occupied during the last three years; and the amount of the gross and net annual rents or income arising therefrom during the same period.

9. The amount of the money (if any) to be received or paid by way of equality of exchange.

10. The manner in which the money (if any) to be so received by the charity is proposed to be invested and secured, or in which any money to be so paid by the charity is proposed to be raised or provided.

11. The name and address of any surveyor by whom the properties to be given and taken in exchange respectively have been or are proposed to be surveyed and valued on behalf of the charity.

Note.—If there is any report or valuation or map or plan of the properties referred to, the same, or a copy of each, should be sent herewith. The commissioners will, if they think fit, require such properties to be surveyed and valued, and the proposed exchange to be reported on or approved, by a surveyor appointed by themselves.

We declare that the foregoing statement is in all respects true according to our information and belief.

Dated this   day of   , 186 .

*

•

* Signatures, professions or occupations, and residences of applicants.

Minutes made by the Board of Charity Commissioners for England and Wales on the 20th Day of November, 1860, relative to the Institution and Conduct of their Proceedings under the Jurisdiction created by the Charitable Trusts Act, 1860.

1. Every application to the Board for an Order under the above-mentioned jurisdiction shall be made in writing, signed by the applicants or by their authorised solicitor or agent (in that declared character); and every such application not made by Her Majesty's Attorney-General shall show that the applicants are competent to apply to the Board under the Act as

(*a.*) Trustees or persons administering or claiming to administer the Charity the subject of the application;
(*b.*) Or persons interested in the benefits of the Charity;
(*c.*) Or two or more inhabitants of some parish or place within which the Charity shall be administered or applicable—

2. Every application shall be intituled, In the matter of the Charity to which it shall relate, by its usual name or designation, and shall state as far as conveniently may be—
The parish or locality for which (if of a local character) it is founded or within which it is administered or applicable;
The endowments of the Charity;
The objects of its foundation;
The amount of its annual or ordinary income;
The actual application of such income;
The names and personal descriptions and residences of the trustees or actual administrators of the Charity;
And all other circumstances material to the specific purposes of the application.

3. If the application shall not be made by all the trustees or actual administrators of the Charity, it shall state whether those who are not parties to it are assenting to or dissenting from its objects.

4. Every application for the appointment of trustees, or for the establishment of a scheme for the administration of any charity, shall be made in general terms for those objects, but may be accompanied by any proposal or recommendation as to the particular trustees or scheme to be respectively appointed or established.

5. The form No. 1. in the subjoined schedule shall be followed as nearly as conveniently may be for the purposes of all applications to the Board under the said jurisdiction.

6. The Board may require any application to be explained, amended, or altered in such manner and so often as they may think fit, and all or any of the statements on which it shall be founded, or any other circumstances material to its purposes to be established by the applicants by sufficient evidences.

7. Notice in writing of every application to the Board stating its objects shall be given by the applicants to all trustees or administrators of the Charity not parties to the application, and when and as directed by the Board, to Her Majesty's Attorney-General, and to all persons to whom in respect of any personal rights or interests liable to be affected by the Order to be thereupon made, or for any other reason, the Board shall think it fit that such notice shall be given.

Such notice may be in the form No. 2. in the subjoined schedule.

Similar notice shall also be published by the applicants for the general information of all persons interested in the matter in all cases in which the Board shall consider it desirable, and shall direct that such publication shall be made.

Such last-mentioned notice may be given in the form No. 3. in the subjoined schedule.

The Board will not proceed in the matter of the application until they shall have been satisfied that every such notice directed by them to be given shall have been given accordingly.

8. The public notice required by the sixth section of the Act of every Order proposed to be made by the Board appointing or removing a trustee or establishing a scheme (if relating to any parochial charity) shall (unless otherwise

directed by the Board in any special case) be given in writing, to be affixed for fifteen days at least to or near some principal door of the church of the parish or district, or of each parish or district (if more than one), in which the Charity shall be administered or applicable, and shall state that any objections to or suggestions on the proposed Order may be made or transmitted to the Board in writing within twenty-one days from the date of such notice.

Such notice may be in the form No. 4. in the subjoined schedule.

9. All objections to any Order proposed to be made by the Board, and all suggestions thereon, shall be made and transmitted to the Commissioners in the first instance, in writing, but the Board so far as the justice of any special cases shall in their judgment require, as well as in the cases provided for by the Act, will at the request of the parties, or at their own discretion, require such objections or suggestions, or the matter of the application, to be heard, in such manner as they shall direct, before themselves or one or more of the members of their Board, or an inspector to be deputed by them for the purpose.

10. The Board shall be at liberty to proceed in the matter of any application, and to make any Order thereon, notwithstanding that these minutes shall not have been fully complied with by the applicants or others, in any cases in which they shall be satisfied that such incomplete compliance is immaterial to the justice of the case.

11. These minutes or any of them may be revoked, amended, or added to by the Board so often and in such manner as they may think fit.

SCHEDULE.

No. 1.

Form of Application to the Board under the Jurisdiction created by " The Charitable Trust Act, 1860."

To the Charity Commissioners for England and Wales.

* Insert the usual name or designation of the charity, and the name of the parish or place for the benefit whereof the same (if of a local character) is founded, or in which it is administered or applicable.

In the matter of the charity called *

in the   of

in the county of

† Under the provisions of the Act applications may be made by any one or more of the trustees or persons administering or claiming to administer the charity, or by any person interested in the charity, or by two or more inhabitants of any parish or place within which it is administered or applicable. The capacity of the applicants under this provision to be here inserted.

The undersigned being †

submit the following statement.

Forms under Act of 1860.

1. The Charity is endowed with the following properties, viz. :—
     1. State the particulars of the endowments.

2. The objects of the foundation are
     2. The objects of the foundation.

3. The ordinary yearly income of the Charity amounts to £   and consists of the following particulars, viz. :—
     3. The particulars and amount of the income.

4. The net income is now applied to
     4. The actual application of the income.

5. The present trustees are
     5. The names, descriptions, and residences of the trustees or administrators.

[*or as the case may be*] the charity is administered by

6.
     6. State whether the trustees or administrators, not parties to the application, are assenting to or dissenting from it.

7.
     State under the following numbers any other circumstances material to the application.

8.

9.

10.

Forms under Act of 1860.

Under the foregoing circumstances the undersigned are desirous of obtaining an Order of the Board for the following objects;

State here seriatim the objects for which the Order of the Board is required. If for the appointment of trustees or the establishment of a scheme, these objects to be stated in general terms.

That is to say,

The appointment of any particular trustees or the establishment of any particular trusts or any other order may be recommended here by the applicants according to the nature of the application.

It is recommended by the applicants

We declare that the above statements are in all respects true according to our information and belief.

Dated this   day of   186 .

(Signed)*

*Add the signatures of the applicants with their personal descriptions and places of residence.

If the application is made by the authorised solicitor or agent of the applicants, it should be signed by him accordingly in that declared character.

Forms under Act of 1860.

No. 2.

Form of personal notice of application to the Board to be given by the applicants.

In the matter of the Charity called
    in the   of   in the county of

Take notice that application has been made on the day of 18 [*or* will be forthwith made, *as the case may be*], by or on behalf of

to the Board of Charity Commissioners for England and Wales for an order for the following objects, viz. :—

> State the objects of the Order sought by the application.

Any objections to or suggestions on the proposed application may be transmitted, in writing, to the said Board at their Office, No. 8, York Street, St. James's Square, London, within 21 days from the date hereof.

    Dated this   day of   186

> To be signed by the applicants or their authorised agent in that character.

No. 3.

Form of general notice of application to the Board to be published by the applicants.

CHARITY COMMISSION.

In the matter of the charity called
    in the parish of   in the county of

By direction of the Board of Charity Commissioners

for England and Wales, notice is hereby given that application has been made on the   day of
[*or* will be forthwith made, *as the case may require,*] to the said Board by or on behalf of
                                        for an Order for the following objects, viz. :—

<small>State objects of the application.</small>

Any objections to or suggestions on the proposed application may be made or transmitted, in writing, to the said Board at their office, No. 8, York Street, St. James's Square, London, within 21 days next after the date of this notice.

<small>To be signed by applicants.</small>

Dated this   day of   186

No. 4.

Form of notice of proposed Order of the Board to be given in pursuance of the Sixth Section of the Act.

CHARITY COMMISSION.

In the matter of the charity called
       in the parish of   in the county of

By direction of the Board of Charity Commissioners for England and Wales, notice is hereby given that an Order is proposed to be made by the said Board after the expiration of one calendar month, to be computed from the publication of this notice, having the following objects; namely,

<small>State objects or sufficient particulars of proposed Order.</small>

Any objections to or suggestions on the proposed Order may be made or transmitted, in writing, to the said Board at their office, No. 8, York Street, St. James's Square, London, within 21 days next after the date of this notice.

Dated this   day of   186

INDEX.

	PAGE
ACCOUNTS OF CHARITIES	
may be required	125
to be rendered	110
how kept by board	160
ACTIONS OR SUITS	
to be sanctioned by board	130
how compromised	134
ACTS OF BOARD, how authenticated	171
ADJUDICATION, powers of the board as to	120
ADMINISTRATION OF CHARITIES	
left to trustees	68—87
advice or direction as to	111—129
ADVERSE CLAIMS	
inquiry as to	129
procedure as to	142
enjoyment, meaning of	43
ADVICE, application for	111—129
ALTERATIONS OF SCHEMES,	
how effected	161
AMOUNT OF INCOME OF CHARITIES,	
how determined	154
APPEALS	
APPLICATIONS TO BOARD	
for general direction	111
for particular purposes	134—140
how made	112
forms of	224—235
To CHANCERY	
how restrained	131
when made	140
how made	143
by whom made	131—133
APPOINTMENT	
of trustees	62
jurisdiction of chancery as to	140
of county courts	143
of officers	87
APPORTIONMENT OF PAROCHIAL CHARITIES	72
ARBITRATION, power of board for	114

	PAGE
ATTORNEY-GENERAL, saving of his rights	. 132
power of board as to	. 133

BOARD
  powers of, generally . . . . . . 108—122
    to give advice or direction 129
    to direct or delay suits . . . . 130—133
    to sanction compromises 134
        documents 135
        leases 136
        sales, &c. 137
        purchases 138

CHANCERY, JURISDICTION OF
  generally 19, 104
  special 104
  as to creation of trusts 18
    declaration of trusts 49
  extension of 75
  administration 81
  under the Act 140

CHAPELS, TRUSTS AS TO 29

CHARGES
  distinguished from trusts 169
  provision for apportionment of 180

CHARITIES, what are so, generally . . . . . 1—18
  incorporated . . . . . . 2—9, 180
  how created . . . . . . 18—51
  definition of 168
  parochial 11, 102, 185
  municipal 11
  societies, &c. 15
  administration of 68
  management of property of 98
  jurisdiction over, in chancery 104
    of county courts . . . 140—144
    of commissioners of charities . . 108, 188
  accounts of 172, 184
  apportionment of benefits of 174
    charges on 180
  recipients of benefits of 112, 191
  vesting of property of 156, 175
  investment of funds of 100, 180
  sales, exchanges, &c. 179

CLAIMS, by or against charities, how settled . . . 134

COMMISSIONERS OF CHARITIES, how appointed . . 123
  their powers . . . . . . 125—140

COMPROMISES, of claims, &c. 134

Index. 239

	PAGE
COUNTY COURTS, jurisdiction of	143—148

DECLARATION OF TRUST
    when material 55
    how made 53
DEEDS, of charities, how called for 126
    where deposited 161
DEPOSIT OF DEEDS 161
DIRECTION
    power of board to give 129, 187
DISMISSAL OF OFFICERS, &c. . . . . . 86, 135—189
DISPUTES
    as to charities within the jurisdiction 129
        exempted 167
DISTRICTS, of parishes,
    charities, how apportioned to 174
    of county courts 191
    of commissioners of bankruptcy . . . . . *ib.*
DIVIDENDS
    of charity stock, &c. 177
DOCUMENTS, issued by board
    how authenticated 171
    of charities 161
DONEES
    how made trustees 24, 25
DONORS
    services for benefit of 31

ENDOWED CHARITIES
    within the Act 169
ENDOWMENTS 24
ENFORCING ORDERS OF BOARD 173
        of county court 148
ENQUIRIES. *See* INQUIRIES.
ENJOYMENT
    adverse to charity 202
    observations on 44
ESTATES OF CHARITIES
    management of, generally 98
    leases of 136, 179
    sales or exchanges 137, 179
    of parochial charities 13, 102
    of municipal charities 12, 157
EXCHANGES
    of charity lands 180, 181
EXISTENCE OR EXTENT OF TRUST
    inquiries as to 151

	PAGE
FORMS. *See* Appendix	216
GRAMMAR SCHOOLS	10
masters of	88, 135, 191
HOSPITALS, ancient	3
nature of	4
evidence as to	6
jurisdiction as to	5—7
right of inmates of	6
provision as to removal from	191
HOUSES	
held by officers of charity	88, 135
or recipients	6
provision as to removal from	191
INCOME OF CHARITIES	
how estimated	154
returns of	184
inquiries as to	125
INQUIRIES	
powers of board as to	125, 173
as to adverse claims	151
persons liable to	172
INSPECTORS	
powers of	125
reports of	132
INSTITUTION OF SUITS	
how sanctioned	133
INVESTMENT OF CHARITY FUNDS	138
JURISDICTION	
of chancery, generally	62
under Romilly's Act	104
under Charitable Trusts Act	140
of county courts	143, 155
of commissioners of charities	125, 140, 169, 179, 187
how determined	154
under Charitable Trusts Act	169
exemptions from	164
of visitors	7
over religious charities	86
LANDS OF CHARITIES	
how let	136—179
or sold	179
or mortgaged	ib.
LEASES OF CHARITY LANDS	107
powers of Board to sanction	136
frame schemes as to	181

	PAGE
LEGAL ESTATE	
in property of a charity	156
of municipal charities	157
of parochial charities	175
LETTING CHARITY LANDS	101
schemes for	181

MASS
   what it is 30
   support of, legal . . . . *ib.*
MASSES for souls of donors . . . . 31—37
MASTER OF SCHOOL
   how appointed or removed . . . . . . , 88
   power of Board as to 135, 191
MINISTERS OF CHAPELS, &c.
   how appointed 87
      removed 88
   power of Board as to . . . . . . 188—191
MORTGAGES OF CHARITY PROPERTY
   how sanctioned 179
   officers of charities 88
      dismissal of . . . . . . 135—191

ORDERS OF THE BOARD
   to render accounts, &c. . . . . . 128—185
   to authorise suits 131
      sales, &c. 179
      transfer of stock, &c. 177
      for investment 181
   by their own powers 186
   how published 188
      authenticated 171
      appealed against 189
      enforced 173
ORDERS OF THE COURT OF CHANCERY
   under Romilly's Act 104
      the Charitable Trusts Act . . . 140
   of the county court 144
   to vest charity property in official trustee . . . 156

PARISH CHARITIES 11
   lands of 102
   apportionment of 174
   schemes for 189
PAYMENT OF MONEY
   orders for 176

242   *Index.*

	PAGE
PERSONAL PROPERTY OF CHARITIES	
how vested	159
PERSONS LIABLE TO BE EXAMINED	126
POWERS OF BOARD	
to make inquiries	127
give advice	129
sanction suits	131
compromises	134
dismissals	135—191
leases	136
sales, &c.	137
purchases	138
demand accounts	185
arbitrate disputes	167
make schemes	188
tax costs	182
require deeds, &c.	183
make original orders	188
PRINCIPAL MONIES OF CHARITY	
how secured	177
PROPERTY OF CHARITIES	
real—how vested	156
how let	136
sold, &c.	137, 179
personal—how vested	159, 175
invested	181
PUBLICATION OF ORDERS	189
of accounts	183
PURCHASES OF LAND FOR CHARITIES	138
REAL ESTATE	
how given for Charity	52
fixed with trust for	25
REAL ESTATES OF CHARITIES	
how vested	156
let or sold. (See LAND).	
RECIPIENTS OF CHARITIES	70
parochial charities	72
rights and remedies of	81, 82, 112, 145
RELIEF, ORDER OR DIRECTION	
how obtained by charities	103
under Romilly's Act	104
the Charitable Trusts Act	106—108
from the Board	187
county court	146
Court of Chancery at chambers	140

Index. 243

	PAGE
REMOVAL OF TRUSTEES	156, 188
officers or recipients	135, 191
RENT-CHARGES OF CHARITIES	103
how redeemed	138
ROMAN CATHOLIC CHARITIES	29
Act	39, 196
ROMILLY'S ACT	
jurisdiction under	204
SALES OF CHARITY LANDS	103
sanction of, by Board	137, 179
SECRETARY OF BOARD	156
accounts of	160
SECURITIES OF CHARITIES	
accounts of	ib.
SCHEMES	
when required	74
how framed	76
in Chancery	140
of the Commissioners	189
by Parliament	161
how authenticated	171
SCHOOLS, GENERALLY	6—10
Grammar	10
masters of	135, 191
religious teaching in	85
privileges of Church of England as to	84
SHARES, STOCK, &c., OF CHARITIES	
how vested	159, 176
SOCIETIES, CHARITABLE	
exempted	165
SPECIAL JURISDICTIONS	152
how determined	154
STOCK, &c., OF CHARITIES	176
how vested	159
dividends on, how received	160
transfers of, how effected	177
SURPLUS OF CHARITY INCOME	77
how applied	77, 81
TAXATION OF COSTS	
provision for	182
TERMS	
interpretation of	168
TRANSFER OF STOCK, &c.	177
TREASURER OF CHARITIES	156, 176

Index.

	PAGE
TRUSTEES	
official	156—176
property transferred to	ib.
TRUST PROPERTY	
what it is	21
transfer of	156
management of (See CHARITY).	
TRUSTEES	
how made	24, 25
appointed	62
removed	63
controlled	64
directed	129
TRUSTEES, POWERS OF	
generally	68
as to letting	101, 178
selling, &c.	103—179
dismissing officers	87
removing recipients	82
TRUSTS, CHARITABLE	
in general	1
how created	18
ascertained	42, 66, 95
discretionary	21, 22, 70
beneficial to donees	23, 44, 78
perpetuity of purpose	26
for chapels, &c.	29
masses	30
of general; how deposed	49
how declared	58
disclosed	60
administered	00
recipients of	82

THE END.

www.ingramcontent.com/pod-product-compliance
Lightning Source LLC
Chambersburg PA
CBHW021343230426
43666CB00006B/392